AMERICA'S
FORGOTTEN
WARS

AMERICA'S FORGOTTEN WARS

The Counterrevolutionary Past and Lessons for the Future

SAM C. SARKESIAN

Contributions in Military History,
Number 40

GREENWOOD PRESS
WESTPORT, CONNECTICUT • LONDON, ENGLAND

Library of Congress Cataloging in Publication Data

Sarkesian, Sam Charles.
  America's forgotten wars.

  (Contributions in military history, ISSN 0084-9251 ;
no. 40)
  Bibliography: p.
  Includes index.
  1. United States—History, Military. 2. United States
—Territorial expansion. 3. Counterrevolutions—History.
I. Title. II. Series.
E181.S27 1984   973   83-26669
ISBN 0-313-24019-1 (lib. bdg.)

Library of Congress Catalog Card Number: 83-26669
ISBN: 0-313-24019-1
ISSN: 0084-9251

First published in 1984

Greenwood Press
A division of Congressional Information Service, Inc.
88 Post Road West
Westport, Connecticut 06881

Printed in the United States of America

10 9 8 7 6 5 4 3 2 1

Contents

Illustrations

Maps

Figure

Tables

Preface

This book is about America's forgotten wars: those counterrevolutionary wars that have occurred from the 1800s to the present time that have been or are being placed on the shelves of forgotten history. Our present concern with missiles, sophisticated aircraft, and electronic battlefields, combined with the continuing "Vietnam syndrome," has created in both civilian and military minds the impression that conflicts in non-European areas (Third World) will surely follow the Vietnam pattern, which was basically an aberration of American policy. This book argues that American involvement in counterrevolutionary conflicts has followed a consistent pattern and that Vietnam was not an aberration, but a conflict consistent with the historical pattern of American wars.

What is so important about such forgotten wars? Simply stated, in the future, military doctrine, political-military policy, and the nature of battles are likely to be patterned after America's forgotten wars. The threats, both actual and potential, facing the United States today may develop primarily in Third World areas. These are not likely to follow conventional patterns of warfare or to erupt in battles across the central plains of Europe. Moreover, they may not follow well-established military guidelines associated with nuclear war or war between major powers. Rather, Third World conflicts are most likely to be associated with revolution and counterrevolution, which are unconventional, protracted, and highly political-social in their content.

One hundred and fifty years ago, American forces found that the best way to defeat the Seminole Indians in Florida was to burn their crops and villages and to establish areas of operations in order to destroy the Indians' economic livelihood. This approach was adopted only after

American commanders learned that conventional tactics were unable to bring the elusive Seminoles to battle. Indeed, a relative handful of Indians had kept American forces running around the interior of Florida for several years. Even with overwhelming manpower and superior firepower, the change in tactics did not bring about the total defeat of the Seminoles for a number of political and geopolitical reasons.

A close study of the Seminole conflict reveals important similarities and parallels with American doctrine and experience in Vietnam. The war in Florida also shows a number of important linkages to the domestic politics and policy of the Vietnam period. Thus, some major mistakes might have been avoided in Vietnam, had civilian and military leaders not forgotten about wars such as the Second Seminole War. Yet, today this early conflict in Florida is simply a sidenote in history. Other such wars—the Spanish–American War, the Philippine–American War, the Punitive Expedition into Mexico, and, more recently, Vietnam—have also been placed in a historical corner.

Particularly disturbing is the American military leadership's narrow view of history. The military is preoccupied with the grand battles of the past and the translation of these into modern battle techniques. Combined with high technology warfare, the professional mind set perceives world threats and confrontations in terms of major wars, both nuclear and nonnuclear. Thus, traditional perspectives are given a modern manifestation; the concern of the 1980s with battles on the plains of Europe is a case in point. Similar criticism can be leveled at most civilian policymakers and elected officials at the national level: few bring to their office a sense of history or keen analytical ability. The end result is both a civilian and a military perspective that rarely relates historical experiences in counterrevolutionary conflict to current issues of political-military policy.

A study of America's forgotten wars will not only help identify future political-military policy, but will also develop military doctrine and a professional capacity to deal with the complexities of counterrevolutionary war. Security challenges that are developing in the Third World and the American military's general unpreparedness to respond to these challenges make this study a critical necessity.

This volume is not a detailed historical account of military tactics or doctrine, or of battles or wars. Nor is it intended to be a comprehensive study of a particular time in American history. Rather, it seeks to synthesize the highpoints of America's past experience in counterrevolution at selected times in history and to bring these into contemporary focus. As such, the study is selective and views the past political-military landscape, rather than delving into the details of the terrain. Underlying this approach is the premise that the key to understanding counterrevolution (as well as revolution) lies in studying not the "shooting" war, but the political, social, and psychological factors that influence political systems involved in the conflict. Thus, the main focus is on the political temper of the times, the state of the military profession and the military's capability, and the character of the conflict in which the United States was involved.

For this study I have relied upon a variety of military, scholarly, and popular sources. In the case of Vietnam, I have also considered my own experience as an Army officer with service in Korea and Vietnam as well as those of a number of military officers with whom I discussed the war at length. The examination of other counterrevolutionary conflicts is based on my studies of historical accounts and on my interpretation of the evolution of American military professionalism.

Counterrevolutionary conflicts are primarily "ground" wars. For the United States this has meant an "infantryman" type of conflict. Combined with my own experience as an infantry officer, this characteristic of counterrevolutionary conflicts has focused my own attention on the role of the U.S. Army, rather than the other services. It is the ground war that sets the direction and determines the outcome of counterrevolutionary conflicts.

Four cases have been selected for analysis: the Second Seminole War (1835–42); the Philippine-American War (1899–1914), which evolved directly from the Spanish-American War (1898); the Punitive Expedition into Mexico (1916–17); and the Vietnam War (primarily the period from 1965 to 1970). (For details on the reasons for these selections, see Chapter 1.) While each of these cases is distinctive, certain common themes link them to form a coherent analytical framework for this study. Moreover, each case is pivotal in understanding and explaining the American counterrevolutionary experience.

This study does not purport to be the final word on American counterrevolutionary policy. But it has the distinction of being one of the few attempts to link American historical experience in counterrevolutionary war with policy guidelines for the future. Equally important, this study shifts the focus from the more traditional studies of American conflicts to counterrevolution and away from the battlefield preoccupation to the political-psychological realm.

Finally, a serious study of the American counterrevolutionary experience as it bears on current issues may prevent American involvement in situations that cannot be resolved either militarily or politically. The development of a historical "sense" may inculcate the kind of sophistication and astuteness which American civilian and military leaders will need to make judicious decisions, if America becomes involved in counterrevolutionary conflict. These observations are particularly appropriate in light of the conflicts in Central America during the period 1983–84, particularly in El Salvador. American interests in the region were clearly stated by the National Bipartisan Commission on Central America (the Kissinger Commission) in a report to the president in January 1984. The report made it clear that not only does America have a vital interest in the area, but that its role must be expanded. This raises the distinct possibility of an American counterrevolutionary role similar to its role in the past. It would be one of the great ironies of history if the mistakes of the past were to be repeated in Central America.

Acknowledgments

I wish to express my thanks to those colleagues, both military and civilian, who encouraged me to write this volume. I also wish to express my gratitude to those few men and women who have been courageous enough to write realistically about revolution, counterrevolution, American policy, and strategy in the context of American democracy without sparing anyone the seriousness of the moral and ethical challenges that these pose to the United States. I have tried to follow in their path.

AMERICA'S FORGOTTEN WARS

1

The Study of American Counterrevolutionary Policy

America's inability to protect its citizens in Iran during the takeover of the American embassy there and the pouring of Soviet troops into Afghanistan in 1979 marked a turning point in American attitudes toward relationships with the outside world. For the president of the United States these events appeared to be traumatic, forcing a rethinking of U.S. policy. At the end of the Vietnam War many Americans, including a vast majority of policymakers and elected officials, came to believe in the so-called Vietnam syndrome. American involvement in Third World areas, it was thought, would surely lead to another Vietnam and a humiliating withdrawal, not to mention the costs in men and material. The policy of human rights and detente appeared to be the best, and indeed the easiest, course of American policy, even though such a policy provided little in the way of coherent strategy and did not provide the economic and military wherewithal to fulfill America's political-military commitments. Only belatedly did the Carter Administration take steps toward some restoration of military strength.

Even with the change in administrations and President Ronald Reagan's commitment to a strong defense posture, there remain fundamental philosophical as well as practical problems in America's defense posture. Whether the American invasion of Grenada in October 1983 (shortly following the terrorist attack on the Marines in Lebanon) signals a basic change in U.S. political-military posture or is only a passing phenomenon remains to be seen. In any case, serious questions remain regarding America's ability and political resolve to successfully intervene in foreign areas, even for cogent security reasons.

In this respect, much of America's expanding defense system in the

1980s rests on strategic considerations and general purpose forces (Rapid Deployment). This has developed primarily because of the fear of Soviet nuclear capability. This fear has been exacerbated by the Soviet use of military power to extend its influence in parts of Africa, the Middle East, Central and South America, and Asia. While the extension of such power is fundamentally a result of the conventional maneuvering of Soviet military forces, many Western observers link it directly to Soviet nuclear capability. The U.S. concern with Soviet nuclear capability is well founded. Nonetheless, a potentially more serious consequence may result from the American preoccupation with the perceived Soviet nuclear capability. A key element in Soviet political-military strategy appears to be based on the deliberate "fixing" of American and Western military strategic concern on a European-type scenario and nuclear technology, in order to afford the Soviet Union political-military flexibility in conventional military contingencies.

This strategic "fixing" of the United States and the West is also the result of a series of counterinsurgency conflicts in which the Western world was handled roughly, that is, the French in Algeria and Indochina, the British in Northern Ireland, and the United States in Vietnam. Even the British victory in Malaya was not as complete as originally presumed. For the United States, these experiences have perpetuated a "never again" mentality. Thus, according to this view, the United States should never again become involved in counterrevolutionary conflicts. In this context, many argue that American involvement in Vietnam was an aberration of policy. The Vietnam syndrome is used as a label for unsuccessful counterrevolutionary efforts and for misguided and ineffective policy. Hence in 1982, for example, Afghanistan was labeled Russia's Vietnam.

For a number of American policymakers, the Western experience has led to a political-military premise that Vietnam-type situations and counterrevolutionary conflicts are, in general, outside the scope of American political-military policy. Even with the current attempts to increase American military capability, the main focus is on Europe or on the Middle East.

Regardless of the views of the American experience in Vietnam and the existence of the "never again" school, one thing seems eminently clear: American involvement in Vietnam was only *one* instance of a relatively long line of counterrevolutionary involvements. Not only was it not an aberration of policy, but it also followed a counterrevolutionary strategy whose pattern was set during the American Revolutionary War period. Moreover, within American military "intellectual" circles a theme focusing on the unconventional has always existed, though admittedly it has usually been overshadowed by the conventional perspective.

American political-military strategy and military tactics have confronted the challenge of unconventional wars on a number of occasions in our history. While the particular conditions differed from one period to the next, the fundamental issues of counterrevolutionary strategy and tactics were the same. Unfortunately, both American political leaders and military professionals have had to relearn the lessons of the past with each involvement in unconventional conflict.

It is sometimes difficult to understand why American professionals continue to neglect some of the most difficult wars of the past, especially when we consider that some of the most serious threats to American national security over the next decade may be from within developing systems in which revolutionary and counterrevolutionary conflicts are most likely to occur. An understanding of the American military profession provides part of the answer. The profession today is primarily oriented toward high technology wars: wars against potential enemies conventionally postured. In addition, counterrevolutionary wars are fundamentally alien to a culture rooted in democratic principles and in the concept of individual worth and justice. Indeed, for the American military profession, it would be less difficult, intellectually and organizationally, to prepare to fight the Soviets, for example, than Asians or Africans in a Third World environment.

What makes the issue even more bewildering is that recent studies make little, if any, reference to past American experience in counterrevolution. While the literature on Vietnam is varied and voluminous, many of the works reflect contemporary and conventional perspectives, neglecting historical dimensions and comparative analyses. As such they lack the historical depth and analytical insights necessary for the development of effective long-range American policy. Moreover, some of the current works create such an ethical, moral, and ideological maze that the ingredients of successful policy are lost.

In this study we will examine America's historical involvement in counterrevolutionary conflict and identify the policy that was followed in prosecuting that particular conflict. We will identify those elements of policy that are relevant to modern low-intensity conflict and will relate them to America's current security problems.[1] Before we begin this examination, however, it is necessary to develop an understanding, as well as an appreciation, of the fundamentals of revolution and counterrevolution. There are many excellent volumes on the principles, theories, strategies, and tactics of revolutionary warfare.[2] A serious examination of these subjects will surely require a close reading of such volumes. Here, however, we will briefly review and highlight the major characteristics of revolution and counterrevolution as a basis for developing an analytical scheme for this study.

REVOLUTION AND COUNTERREVOLUTION: AN OVERVIEW

Historically, revolution has meant the violent overthrow of an existing regime by the masses. In more modern terms, it has also come to mean the existence of a revolutionary political system, an ideology, and a core of revolutionary leaders capable of mobilizing segments of the population against the existing regime. The tactics of revolution cover the spectrum from assassination to unconventional warfare. Obviously, revolutionary leaders would prefer a tactic that allows economy of force and quick overthrow of the existing system. However, in many cases, revolution requires protracted war using unconventional tactics. In the process of this protracted war, a countergovernment needs to be established challenging the legitimacy of the existing system. Mao Tse-tung's three-phase revolutionary warfare is usually cited as the basis for many revolutionary guidelines.

Since Mao's revolution in China, much has been written about revolutions and revolutionary principles. In the post-World War II period, a variety of revolutions have taken place in Africa, Southeast Asia, and Latin America, and they have more or less followed the general patterns of the Chinese revolution. There are distinctions, of course, between the Huk revolution in the Philippines, the Castro revolution in Cuba, African revolutions in Angola and Mozambique, and the Vietminh and Vietcong revolutions in Indochina and Vietnam. In the main, however, all of them share general characteristics. The revolutionaries developed a reasonably effective alternative to the existing regime, there were many grievances against the existing system, there was an alternative ideology which appealed to the masses, and the revolutionaries had a core of leaders and cadre capable of conducting revolutionary war. The tactics used varied, but the purpose and principles remained the same: the overthrow of the existing system by the use of protracted war conducted by a revolutionary system.

In the end it will be a question whether the government falls before the military is destroyed in the field, or whether the destruction of the military brings about the deposition of the political regime. The two processes are complementary. Social and political dissolution bleeds the military, and the protracted and futile campaign in the field contributes to the process of social and political dissolution, creating what I have called elsewhere "the climate of collapse." This is the grand strategic objective of the guerrilla: to create the "climate of collapse." It may be taken as the key to everything he does.[3]

Counterrevolution is the handmaiden of revolution. In simple terms, counterrevolution usually occurs only after the revolution begins. This in turn usually means that the counterrevolutionaries face more difficult problems than the revolutionaries. While the major purpose of the revolution is to demonstrate the ineffectiveness of the existing government and undermine its determination to carry out policies against the revolutionaries, the purpose of the government is to combat the revolutionaries and yet remain within the realm of law, and reflect the aspirations, values, and beliefs of the people; it must be legitimate if there is to be hope of success in earning and keeping popular loyalty. In psychological terms, the revolutionaries can resort to extralegal means more easily since they are defined as outlaws in the government's eyes, while the very conditions that allow the growth of revolutionary movements tend to "legitimize" extralegal activities. In addition, counterrevolution is usually based on the specifics of revolutionary strategy and tactics. What makes it even more difficult for the counterrevolutionary system is that the very basis for combatting the revolution may lie in instituting all the political, social, and economic programs associated with revolutionary purposes.

That better government and economic development are the best measures for countering revolution has become a well-worn observation. Yet it is true. The problem is how to have better government and economic development in an orderly fashion, satisfy expectations, and still maintain a legitimate and credible posture vis-à-vis revolutionaries or internal dissidents. Moreover, government policies and perspectives usually aim at countering revolutionary tactics and neglect long-range strategic objectives. While a response to the immediate threat of the revolution is important, political-military plans for the "long haul" are equally vital.

The best counterrevolutionary posture is the existence of a political system that is responsive to grievances, has an established procedure for effective political participation by a variety of groups, and provides a reasonably effective economic structure. In developing systems, these mechanisms are the most difficult to accomplish. In a developed democratic system, however, they are well established, making it extremely difficult for dissident groups or revolutionary movements to achieve any real success. Democratic ideology, if purposefully applied to the operation of the political system, can usually erode any appeal of revolutionary ideology. Moreover, an established system is most likely to have the effective instruments of a modern state to combat radical groups or those groups intent on using violence. A former chief of staff of the U.S. Army has written:

One of the key strategies of insurgency, or "wars of national liberation" is initially to create disorder which can later be exploited, penetrating every institution to the maximum degree possible to promote confusion, disagreement, and uncertainty. The counter insurgent's task is to maintain the established order while in fact waging war against the insurgents who are spread among the population.

The counter insurgent is thus restrained against the use of force which would normally be acceptable against a completely hostile population. The arms of the government must be long enough to reach out to all of the people, firm enough to give them support, and strong enough to protect them from coercion and outside influence.[4]

In brief, a well-balanced combination of military and nonmilitary instruments and measures appears to be the best road to counterrevolutionary success: "One must constantly keep foremost in mind that military action is only a part of counter-insurgency and that a well-integrated 'team' can often compound a military success or minimize failure."[5] Yet, it is a historical truth that even with recognition that political and social issues may be paramount, many counterrevolutionary systems react with a heavy-handed military instrument. Furthermore, they tend to view the revolutionary effort through a military lens.

A revolution is made possible partly by the administrative and political weaknesses of the existing system. It follows that the more effective the government and the more responsive it is to the needs of the populace, the more likely that a revolution can be limited or prevented. To a large degree therefore, effective counterrevolutionary measures are essentially those connected with effective government. Generally, military actions are effective only when they are conceived and implemented in the context of effective government.[6]

In sum, there appears to be no particular model of counterrevolution except perhaps the need for the government to demonstrate its determination and capacity to win, while at the same time providing a legitimate framework within which the aspirations of the people can be achieved. Therefore, the counterrevolution must not only prevent the revolution from growing, but must also take the necessary political, social, and economic measures that will create a government-controlled revolution against the revolutionaries.

It is urgent to lay stress on the fact that to destroy them (guerrillas) with military might . . . will always fail as long as the guerrilla fighters can conceal themselves among the people and call for help, as long as they have their base within the people. It is this that is not primarily a military matter, but largely a matter of political, psychological and socio-economic concern.[7]

The history of counterrevolution suggests that the initial military posture and threat perceptions of the government determine, to a great extent, its long-range counterrevolutionary policy. That is, these initial decisions create the boundaries within which subsequent policy is formulated and determine perceptions regarding the conflict. Once such a policy is established, it is difficult to make major changes in direction or in the way it is implemented.[8]

An important consideration in counterrevolutionary war is the role of the third power. Struggles between revolutionaries and counterrevolutionaries can be markedly influenced by an intervening power, particularly when such a power is either a major or superpower. The third power role can take on a variety of forms, from direct involvement (that is, the dispatch of ground combat troops such as the U.S. involvement in Vietnam and the Soviet Union in Afghanistan), the use of proxy armed forces (that is, the Soviet Union working through Cuba to influence politics in Africa and Latin America), to a number of lower visibility methods such as military assistance and economic aid. Each type of involvement requires certain mixes of military participation and economic assistance. In addition, each type of involvement stimulates different kinds of political reactions and forces within the third power, as well as within the target area. Since our primary concern here is with American counterrevolutionary involvement, little needs to be said about the differences in these issues between democratic and authoritarian systems in terms of third power involvement.

Third power involvement (particularly when it includes the commitment of ground combat units) exposes the power to political and military pressures associated with the indigenous counterrevolutionary system. Such involvement usually complicates the conflict and exacerbates political and social tensions within the target area.

These observations apply to America's counterrevolutionary role. The democratic and moral demands of American policy usually mean that the success of America's counterrevolutionary policy is linked to the degree of legitimacy and relative efficiency of the system on whose behalf America intervenes. At the same time, America's interventionist role is conditioned by the degree of support it receives from the counterrevolutionary system. As we learned in Vietnam and should have learned in Mexico in 1916, lukewarm or conditional support can lead to outright antagonism by the very system American policy was intended to support. Most important are the constraints which the American people themselves may impose. These constraints can limit the kinds of doctrine and strategy employed by American forces, since the American people expect their military men to behave in general accord with the norms of society. Thus, society's values must be reflected in military professional ethics and behavior, even on the battlefield. On some occasions democratic constraints have been disregarded for the purpose of quickly defeating revolutionaries or of meeting the battle imperatives of the moment. However, military necessity as a rationale in counterrevolutionary conflicts usually precipitates American reaction. Even so, in some counterrevolutionary conflicts American forces have exhibited questionable battlefield behavior without eliciting much notice. There are at least two explanations for this situation: the confusion inherent in any military conflict; and the fact that the conflict touches only a small segment of the American people, and thus falls outside the political mainstream.

Our concern with democratic systems should not obscure the fact that authoritarian systems may be better prepared to counter revolutionary movements. Using police, military, and government-initiated terror tactics, authoritarian systems can successfully counter revolutionary movements as long as such movements are identified early and effective action is undertaken. This, of course, presumes the existence of reasonably effective police, military, and bureaucratic instruments in support of the authoritarian political system. Indeed, an efficient authoritarian system is usually in a position to defeat revolutionary movements before they can seriously undertake revolutionary activity.

ANALYTICAL SCHEMES

A variety of frameworks can be used to examine America's forgotten wars. Violence and revolution are political phenomena that provide a multitude of case studies and theories. In the modern era, many scholars, practitioners, and commentators have examined and analyzed these matters, developing a variety of categorizations, concepts, and definitions. Many of the studies emphasize that revolution is a multi-faceted and complex political, social, economic, and psychological phenomenon that defies one conceptual scheme or universal theory. Moreover, such studies show that many aspects of revolution are not only immeasurable, but also imponderable, defying categorization. Yet, in the name of scholarship some authors oversimplify these concepts to explain both revolutionary phenomena and politics in general. The concepts have not been satisfactorily defined, however:

Recent years have brought a plethora of writings on unconventional wars, ranging from purely military studies at the level of the smallest troop units to the analysis of nation-building. Useful as they have been, they reveal a lack of agreement on basic definitions and terminology. Revolutionary war, civil war, internal war, insurgency, resistance movements, guerrilla war, wars of national liberation, stability operations, internal defense, counter-insurgency—these are but a few examples of the proliferating terminology.[9]

A number of studies on revolution also tend to reflect the intellectual biases of the scholar. Historians tend to use the principles that evolved from the "Great Revolutions" of the past as criteria for the study of all revolutions; sociologists generally focus on social class and order as well as societal grievance as the primary bases for revolutions; while political scientists may direct their attention to coercion, violence, and power associated with institutions and systems. Aside from the disciplinary orientation, there is a problem of scope. While some scholars prefer the narrow definition of revolution, restricting its application to civil disorders and violent upheaval, others accept a looser definition encompassing, among other things, the scientific and technological revolution— which after all, they argue, is no less earthshaking than the Cuban or Iranian revolutions. Some of the most recent works are eclectic and borrow from a range of social sciences. The behavioralist approach focusing on revolutionary mentality and economic models suggests that revolutions stem from perceived economic deprivation and have a greater empirical susceptibility than traditional theories. There is much work in progress to develop theories dealing with cross-national analysis of revolution. Finally, there are numerous ideological interpretations, representing all shades of political outlooks. In any case, any one-dimensional view of revolutions presupposes relatively clear and differentiated political, social, and economic systems—and clearly identifiable human motivations—which is hardly a realistic assessment. Yet, some characteristics can be used as a conceptual framework:

Despite the ambiguities, some characteristics are common to all of these efforts; the use of force; the objective of changing the composition of government; revolutionary goals; organization; and the fact that the participants are apt to appear to be civilians and avoid conventional battle tactics. Unconventional warfare may include the entire range of activities from sabotage and ambush to operations involving organized units on a larger scale, employing tactics of dispersion, rapid assembly, surprise attack, and dispersion. But the decisive element is the departure from the use of always visibly distinguishable combatants in formal battle order.[10]

In the final analysis, policymakers in counterrevolutionary systems are placed in a quandry. While studies can be made of revolutions, frameworks developed, and revolutionary phenomena intellectualized, counterrevolutionary policy remains primarily reactive. Revolutionaries take the initiative with counterrevolutionaries usually responding. Thus, regardless of the intellectualizing and the analysis of historical experience, counterrevolutionary strategy is linked to revolutionary strategy. Thus, in order to study counterrevolutionary policy one must make an intellectual as well as operational synthesis between revolutionary and counterrevolutionary systems.

The analytical scheme used in this study is based on the premise that political-social dimensions are most important in analyzing counterrevolutionary policy. It must, therefore, be stressed that the analysis here is not a history of any particular conflict. The actual battlefield will not necessarily hold the answers, nor is it the main area of attention. Battlefield strategy, tactics, and specific battles are examined only inasmuch as they provide insights into counterrevolutionary policy and military posture in carrying out that policy.

The analytical scheme comprises three components: state of the nation, military posture, and nature of the conflict. The first component, state of the nation, entails a study of four elements: review of the politics and policy issues of the period in question; study of the quality of presidential leadership; assessment of the nation's will and political resolve to carry out counterrevolutionary policy; and socioeconomic patterns. A review of the politics and policy issues of the day will provide indicators of the dynamics of the times and the main concerns of the American people and their elected officials. Did domestic or foreign policy issues occupy the attention of the American people? How did Americans view their country's role in foreign policy? Investigating such questions will assist in judging how the American political system responded to counterrevolutionary conflict and their ability or willingness to sustain counterrevolutionary efforts.

With regard to the second element, the quality of presidential leadership, the presidential character, personality, and leadership style is particularly important in a democracy, not only because of the need to mobilize opinion, but also because the policy is partly a function of the president's ability to develop and maintain a consensus. In addition, the president's ability to control the bureaucracy and provide directions for the military is essential to the coherency of policy and the degree to which it is aggressively pursued:

It makes a difference who is there at a given moment. This is particularly true when high threat, surprise, and short decision time combine to form a crisis situation. Under such conditions, a leader's personality—his character and values—may even be decisive. Stated in another way, if the decision maker had been a different person, the course of events might have taken a different turn.[11]

The leader's character and personality also influence the nation's policies:

In our time, a person who makes foreign policy may hold our future in his hands. *His* personality may be *our* destiny. A leader's character may spell the difference between war and peace, destruction and survival. The United States is a government of laws and not of men in its relations to its citizenry. But in its foreign relations in this century, the United States has been a government of men—a handful of men.[12]

The third element, an assessment of the nation's will and political resolve to carry out counterrevolutionary policy, is also important in assessing the state of the nation. In actuality, this element is a function of the first two. The political-social environment of the period in question, and the quality of presidential leadership, are the basis for the nation's will and the political resolve to pursue counterrevolutionary policy. For example, while these elements may be initially steadfast, they may erode or waiver as the conflict wears on. In this respect, reports from the battle area, for example, have an impact on national will and political resolve. However, the quality of presidential leadership has a greater correlation to the degree of national will and political resolve to carry on with the counterrevolutionary effort than most other factors. In this respect, national will is based on the degree and intensity of support which the American people give to national policy. Political resolve refers to the determination of those in policymaking positions to adopt and implement a particular policy.

Finally, an overview of the state of the nation must include some attention to socioeconomic patterns. There is a close relationship between politics, policy, and leadership, and the character of the socioeconomic patterns within the country. Thus, if economic distress and social dislocation occur at the same time that Americans become involved in counterrevolutionary conflict, socioeconomic dissatisfaction is likely to limit the kinds of policies and programs developed to respond to conflict.

All of these elements are interrelated and are linked to policy formulation and implementation. A coherent and aggressive policy, formulated and carried out by an active president, requires a political-social environment supporting such leadership, and a political resolve and national will supporting and perpetuating such policies and leadership. A failure or weakness in one area is likely to result in vacillating and unsuccessful policies.

The second component of the analytical scheme, military posture, is studied here in order to determine the degree of military capability and effectiveness in carrying out counterrevolutionary policy. To grasp the essentials of military posture at any given time in history, one must first understand the character of the military profession. American military professionals see the world through certain military lenses. Their view of the world affects how they feel wars should be fought and the needs of the military. Professionalism is also based on the training and education of the military, which in turn determines the kinds of wars that the military is prepared to fight. In this respect, a study of the strategy and tactics of counterrevolution will provide a criterion to judge the relative effectiveness not only of military professionalism, but also of the military instrument as a whole. Part of military posture stems from the relationships between civilian and military leadership, and from the view of the people regarding the status and effectiveness of the military instrument. Finally, many political-social characteristics of society condition the shape of the military instrument and affect those who serve. This consideration has an effect on how well the American military was (and is) able to conduct counterrevolutionary wars, and is an essential part of military posture.

The third and final component of the scheme used in this study, the nature of the conflict, includes a study of the political-military capability of the revolutionaries, their purposes, goals, and organization, and the nature of the conflict as perceived by the revolutionaries. Such an assessment will provide the background and context within which an examination can be made of the relationship between the first two components of our analytical scheme and the revolutionary system. The ability of the revolutionary system to carry out political-military operations against American forces is an indicator of the relative success or failure of American strategy and tactics. The general consequences of America's counterrevolutionary role are reflected not only in the final outcome, but also in the direction and progress of the conflict itself. Thus, the reaction of both military men and civilians to the ongoing battles, and the kinds of policy decisions, both civilian and military, made in response to revolutions reveal the tensions, relationships, and political-military dynamics within the American system.

The analytical scheme does not include all subjects within the scope of counterrevolutionary policy. But it identifies key indicators of the direction and effectiveness of policy. These three components evolve from fundamental premises of democratic political systems that are specifically connected to capabilities of revolutionary and counterrevolutionary warfare. These premises are as follows:

1. Military intervention and the conduct of military operations must have some degree of support from and approval of political actors and the public. The military in democratic systems depend upon the psychological as well as material support of a wide range of political actors. The withdrawal or withholding of such support can lead to the erosion of the military's sense of mission and decreased combat effectiveness, as was the case in Vietnam.

2. The leadership style and commitment of the president to particular policy goals help determine the character of the policy process and the quality of the implementation of counterrevolutionary policy. An active and aggressive assertion of presidential leadership in developing the necessary consensus in Congress and the public, combined with forceful application of presidential duties as commander-in-chief, are essential for effective use of the military in counterrevolutionary struggles. Effective presidential leadership must be maintained throughout the course of the counterrevolutionary involvement.

3. A democratic military system reflects to some degree the political-social character of the society it serves. The continual influx of young men and women into the military institution and the civil-military traditions of a democratic system instill a cultural value system that is based on moral and ethical imperatives of democratic ideology, that is, individual worth,

political system in general. Although the means employed to achieve policy goals may vary within systems, the elements of counterrevolutionary policy remain valid criteria in determining success or failure in counterrevolutionary war.

One must be extremely careful in making historical comparisons, particularly with respect to conflicts separated by many years and affected by a different set of political and social forces, both domestically and internationally. Yet, the presumption that comparisons are valid only when there are identical conditions, as if somehow history can be compared in accordance with laboratory conditions, poses a danger of neglecting the lessons of history. A more practical, common sense approach rests in seeing the differences between historical periods, assessing and comparing these differences according to the particular forces of the times, and drawing conclusions in the form of general guidelines that can be applied without straining historical analogies.[17]

There are, to be sure, dissimilarities between these conflicts, particularly in terms of the political-social forces of the times; these dissimilarities are briefly addressed in the various chapters. Nonetheless, the main focus of attention is on the patterns of politics, socioeconomic developments, political-military policy, and the nature of the conflicts, which can provide general directions and boundaries for the future. In brief, dissimilarities are recognized, but they do not preclude identifying patterns of conduct and developments that may be appropriate in analyzing current American policy.

Finally, this study attempts to follow the path of scholarly objectivity, even if the outcome may not be totally acceptable by various democratic criteria. Although the final chapter addresses the elements of successful counterrevolutionary policy, this should not be seen as advocacy of one way or another. The successful elements of counterrevolutionary policy may well incur too high a cost for any democratic political system.

NOTES

1. See the discussion in Sam C. Sarkesian, "American Policy and Low-Intensity Conflict: An Overview," in Sam C. Sarkesian and William L. Scully (eds.), *U.S. Policy and Low-Intensity Conflict: Potentials for Military Struggles in the 1980s* (New Brunswick, N.J.: Transaction Books, 1981), pp. 1–15.

2. See, for example, Crane Brinton, *Anatomy of a Revolution* (New York: Prentice-Hall, 1957); General Vo Nguyn Giap, *People's War People's Army* (New York: Praeger, 1962); David Galula, *Counterinsurgency Warfare: Theory and Practice* (New York: Praeger, 1964); Robert Taber, *The War of the Flea* (New York: Lyle Stuart, 1965); and Sir Robert Thompson, *Defeating Communist Insurgency* (New York: Praeger, 1967). For a useful commentary on sources for the study of revolution, see A. Thomas Ferguson, Jr., "Sources for the Study of Revolutionary Guerrilla Warfare," in Sam C. Sarkesian (ed.), *Revolutionary Guerrilla Warfare* (Chicago:

Precedent Publishing, 1975). A recent historical study of revolution is James H. Billington, *Fire in the Minds of Men: Origins of the Revolutionary Faith* (New York: Basic Books, 1980).

3. Taber, *War of the Flea*, p. 29.

4. Richard L. Clutterbuck, *The Long, Long War* (New York: Praeger, 1966), pp. viii–ix.

5. Ibid., p. ix.

6. C. C. Too, "Some Salient Features in the Experience in Defeating Communism in Malaya, with Particular Regard to the Method of New Villages" (Paper presented at the International Seminar on Communism in Asia, June 19–25, 1966; Onyang, Korea), p. 3.

7. Abdul Haris Nasution, *Fundamentals of Guerrilla Warfare* (New York: Praeger, 1965), p. 59.

8. Lucian W. Pye, "Lessons from the Malayan Struggle Against Communism" (Unpublished MS, n.d.), p. 57.

9. Sarkesian, "American Policy," p. 4.

10. Ibid., p. 7.

11. John G. Stoessinger, *Crusaders and Pragmatists: Makers of Modern American Foreign Policy* (New York: Norton, 1979), p. 287.

12. Ibid., p. xiv.

13. See, for example, Barry M. Blechman, et al., *Force Without War* (Washington, D.C.: Brookings Institution, 1978).

14. Russell F. Weigley, *History of the United States Army* (New York: Macmillan, 1967), p. 160.

15. One of the few studies that examines the entire Seminole period and the Florida conflicts is Virginia Bergman Peters, *The Florida Wars* (Hamden, Conn.: Archon Books, 1979). Using a variety of primary sources, the author provides an excellent as well as interesting account of the long conflicts between the United States and the Seminoles.

16. Richard E. Welch, Jr., *Response to Imperialism: The United States and the Philippine-American War, 1899–1902* (Chapel Hill: University of North Carolina Press, 1979), pp. xiii–xvi.

17. Ibid., p. xiv.

2

State of the Nation

THE JACKSONIAN ERA AND THE END OF REVOLUTIONARY AMERICA

The Jacksonian period is generally viewed as a watershed in American politics. Andrew Jackson brought to the White House a vigorous and overpowering leadership style, which he nurtured by consistently relating his office to the people. Strengthened by his populist image, he expanded the concept of the presidency and established what many consider the beginnings of the modern presidency. Although there is some disagreement regarding the meaning of the Jacksonian presidency, it seems clear that Andrew Jackson linked the power of the office to a popular mandate and presided over an important period in American history. The age of Jackson was marked by major changes in politics, demographics, and socioeconomic patterns. At the same time it opened the doors for the expansion of the United States across the continent and laid the groundwork for industrial development.

The War of 1812 established Jackson's national reputation, which he used as a springboard to the presidency. In the aftermath of the war, America shed its revolutionary past, creating the groundwork for its own particular political and economic system. As a result, the presidency emerged as the dominant national office. This dominance was also the result of the strength of the presidential political party and of those who occupied the office: John Adams, Thomas Jefferson, James Madison, James Monroe, and Andrew Jackson. By the second decade of the nineteenth century, the president had secured the primary role in determining the direction of policy. This role was a far cry from what the

Founding Fathers had envisioned when they offered the presidency to George Washington. Presidential influence on policy and the vigor of its implementation were particularly important during the Second Seminole War.

The Jacksonian era was preceded by important changes in the political party system. From the presidency of John Adams until Jackson, the presidential party, the Democrat-Republicans, controlled Congress. In 1816 the Federalist party disappeared to emerge as the National Republicans in 1820, later as Whigs, and finally as Republicans in 1856. By the election of 1828, the Democrat-Republicans had split into Jacksonians (the Democrat-Republicans) and the Adamsites (the National Republicans). Thus, while Jackson as an individual had an important impact, changes were already in the making when he came to office.

POLITICS AND POLICY ISSUES

The War of 1812 was not necessarily a glorious chapter in American history, but it did develop a sense of national unity and tested the nation's military in its first war against a foreign foe. The changes following the war presented the government with a variety of policy issues, including military policy. As Robert V. Remini notes, "After the War of 1812 the country slowly freed itself from its economic dependence upon Europe and began to build a viable domestic economy, not one based exclusively on international trade."[1] The focus of most Americans on newfound opportunities in politics and in the economy, and with them a host of new problems, swept aside any serious concern for the plight of the Indians, particularly those in Florida. It was the misfortune of the Indians that their "homelands" stood in the way of the westward migration, at a time of major changes and expansion of the American political system.

An economy oriented towards the small craftsman, farmer, and merchant was changing into a commercial and industrial one. But before this new system could take hold the prices for cotton and other commodities dropped drastically on the world markets. Banks closed, debts could not be paid, and the economy plummeted. Workers lost jobs and homes; farms and businesses failed. Political changes followed on the heels of the economic crisis. Sectional interests, concern about faltering businesses, and the general attention to the common interests of the people, combined with the apparent inability of those in power to deal with these new concerns, eroded confidence in the established political order. Many looked to political participation as a means of affecting these economic and social issues.[2]

The stage was set for Jackson. As John C. Calhoun observed in the spring of 1820, people were in distress everywhere, and there was a "general mass of disaffection to the Government not concentrated in any particular direction, but ready to seize upon any event and looking out anywhere for a leader."[3] Andrew Jackson seemed to be that leader.

The West's experience in the panic of 1819 provided an appropriate background for Jackson's presidency. The panic generated grass-roots political activity, inspired attacks against special privilege, reawakened a Jeffersonian animus against lawyers and bankers, and renewed latent misgivings about a national government both remote and unresponsive.[4]

Jackson's election victory in 1828 was preceded by important changes in the American political map characterized by struggles within the various political parties. These surfaced during the administration of President Monroe. In an attempt to reconcile these differences, an "Era of Good Feelings" was instituted to maintain national unity within the Democratic-Republican party, a unity that was based on the revolutionary past.

The decade of the 1820s was a period of party change and realignment. The rise of the Republican party seemed to establish a one-party system, with the collapse of the Federalist party. The disappearance of visible opposition at the national level gave the appearance of harmony and unity. This turned out to be a superficial harmony.[5] The efforts of President Monroe and the Republican party could not hide the sectional differences and factional disputes within the party. During the presidential election of 1824, sectional and factional rivalries emerged for the first time to challenge the old style of selecting a president. Up to this time, the Democratic-Republican senators and representatives had met in a caucus in Washington to determine who would be their presidential candidate. During the previous two decades, nomination in the caucus meant, for all practical purposes, election as president. The election of the president in 1824 was determined more by voters, whose numbers had increased as a result of extending voting privileges to most males. Equally important, parties began to recognize the importance of organizing at the local level for the purpose of capturing the presidency.

In 1824, the Tennessee legislature supported a fellow Tennessean, Andrew Jackson, for the presidency. A war hero and conqueror of Indians in the First Seminole War (1810–1818), General Jackson had gained a great deal of fame among Southerners and Westerners. While Jackson had no real program and had not taken a stand on public issues, he caught the popular imagination and stood as a leader not connected with the Republican old guard.

The election became a serious four-way fight between John Quincy Adams, Andrew Jackson, John Calhoun, and Henry Clay. It ended with no one receiving a majority, although Jackson led the four-man field.

The election was thrown into the House of Representatives, resulting in the victory of Adams by a narrow margin, after Clay threw his support to Adams. Jackson and his supporters felt cheated, particularly after Clay was appointed secretary of state in the Adams Administration. There followed a bitter four-year period which continued through the election of 1828.[6]

John Adams' presidency, 1824–1828, evolved out of the collapse of the Federalist party and the rise of the National Republican party and the Jacksonian Democrats. Presidential politics were still mainly a result of party caucuses. Challenged by Jacksonians throughout his presidency, John Adams did not compile an enviable record. However, as president he laid the groundwork for the Seminole War and the eventual defeat of the Indians in Florida. Aside from his inability to deal effectively with the British over West Indian trade and his ineffectual policies with respect to Latin America, President Adams was seriously challenged by the state of Georgia over the issue of the Creek Indians.

A treaty with the Creeks in 1825 was supposed to cede much of their land to Georgia, abrogating a 1791 treaty between the United States and the Creeks which guaranteed the Creeks their land. Adams refused to enforce the 1825 treaty on the grounds that it was unconstitutional. Nevertheless, the governor of Georgia went ahead with Indian removal plans. In 1827 another treaty was signed in which the Creeks yielded their claims. Their power broken by the war of 1810–18, the Creeks realized they could not continue their struggle. In 1821 the Spanish ceded Florida to the United States, thus opening the way for the incorporation of Florida and other Indian lands east of the Mississippi into the American state system. In any case, President Adams' administration was not popular with the Southerners, especially the Georgians. Nor was it popular with the Jacksonians who supported Jackson's view that the land east of the Mississippi belonged to the United States, not the Indians.

The elections of 1828 brought Andrew Jackson to the presidency on a wave of populism, sweeping aside elite control of presidential politics. His victory was widely interpreted as a signal of change: "Everyone agreed—the opposition included—that something extraordinary had happened. Not all would accept Jackson's interpretation of his election but they did acknowledge that something unique in the annals of American politics had occurred."[7]

The campaign of 1828 was bitter and full of personal attacks against both Adams and Jackson: "The campaign left an aftermath of ill feeling, an extreme contrast with the so-called good feelings that had followed Monroe's first election. Not long after Jackson's victory at the polls, his wife died and he blamed her death upon his political opponents . . . and embittered him against his party foes."[8]

The Jacksonian presidency was marked by major domestic policy issues such as the Bank issue, tariff policy, nullification, the spoils system, the Missouri Compromise, and another economic panic. These were accompanied by important changes in politics and demographic patterns. In addition, the westward movement continued unabated, while relationships with foreign countries reflected a brashness evolving from uncertainty and a newfound sense of American nationhood.

Although most of the Second Seminole War took place during the Martin Van Buren presidency, it was during Jackson's administration that Indian policies were set and were to be followed throughout Van Buren's tenure and into the Tyler Administration. Moreover, it was during Jackson's second term that serious questions emerged regarding military leadership and operations in Florida. This set the tone for the succeeding years.

Jackson's vigorous pursuit of the Indian removal policy was motivated primarily by his view that the states had sovereign rights in controlling their own land and inhabitants. Combined with his tendency to perceive the actions of government from a Western perspective, Jackson felt that the best method to deal with the Indians was to remove them from areas of confrontation with Americans. His own military operations against the Creeks a decade earlier left little doubt that he had little use for those who stood in the way of the exercise of legitimate government power— but this was viewed primarily in terms of the power of the individual state. Yet, it is also clear that Jackson considered the power of the individual states subordinate to the maintenance of the Union. In light of other major national issues that emerged during the Jacksonian presidency, the issue of Indian removal was considered a foregone conclusion and thus was a matter of implementation rather than serious debate. Most of the focus of American politics was on issues far removed from the Seminoles in Florida. The Second Seminole War did become a part of the national political scene, but this was primarily a result of its connection to other major issues and to criticism of the administration for its lack of aggressive prosecution of the war.

Van Buren was Jackson's hand-picked successor. Serving earlier as Jackson's secretary of state, Van Buren had become a staunch Jacksonian. He won election as vice-president in 1832, thereby becoming "heir apparent,"[9] and he was the Democratic nominee for president in 1836. When Jackson retired to the quiet of "Hermitage" near Nashville in 1837, he left the Democrats and Van Buren with economic problems that led to the depression and great panic of 1837. During the next four years Van Buren grappled with these economic problems. Much of the country's attention was also on these issues, and little serious thought was given to the consequence of the policy in Florida.

Although financial hard times worked to the disadvantage of the Democrats, the Whigs' campaign strategy in 1840 was the real basis for the victory of their candidate William Henry Harrison. Stressing the concern for the common man and Harrison's hero image, the Whigs were able to charge that the Democrats and Van Buren were insensitive aristocrats living in White House splendor.[10] It did not help the Democrats that Van Buren ran on his record, which included a statesman-like approach and a long-range solution to the country's financial problems rather than immediate and politically expedient solutions. Interestingly enough, the Second Seminole War had little impact on the 1840 presidential election.

The end of the Seminole War was proclaimed during the Tyler Administration. (Tyler had been sworn in as president after Harrison's death in office.) Again, policy matters other than the Indians in Florida occupied the attention of national leaders. The Second Seminole War appeared to slowly die out with a whimper by 1842.

PRESIDENTIAL LEADERSHIP

Andrew Jackson's style of leadership, his personality, character, and perceptions of the presidential role, did much to strengthen the efforts and spur the removal of Indians east of the Mississippi. Views regarding Andrew Jackson as a man vary. There appears to be a consensus, however, that, although lacking in formal education and generally viewed as a frontier character awash in a sea of uncouth frontiersmen, Jackson was a complicated man, and his mind was shrewd:

Nor was Jackson quite the roughhewn frontier character he sometimes seemed. He could not spell (again, like Washington), he possessed the unsavory habits of tobacco chewer, and he had a violent temper. But his manners were those of a southern planter, his judgment intuitive but usually sound. Even his reputation for unbridled irascibility was not really deserved. His frequent rages were often feigned—designed to accomplish some carefully thought-out purpose.[11]

Jackson brought to the presidency a commitment to equality of opportunity; he had a deep mistrust of privileged status and of those entrenched in power. This was reflected in his struggle against the Bank of the United States and its director, Nicholas Biddle, whom he considered one of those entrenched in power against the public good. Thus, as Remini concludes, "if Jacksonian Democracy means anything at all, the definition must begin with what the Democrats believed was a crusade against political and economic privilege. The principle—and Jacksonians were committed to it as principle—was incessantly repeated."[12]

Jackson also had a deep mistrust of strong central government, convinced that states were the proper focus of most governmental activity. Nevertheless, he was committed to the Union. During the nullification crisis, he responded to South Carolina's attempts to nullify acts of the federal government (and threats of secession) by declaring "The Union will be preserved." Yet, Alexis de Tocqueville sees in Jackson an individual sensitive to the views of the mass of people:

Not that he is by nature either weak or hostile to the Union; once the majority had pronounced against the pretensions of the southern nullifiers, we have seen him put himself at its head, clearly and energetically formulating the doctrines it professed and being first to appeal to force. General Jackson, if I may use terms borrowed from the vocabulary of American parties, seems to me *federal* by taste and *republican* by calculation.[13]

In foreign affairs, Jackson vigorously pursued a policy based on nationalistic self-interest, bordering on brashness. Although he succeeded in concluding favorable trade agreements with Great Britain and in pressuring the French to resolve claims dating back to the Napoleonic Wars, he was viewed by foreign states as an arrogant leader of a country that "was a rash young country with a chip on its shoulders and pathologically mistrustful of the good faith of other powers."[14] Yet, his dealings with foreign powers reinforced the view held by most Americans that he was a strong leader. These convictions and behavior were a reflection of Jackson's personality and character. Attuned to the vigorous life of a frontiersman—a man of action—Jackson did not hesitate to vigorously pursue a particular policy once he decided on its necessity. But this was not based on a precipitous, spur-of-the-moment reaction; rather, it was generally a deliberate and carefully formulated policy.

Jackson was a man of action and impulse, and no one would claim that he was an original thinker. . . . It is equally evident that Jackson was an astute leader who consulted widely on matters of policy and politics. He sought aid from cabinet members, noncabinet officials, members of Congress, and friends and acquaintances outside of government. His advisory system was flexible, pragmatic, and perfectly consonant with his determination to control his administration.

. . . Throughout his presidency, Jackson sought counsel from western advisers and displayed a concern for maintaining western strength in the Democratic party. Moreover, to some degree western experiences shaped the programs and rhetoric of his administration, particularly its concern for the farming and mechanic population and its endorsement of hard-money, anti-banking, and egalitarian principles.[15]

In his exercise of presidential power and his vigorous prosecution of his policies, Jackson created a number of enemies. Although he had wide popular support bordering on adoration (some called it charisma), there were those who strongly opposed him for fear of executive despotism and tyranny.[16]

Although Van Buren, Jackson's successor, remained closely wedded to Jackson's politics, his personality differed considerably from that of his predecessor.[17] Recognized for his brilliance as a politician, Van Buren was also known for his statesmanship. By being cautious in his political activities, he remained flexible and independent in dealing with special interest groups. Van Buren was pragmatic in his approach, although he considered himself a Jeffersonian committed to the idea that state, rather than federal action, was in keeping with "good" government.

Nonetheless, Van Buren was widely known for his evasiveness. Even when he decided on a course of action, he tended to avoid taking a stand in public. With his unimposing figure and inability to project an image of a determined and strong leader, his administration became a shadow of the Jacksonian presidency. Indeed, according to Julius W. Muller, even Van Buren himself realized he had been a "colourless successor" to Jackson.[18]

POLITICAL RESOLVE AND NATIONAL WILL

As we have seen, the Jacksonian period was characterized by a great deal of political and social change, as the country developed a sense of nationalism and shed its revolutionary past. While there was much disagreement and political debate over domestic issues (particularly those issues related to the nature of the Union), the general feeling was that the United States was growing stronger and needed to exercise its power and strength, particularly over its own territory. This attitude combined with Jackson's popularity provided the basis for a determined pursuit of an Indian removal policy. Criticism of this policy did emerge but was based more on lack of effective implementation than on the substance of policy. Others used the Indian removal policy as a way of attacking Jacksonian domestic policies, with little real concern for the plight of the Indians.

This is not to say that the Indian removal policy was totally obscured by other issues. Debate over such policy was usually addressed in terms of broader issues, and not the specifics of the Indian problem. In the main, Jackson's Indian policy was rationalized in constitutional terms, based on states' rights. As de Tocqueville observed,

The constitution gave the Union the privilege of treating with foreign peoples. The Union had generally considered the Indian tribes bordering its territory from this point of view. So long as the savages agreed to fly before civilization, this federal right was not contested; but as soon as an Indian tribe attempted to fix its residence on any given spot, the adjacent states claimed possession of the land a right of sovereignty over the people living there. The central government hurriedly recognized both claims, and whereas it used to treat with the Indians as with independent peoples, it then handed them over as subjects to the legislative tyranny of the states.[19]

Using the Seminole War as a case in point, abolitionists argued that the Southerners were able to get the United States to commit its forces against the Seminoles in order to defeat the Indians and return slaves to their rightful owners, the Southerners. Georgians and Southerners countered that slaves were the rightful property of slaveowners. According to many Southerners, not only had the Seminoles deprived white men of their property, but also their continued presence along the borders of Georgia and Florida constituted a threat to civilized society.

Although Van Buren was elected president rather easily in 1836, things were different in 1840. The Panic of 1837 had serious economic consequences for business and workers. Regional tensions increased, differences between workers and management surfaced, and a host of social issues emerged. Hundreds of banks failed, workers lost jobs, and bankruptcies occurred in many businesses and in agriculture. The depression was a key issue in the election of 1840. While the Seminole War was incidental, it was used as a basis to criticize the administration for extravagance and incompetence in the war effort. In combination with a variety of other major issues, the conduct of the Seminole War emerged as a campaign issue.

The Whigs swept into power with William Henry Harrison, who died in office exactly one month after he was inaugurated. John Tyler, the vice-president, moved into the president's office. Only later was it clear that Tyler was more a Democrat than a Whig. In any case, in 1842 Colonel William Worth, then in command in Florida, was told to bring the warfare in Florida to an end. In August 1842 he declared the end of hostilities, although they continued sporadically through 1843.

Standard treatments of the Jacksonian era have very little to say about the Second Seminole War and the Indian removal policy. Their focus is on Jackson's excursions into Florida during the Creek Wars rather than on his administration's policies and programs regarding the Indians.

This emphasis is perhaps to be expected, for, as noted earlier, the major events of the Jacksonian period had little to do with the Seminole Indians. The greatest concerns of the Jackson presidency were the general state of the American economy, the new politics, and especially the westward movement, which became an ingrained part of the American psyche:

There was nothing new about the westward movement. That was part of a larger American experience. What was special to the Jacksonian era was the rationalization applied to it by spokesmen of the Democratic party. John L. O'Sullivan's phrase about "Manifest Destiny" was quickly adopted by most expansionists who blithely insisted that the country had some sort of divine right to lands claimed by Indians, Mexicans and British.[20]

Two major pieces of legislation reflected Jackson's attitude toward the Indians and established a policy that ultimately sparked the Second Seminole War. Jackson's commitment to the Union, his Western-oriented perceptions regarding Indians, and his view of the power and sovereignty of the individual states were the basis for the passage of the Indian Removal Act of 1830, and later the Indian Intercourse Act of 1834. The earlier act was designed to exchange tribal lands east of the Mississippi for lands west of the Mississippi. The later act marked off Indian lands and provided for the establishment of a series of forts which would keep the Indians inside their lands and the white men outside. The president was instrumental in the passage of these bills and in use of the Army to force the movement of Indians across the Mississippi.

Jackson's attempt to pass the Indian Removal Act of 1830 sparked the first major battle of his administration. The battle in the Congress was generated more by the issue of federal versus state power than by concern over Indians. Nevertheless, Jackson's opponents, even some from within the Jacksonian ranks, argued against the coercive aspects of the plan and criticized the Southerners' motives. Moreover, fears of executive dominance surfaced during the debates on the bill.

Part of the complexity of the Indian Removal Act stemmed from its linkage to the Maysville Road bill, which Jackson vetoed. The Maysville bill provided for federal government involvement in constructing a road from Maysville to Lexington in the state of Kentucky. It was expected that the federal government would buy stock in a corporation planning to construct the road. The Democratic party was split on the bill. Most Southerners were opposed to it because it would lead to expanded federal power. Democrats from the West supported the bill as a measure that would provide better transportation and assist the economy. Jackson's commitment to the sovereignty of states dictated his veto of the bill. Moreover, he felt that the bill unconstitutionally expanded federal power, that the project was uneconomical, and that there was no real basis for federal involvement in internal improvements.[21]

The Indian Removal Act was passed by the Congress where it received most of its support from the Southeast, Southwest, and West. Even in those areas that opposed the bill such as New England, several states did vote in favor, for example, New Hampshire and New York. The debates over the Maysville Road spilled over into the debates over the Indian removal policy.

To prevent reaction over the Maysville issue from affecting support of his Indian policy, Jackson maneuvered the Indian removal policy bill to the forefront. Voting on it first, Congress passed the bill before turning its attention to the Maysville bill. It was passed but was vetoed by Jackson. In any case, the arguments over the Maysville Road bill as well as the Indian policy were rooted in the concern over the extent of executive power and federal versus state power: "Whatever the Indians' fate in the West, however, Jackson was adamant that the states had full sovereignty over their lands and population, and that the central government must protect this right even if it meant reducing its power in areas where some claimed it could act legitimately."[22]

The policy of the Jackson Administration regarding Indian removal is well expressed in the following instructions from Secretary of War John H. Eaton to Generals William Carroll and John Coffee dated May 30, 1829.

Sir: A crisis in our Indian affairs has arrived. Strong indications are seen of this in circumstances of the Legislatures of Georgia and Alabama extending their laws over Indians within their respective limits. These acts, it is reasonable to presume, will be followed by the other States interested in those portions of their soil now in the occupancy of the Indians. In the right to exercise such jurisdiction the Executive of the United States fully concurs; and this has been officially announced to the Cherokee Indians. The President is of the opinion that the only mode left for the Indians to escape the effects of such enactments, and consequences more destructive and which are consequent on their contiguity to the whites, is *for them to emigrate*.
. . . The President views the Indians as the children of the Government. He sees [sic] what is best for them; and that a perseverance in their refusal to fly dangers that surround them, must result in their misery, and final destruction.[23]

Yet, there is some disagreement regarding Jackson's views of the Indians. While he may have felt that the only way for the Indians to survive was to migrate, there appears little question that he viewed the Indians with prejudice as did many Westerners of that time.[24] Jackson's actions immediately following the War of 1812 and his influence with President Monroe regarding an Indian policy clearly show his "Western" thinking on Indian matters. Thus, he came to the presidency with clearly established views on what to do with the Indians, and he followed a policy of removal that coincided with his earlier actions.

Following the War of 1812, Jackson was involved in a number of Indian treaty negotiations and had a major role in determining federal Indian policy. He influenced President Monroe's dealings with the Indians, arguing that national security dictated the removal of Indians to the West and concentrating smaller tribes in the East. He felt it necessary to have civilized society replace areas controlled by the "savages." Thus, by the time Jackson became president, Indian removal had become a well-established American policy.[25]

This policy provoked a number of clashes with the Indians following

Jackson's election as President. The Black Hawk War of 1832 resulted in the slaughtering of Sac and Fox Indians by militiamen and Regulars. The defeat of the Creeks was followed by the Second Seminole War. The Cherokees in Georgia were also deprived of their homelands. Unlike most other Indian tribes, the Cherokees were considered a civilized people with a written language and a settled way of life. After great pressure by Georgians to remove them, the Cherokees appealed to the Supreme Court, and in two cases Chief Justice John Marshall upheld the Cherokees' contention that the lands in Georgia belonged to the Cherokee Nation. This brought a now classic retort by President Jackson: "John Marshall has made the decision; now let him enforce it."[26] In the end the Cherokees were coerced into signing a treaty and eventually were moved to Oklahoma at bayonet point. A number fled into North Carolina where they were finally given a reservation.

These policies and programs made it clear that the federal government intended to clear the land east of the Mississippi of Indians or at least gain total control of all lands occupied by the Indians. The Seminoles in Florida proved to be the greatest challenge to this policy. Congress and the country appeared to approve of these Indian removal policies. As expected, in the South and Southwest, the policy received strong support since it promised to rid the area of a population that was considered inferior and an obstacle to the white man's advancement. Moreover, Jackson's view that the states had sovereignty over their own lands and population nurtured the idea of states' power and lessened the fear of a tyrannical central government. Yet, some historians consider Indian removal policy to be unique in the Jacksonian era. As Richard B. Latner notes, "Indian removal stands apart from most of Jackson's other programs. . . . Jackson seems to have treated Indian removal as distinct from the general impulse of his presidency to restore Jeffersonian principles to government."[27]

Jackson and his supporters, convinced that removal of the Indians was the only realistic policy, pursued it vigorously. This was reflected not only in his use of the military to subjugate the Seminoles in Florida, but also in what Jackson's administration accomplished in the overall impact of his Indian policy. By the end of Jackson's eight years in office, Latner reports that "the United States ratified some seventy treaties and acquired about 100 million acres of Indian land at a cost of approximately 68 million dollars and 32 million acres of land in the West."[28] Throughout these eight years, Jackson received a great deal of public support for his Indian policy, which allowed him to pursue policies and programs in Florida that were relatively free from serious civilian oversight. Although domestic criticism emerged, much of it revolved around the perceived lack of vigorous pursuit of Indian removal.

Van Buren continued Jackson's policy of trying to subdue and then remove the Seminoles from Florida. Again, most of the national attention during his administration was on other issues, considered to be more important. In any case, the policy established during the Jacksonian period with respect to the Seminoles continued throughout the Van Buren and Tyler administrations.

In his Second Annual Message in 1838 Van Buren devoted most of his attention to domestic economic issues, but he did note the problems of the Second Seminole War.

The case of the Seminoles constitutes at present the only exception to the successful efforts of the Government to remove the Indians to the homes assigned them west of the Mississippi. . . . The continued treacherous conduct of these people; the savage and unprovoked murders they have lately committed, butchering whole families of the settlers of the territory without distinction of age or sex, and making their way into the very center and heart of the country, so that no part of it is free from their ravages . . . leave the Government no alternatives but to continue the military operations against them until they are totally expelled from Florida.[29]

In his Fourth Annual Message on December 5, 1840, Van Buren referred in greater length to the Seminole problem. After reviewing the history of the American response to the Seminoles, Van Buren concluded:

The Indians having been defeated in every engagement, dispersed in small bands throughout the country and became an enterprising, formidable, and ruthless bandit. . . . hostilities have been renewed throughout the whole of the territory. . . . we must look for the causes which have so long procrastinated the issue of the contest in the vast extent of the theater of hostilities, the almost insurmountable obstacles presented by the nature of the country, the climate, and the wily character of the savages.[30]

Americans adopted a tolerant attitude and supported the military operations against the Indians. Indeed, such operations were not an unusual feature of domestic politics; they accompanied territorial expansion and were considered acceptable political occurrences. As we will see later in this volume, the military was relatively free to pursue tactical operations and adopt military methods, which in modern terms might be considered contrary to established democratic norms.

SOCIOECONOMIC PATTERNS

Social and economic changes during the Jacksonian era paralleled and were linked to the changing pattern of national politics. The dramatic changes in political outlook fostered by the Panic of 1819 were reinforced by the expanding population and the extension of the franchise. In 1790

Table 1
U.S Population Growth and Characteristics, 1790-1840

Year	Total	Urban	Rural
1790	3.9	0.2	3.7
1800	5.3	0.3	5.0
1820	9.6	0.7	8.9
1840	17.1	1.8	15.2

Source: U.S. Bureau of the Census, Bicentennial
       Statistics (Washington, D.C.: Government
       Printing Office, 1976).

the population of the United States was almost 4 million. By 1820 this figure was almost 10 million, and by 1830 the population had reached 13 million. A decade later (1840), the population stood at about 17 million. In a period of fifty years the population of the United States had more than quadrupled (see Table 1).

With the expanding population, there was an upsurge in the economy. But the third decade of the nineteenth century found most Americans living on farms or in small towns. While the roots of industrialism had taken hold, most products were still made by craftsmen supervising small numbers of apprentices. The United States remained a nation of farmers and a great many property owners.[31]

Western lands were open for homesteading, attracting settlers from the East. This movement not only pushed the frontier farther west, but it also brought the inevitable conflicts between Indians and white men. This westward migration was matched by the move to towns and cities—the first signs of an urbanization process in America. At the same time there was great improvement in the communications system. New roads and railroads were being constructed, and there was an increase in inland waterways traffic as new canals were opened.[32]

In the North and Northeast, the bases for industrialization and commercialization were being developed. The Northwest was in the process of developing a great agricultural area, while the South's economy became increasingly dominated by the cotton and slave economy. Many other social changes were occurring, which had an impact on political affairs:

Certain social changes also reflect a new way of looking at political affairs. The final disestablishment of churches . . . the beginnings of the free school movement, the earliest glimmerings of interest in adult education, the slow spread of secondary education. . . . The rapid increase in the number of newspapers. . . and their ever greater concentration on political affairs. . . . All these changes emphasized the idea that every citizen was equally important.[33]

Table 2
Federal Receipts, Expenditures, 1789-1840 (in millions of dollars)

Year	Receipts	Expenditures Total	Defense
1789-91	4.4	4.3	0.6
1795	6.1	7.5	2.9
1800	10.8	10.8	6.0
1810	9.4	8.2	3.9
1820	17.9	18.3	7.0
1830	24.8	15.1	8.0
1840	19.5	24.3	13.2

Source: U.S. Bureau of the Census, Bicentennial
        Statistics (Washington, D.C.: U.S. Government
        Printing Office, 1976).

As John A. Garrity concludes, Andrew Jackson was the first product of this new system to become president: "He was chosen because he was popular, not because he was experienced in government."[34]

Accompanying the economic and social ferment, and the changing nature of politics, was a growth in the federal government. While this growth may appear minor in comparison with the size of the federal government in modern times, it was nevertheless important, particularly when one considers the fact that federal expenditures more than doubled over a ten-year period (see Table 2) and the federal bureaucracy more than doubled in slightly more than a ten-year period (see Table 3). Thus, during the Jacksonian era the role of the federal government increased, and the federal bureaucracy began to overshadow local and state sys-

Table 3
The Growth of Federal Civilian Employment, 1816-1841 (in thousands)

Year	Total	Executive	Legislative
1816	5	5	x
1821	7	7	x
1831	12	11	x
1841	18	18	1

x = fewer than 500.

Source: U.S. Bureau of the Census, Bicentennial
        Statistics (Washington, D.C.: Government
        Printing Office, 1976).

Note: Data for legislative includes judicial.

tems. The federal government also provided a more powerful weapon to the president to implement his policies.

SUMMARY

Convinced of the need to gain control over Indian lands east of the Mississippi, Jackson was instrumental in passing the Indian Removal Act and in setting the stage for the Second Seminole War. These policies continued through the administration of Martin Van Buren, Jackson's hand-picked successor. Van Buren had little time to formulate alternate policies in Florida inasmuch as the economic problems stemming from the Panic of 1837, his struggles with Congress, and the 1840 election campaign absorbed his administration. Most of the military strategy and tactics used against the Seminoles were already well established by the time he took office. It was during his administration, however, that tactics developed which ultimately led to the official end of hostilities.

Although the Seminole issue did emerge periodically in political debates, it was primarily as an adjunct to other national issues. For all practical purposes there was no serious public debate on the Seminoles; rather, there was a narrow sectional interest in pursuing an aggressive policy to remove the Indians from Florida. This policy was supported by the general Southern view that the Seminoles were harboring fugitive slaves. Americans were relatively unconcerned about the Seminoles. Most supported the actions of the Jackson Administration in trying to remove the Indians and in conducting military operations to clear Florida. Jackson justified the Indian removal policy on both constitutional and humanitarian grounds. A deeper political issue was also involved in his Indian policy: removal of the Seminoles from Florida would also remove the major reason for antagonism between his administration and many Southerners. The emotions that developed over the slavery issue and the involvement of the Seminoles could be tempered by simply removing the tribes from Florida. Combined with Jackson's own attitude toward the Indians, these were compelling reasons to pursue an aggressive policy toward the Seminoles.

At the same time many changes were taking place in the socioeconomic structure of the United States. The end of the War of 1812 led to a break from the revolutionary past, developing a sense of American nationalism and an outpouring of energy toward commerce, industry, and westward expansion. Furthermore, the population had quadrupled since 1800, and the urban population had increased from about 300,000 to over 1.5 million. America was well on its way to commercialization, industrialization, and urbanization.

From the end of the Second Seminole War to the Civil War, most domestic issues were associated with the slavery problem. Although the

Mexican-American War in the middle of the century shifted attention to the Southwest and foreign intervention, the slavery issue quickly regained the spotlight. As a variety of alternatives were debated, discussed, and hotly discarded, the nation creeped closer to conflict. One manifestation of the slavery issue was nullification, the same issue Jackson had dealt with in his administration. The Civil War seemed to settle the issue of union and slavery once and for all. As we will see in the following sections, other major political, social, and economic problems soon emerged.

THE SPANISH-AMERICAN WAR AND THE BEGINNINGS OF EMPIRE

The Spanish-American War has been called "the splendid little war" by a number of American historians. As T. Harry Williams has written, "to all Americans with the possible exception of the enlisted men who fought it, it was almost an ideal war."[35] This was true with respect to both the geopolitical character of the war and the humanitarian motivations. However, what started as a seemingly moralistic and simple affair for the United States ended with major implications for international politics. The United States became a world power, and Spain lost its colonies and status in the Old World. For the United States, this was accomplished with little effort and in a short period of time. No wonder it appeared to be a "splendid little war."[36]

If we limit the official period of the war with Spain to the years 1898 and 1899, then we can agree with the general view that the war was indeed splendid and little. However, a broader perspective shows that the war extended from 1898 until 1914, with the enemy being variously the Spanish, the Filippinos, and the Moros. As will be seen in the following examination, it was more complex, longer, and more costly than most people assume.

POLITICS AND POLICY ISSUES

The post-Civil War period witnessed political, economic, and social changes which pushed America onto the world stage. The last years of the nineteenth century saw the culmination of deep-seated changes within the American system. In addition, new currents of intellectual thought and military strategy provided a rationale for America's involvement in world affairs. This period also brought to the presidency a leader whose strength of personality had not been seen since Abraham Lincoln, a leader who was committed to the outward projection of American power.

After the end of the Civil War, national attention focused on Reconstruction and the consolidation of federal control over all areas in the country. The end of the Civil War also brought with it the entry of the United States into an industrial and agricultural revolution which laid the groundwork for modern America. In the political arena, there were two major developments: the resurgence of congressional power and the relative equilibrium between the two major parties. During Reconstruction, Congress dominated the executive, with the Senate being the more powerful body. Although the Democrats had been badly hurt by the Civil War and Reconstruction, they remained a viable party and easily won many congressional elections. The Republican party thrived at the national level and held the presidency for most of the period after the Civil War.

The relative balance between parties in their struggle over control of the Congress made it necessary for each to court a variety of interest groups and to form various coalitions. Yet, each party had its consistent supporters: the Republicans were supported by Union veterans, freed slaves, Northern industrial and commercial interests, Midwest farmers, and Protestants, while the Democrats received most of their support from the "Solid South" and immigrants (who were ignored by Anglo-Saxon oriented party workers). The Democrats became a party of protest: they opposed high tariffs and favored cheap money.[37]

By the 1880s, however, the excesses and ineptitude of the Grant Administration, together with the Democrats' increased strength, made it appear that Republican rule was at an end. In the presidential election of 1876 both parties in the Southern states applied pressure on freed slaves to vote one way or another. After conflicting election returns, the whole issue was referred to an electoral commission which finally declared Rutherford B. Hayes, the Republican candidate, president. This choice was accepted only after Republican leaders and conservative Democrats struck a deal, the Compromise of 1877, which provided for the withdrawal of American troops from the remainder of the Southern states if the Democrats accepted Hayes as president. During the following years, attention was focused on a variety of domestic issues such as civil service reform, the tariff, problems of inflation, and machine politics.

For most, the Hayes Administration was a failure. Convinced that the best way to perform his duties as president was to take a noncontroversial posture, Hayes adopted a caretaker approach on the assumption that Congress was the main actor on the national stage. The administration of James Garfield followed. He was in office only four months before being shot and killed by an assassin. Within that short period, Garfield had already been seen as an ineffective and vacillating leader. Chester A. Arthur assumed the duties of the presidency and to the surprise of most Republicans and Democrats proved to be a reasonably effective president. Nevertheless, he alienated many reformers within the Republican party because of his moderate stand on the tariff and because of his attempt to regulate the railroad industry.

In the 1884 presidential election the Democrat Grover Cleveland and the Republican James G. Blaine became involved in a mudslinging campaign. But the populace tired of the Republicans, and Cleveland's perceived honesty gave the Democrats a narrow presidential victory.[38] Cleveland's first administration was reasonably effective, but he did not appear to be a "strong" president. He viewed the presidency in narrow terms and felt that the exercise of federal power was limited by both constitutional and congressional prerogatives. Faced with strong pressures from the Democrats for patronage and their demands for lowering the tariff, Cleveland did as well as could be expected. He did not throw Republican officeholders out simply because of their political affiliation, and he attempted to reduce the tariff. The House of Representatives controlled by the Democrats passed a lower tariff, but it was rejected by the Republican-controlled Senate. Perhaps the major impact of Cleveland's first administration was in focusing public attention on the tariff and making this a major issue between the two parties.

Thus, the election of 1888 was the first election since the Civil War which was fought on specific issues. Not only the difference in economic status between the parties but also the tariff issue was stressed. This campaign was one of the most corrupt in American history, and both parties engaged in a variety of fraudulent tactics. What seemed to outrage most Americans, however, was the publication of a letter by the British minister in Washington that Cleveland's reelection would favor the British. In any case, the Republicans regained the presidency, and Benjamin Harrison, the grandson of President William Henry Harrison, was elected. This victory was achieved with the help of the votes of Civil War veterans who were incensed over Cleveland's veto of veterans' pensions.

Harrison's conservative approach to fiscal policy led to high tariffs but to few other changes. As T. Harry Williams, et al., state, Harrison and Cleveland had a good deal in common: "Both were politicians of a transitional age that was about to end. Neither understood the rumblings of protest that would shortly shake both urban and rural America."[39]

Cleveland returned to the presidency after the 1892 election, but his second administration was a disaster and set the stage for the return of the Republicans. As noted earlier, one of the major political thrusts after the Civil War was the power of Congress and its dominance over the presidency. With the election of Cleveland in 1892, some felt that the chief executive still had too much power.[40]

The devastating depression of 1893 and the continuing controversy over financial issues combined with the rise of protest groups eroded the strength of the Democratic party. What was particularly damaging to the party was Cleveland's apparent blunders with respect to policy and administrative processes, especially in trying to come to grips with patronage and a variety of economic issues. His policies increasingly alienated members of the Democratic party. These political forces together with the major social changes taking place in the country were beyond the ability of the Cleveland Administration; they changed the character of American politics in the last decade of the nineteenth century.[41]

In the years following the Civil War until the 1880s, the presidency was dominated by the Republican party, and there were few apparent differences between the two major parties. As each party became focused on geographical and economic distinctions, the relative party balance in Congress and the similarity in platforms disappeared and the parties began to battle over specific issues. Although the Republicans came to power in 1889, "the voters unhappy with activism and the threat of higher prices, responded with a crushing defeat for the GOP in the congressional elections of 1890."[42] Campaign rhetoric and issues rarely included foreign policy issues, reflecting a lack of concern for what was going on beyond the borders. There were, of course, some exceptions to this generalization, particularly with respect to the Northern Hemisphere.

The Republican party went into the campaign of 1896 with high hopes. The political environment favored their party. Cleveland's second administration had proved disastrous to the Democratic party, and it had raised a storm of protest in the South and West, particularly among farmers. Cleveland's stand against silver and the confused tariff issue simply exacerbated the situation. The congressional election of 1894, won easily by the Republicans, was a sign of things to come.

By 1896 economic and social issues divided the parties, and changes within the country forced sectional and regional issues into the political arena. A political climate previously dominated by business and industrial interests was now being challenged by labor issues. Reinforced by intellectual currents and the end of the frontier, Americans began to look beyond their continent.

The see-saw battle for control of the presidency from 1884 to 1896, the nature of the political campaigns, and the quality of presidential leadership seem to confirm the conclusions of a number of historians that there was no effective presidential leadership from the time of Lincoln until Theodore Roosevelt. The problems of such leadership were compounded by the dominance of Congress, particularly the Senate, over national matters and the dramatic economic and social changes taking place within the country.

The election of 1896 was probably the most important since 1860. It produced new political alignments and raised politics to high emotional levels. It also created an environment and a political orientation which thrust the United States into the world arena. The dramatic internal changes led to protests and changes in the political system, spilled over into the foreign arena, and were, in no small measure, the basis for America's muscle flexing and involvement in the Spanish-American War.

William Jennings Bryan, the Democratic choice for president, proved to be a strong opponent and carried on a campaign that eroded much of the Republican advantage. Bryan, fighting on a platform of free silver and opposition to the protective tariff, flayed at the Republicans and their candidate, William McKinley. According to T. Harry Williams, "There never has been a campaign like the one in 1896. It had unequalled drama, intense excitement, a clean-cut issue, and a David and Goliath theme: the boy orator Bryan contending against the powerful boss Hannah."[43]

McKinley's victory in the presidential election of 1896 opened a long period of Republican control of the White House. He won by putting together a coalition of the urban North, farmers, industrial workers, and ethnic groups.[44] He received over 7 million popular votes to his opponent's 6.5 million, with over 78 percent of the eligible voters actually voting. During his administration, a number of important domestic policy issues emerged. But in contrast to Jackson, McKinley had to deal with major foreign policy issues and a foreign war that resulted in the overnight acquisition of colonies. Domestic politics limited the presidential policy options, particularly in the area of race relations, labor regulations, banking and currency, civil service, and trusts.[45] At the same time, a great deal of McKinley's time and energy had to be devoted to the Spanish-American War and the subsequent Philippine-American War.

From the War of 1812 to almost the end of the nineteenth century, Americans remained relatively isolated from world affairs. Most serious policy debates and interests were focused on continental expansion and consolidation and economic grwoth. Preoccupied with the industrial and agricultural revolution following the Civil War and a massive Western movement, Americans had little time or inclination to worry about the outside world. The outside world was viewed as old, worn-out, and run by a number of world powers who were imperialistic, monarchical, and unsympathetic towards America. Nevertheless, during the nineteenth century, America did venture into the outside world, particularly in the late years of the century. The early part of the century had seen the Louisiana purchase, President John Quincy Adams's struggle with the British and the Spanish over Florida, and President Jackson's handling of both Britain and France. Finally, the Monroe Doctrine became a major element of American foreign policy and led to an attempt to "police" Latin America, an area that many Americans felt was a North American rather than a foreign concern. During the latter half of the century, America engaged in serious negotiations with Russia and acquired Alaska in 1867; attempted to annex Hawaii; established trade relationships with Japan, China, and Korea; exhibited continuous concern about Spanish rule in Cuba; and, of course, was frequently involved with Mexico, including demanding the removal of French occupation troops following the Civil War.

Immediately after the Civil War, most Americans focused on domestic politics and gave little attention to the international scene. But by the time of the Cleveland presidency Americans had adopted a more international perspective.[46] Continental expansion had been virtually completed, and there was an increasing undercurrent of opinion regarding America's role in world politics. Indeed, when Cleveland rejected the Hawaiian treaty, members of Congress in both parties as well as the press criticized his actions. On the other hand, when Cleveland stood up to Great Britain in the dispute over Venezuela, he received strong bipartisan support.

Most historians consider the McKinley period as marking the end of the isolationist period in American foreign policy, although Americans were clearly becoming accustomed to focusing on foreign affairs even before McKinley's presidency and long before the Spanish-American War. The war and the McKinley Administration were instrumental in plunging America into world affairs. Aside from diplomacy and trade, a number of intellectual currents surfaced, rationalizing America's involvement in world affairs and in expansionist policies. Charles Darwin's *The Origin of the Species* (1859) followed by the *Descent of Man* (1871) advanced the theme of the "survival of the fittest." This theme was quickly applied to the environment in world politics and competition. Americans, with their self-perceived superior values and ability, easily adapted such a doctrine, since they were sure of their success as the fittest in the international arena. Darwin's concepts reinforced the concept of "manifest destiny" by which America felt it was destined to have a major role in world politics.

There were other reasons for this outward look. The imperialistic activities of European powers, particularly in Africa and the Far East, concerned Americans who felt that European control of these areas would deprive American commerce. Military and strategic arguments and theories were advanced in support of the new manifest destiny doctrine. Alfred Mahan's books on sea power had an important impact in rationalizing the outward projection of military power. His volumes, *The Influence of Sea Power Upon History* (1890) and *The Influence of Sea Power Upon the French Revolution and Empire* (1892), provided a military concept for developing a strong navy and acquiring colonies and coaling stations to support such a navy. Advocates of trade expansion looked upon a strong navy as a way of protecting American sea lanes and fostering trade.

American contempt for Europe and support of the Cuban revolution against Spain provided a focal point for galvanizing all of the currents regarding foreign affairs and American expansionism.[47] The completion of American expansion in the continent provided a natural base to look outwards. As early as the John Quincy Adams Administration, territorial expansion and consolidation, and a major role in world affairs, were contemplated. Adams felt that the treaties with Great Britain following the War of 1812 would eventually lead to American expansion across the entire continent. The presence of European countries on the continent was, according to Adams, contrary to the natural order of things.[48]

The United States' acquisition of empire and its intervention in Latin America and the Philippines were not without its detractors. Although the anti-imperialists spoke out against American involvement, it was not until the Spanish-American War and America's acquisition of the Philippine Islands that the debate between imperialists and anti-imperialists became heated. After the defeat of Spain, treaty negotiations included the ceding of the Philippines to the United States for a sum of $20 million. It also became apparent that annexation would have to be accomplished by the use of force.

In November 1898 opponents to the treaty and to American intervention formed the Anti-Imperialist League. They unsuccessfully fought against the treaty, where it cleared the Senate by a narrow margin. After hostilities broke out between American and Filipino forces around Manila, the Anti-Imperialist League became active in publicizing American atrocities and the plight of the Filipino. Most revealing about the disagreements concerning America's role in the Philippines was the investigation launched by a Senate committee in 1902. Senator Albert J. Beveridge defended the administration's position:

We will not renounce our part in the mission of our race, trustees under God, of the civilization of the world. And we will move forward to our work, not howling our regrets like slaves whipped to their burdens, but with gratitude for a task worthy of our strength and thanksgiving to Almighty God that he has marked us as his chosen people, henceforth to lead in the regeneration of the world.[49]

The hearings, although closed to the public, later revealed the extent of American disagreement over its role in the Philippines. More important, it showed a deep division between the democratic ideals, acquisition of colonies, and involvement in counterrevolutionary operations:[50]

[The hearings,] showed the inherent awkwardness—to which most imperialists were blind—in seeking to impose the cultural outlook of the conqueror upon the conquered. . . . They show in lessons only partially learned at the time the severe limitations even of advanced military technology in cooling the molten nationalism then beginning to flow in non-industrial lands . . . the hearings reveal the deep conflict in the American mind between respect for republicanism and lust for imperium.[51]

PRESIDENTIAL LEADERSHIP

William McKinley brought to the presidential office a style of leadership and a personality and character whose impact on the presidency are still unclear. Initially, historians viewed McKinley as a weak, indecisive president, strongly influenced by Mark Hanna, who capitulated to a "yellow" press advocating war with Spain over Cuba and a hysterical public opinion demanding war. Later historians, however, have proposed that, on the contrary, McKinley was a "Machiavellian and cunning executive, bent on expansion and heedless of the interests of Cubans and Filipinos, whom Americans believed they were assisting."[52] A more sympathetic view has emerged. But according to one of McKinley's biographers, Lewis L. Gould, neither view is accurate:

Neither of these portrayals does justice to the complexity of the diplomatic problems that Spain and the United States encountered over Cuba between 1895 and 1898, and neither captures how McKinley sought, in the end unsuccessfully, to discover a way out of the impasse in which both nations found themselves.[53]

McKinley's handling of the Spanish-American War and the subsequent problems with the Filipinos suggest that the sympathetic view is closer to the truth. An examination of the conflict and the military posture of the United States later in this volume shows how complex the conflict was, belying the standard view of the Spanish-American War. Such an examination also points out the difficult decisions faced by the administration in coming to terms with Spain, while trying to respond to the demands of the Filipino nationalists.

Although McKinley's private world was, in the main, closed to public view, some people idolized him, primarily because of the way he handled personal tragedies. His wife was a virtual invalid, and two daughters died at a very early age. Many of these people considered McKinley a kindly, dignified gentleman who separated his private from his public life. McKinley had attained a sort of martyr status which he handled with sensitivity and reserve.[54]

McKinley has been variously seen as vacillating and weak or shrewd and cunning. He has been labeled cold and stoic as well as kind and understanding. He did have ambition and was keenly aware of the historical significance of the presidency. But, as Lewis L. Gould notes, "As a political leader, McKinley had the defects of his qualities. Charisma was not a concept that McKinley would have understood. . . . When McKinley died, his political approach disappeared, leaving large results but few traces of their architect."[55] Perhaps this was the essence of the leadership style. During a war which caught the imagination of many Americans and proved to be a dramatic turning point in American history, many sought a charismatic leader, one who could issue dramatic announcements of the moral quality of America's battles and one who could galvanize Americans into swift and determined action.

The McKinley Administration was at first glance moved more by journalistic urging and popular passions than by purposeful leadership. Yet, on closer examination, it is clear that there was purpose behind policies and a sense of what America's role should be in world affairs.

While the McKinley Administration was responsible for American policy during the Spanish-American War, the presidency of Theodore Roosevelt established policies toward the Philippines and was responsible for pacification of the islands. In his Annual Message to Congress in 1906, President Roosevelt spelled out his view of America's role in the Philippines. He considered America's role as beneficial to the area:

So far our action in the Philippines has been abundantly justified, not mainly and indeed not primarily because of the added dignity it has given us as a nation by proving that we are capable honorably and efficiently to bear the international burdens which a mighty people should bear, but even more because of the immense benefit that has come to the people of the Philippine Islands. In these islands we are steadily introducing both liberty and order, to a greater degree than their people have ever before known. We have secured justice.[56]

Roosevelt overlooked the law in the interest of achieving a particular end. Inherent in the office of the president, according to this view, was the prerogative to seek just ends whether or not the power to do so was in the Constitution or otherwise defined by law—a precedent set by President Lincoln.[57] Roosevelt felt that civilized nations had to use force in order to bring peace and civilization to the world: "In the long run civilized man finds he can keep the peace only by subduing his barbarian neighbor; for the barbarian will yield only to force . . . without force fair dealing usually amounts to nothing."[58]

While Roosevelt's foreign policy was not always resolute—reflecting the conflicts between political reality and his own sense of purpose and idealism—there was no question that Roosevelt favored a strong national defense posture. In this context, he easily justified America's role in world affairs. Roosevelt's personal life reflected much of his public posture. Socialized into a traditional value system, Roosevelt felt that an honorable and just man must perform his duty under obligations to his community and family:

Man was, or ought to be, a socially responsible being; and as such, his obligations to family, work, and community took precedence over his individualistic drives and wants. If there was a war, the responsible citizen was obliged to fight it. If there was a reform to be enacted, he was constrained to support it. If there was a corruption in government, he was bound to expose and destroy it.[59]

Many historians characterize Roosevelt as egotistical, at times ruthless, and aristocratic. That he was energetic, egregious, and dynamic in the performance of his duties is well documented. Roosevelt, in contrast to McKinley, was seen as knowing where he was going, cognizant of the role of Americans in the world, and aggressive in applying the power of the presidency in the interests of the United States. Throughout his life, Roosevelt admired men who were bold: "I felt a great admiration for men who were fearless and who could hold their own in the world, and I had a great desire to be like them."[60]

While presidential prerogative was the key to Roosevelt's presidency, his view on power was tempered considerably by his sense of justice, duty, and morality. These values and the drive for power were conditioned by the political realities, which Roosevelt viewed as the art of the possible.[61] In his dealings with the Philippine–American War, however, the sense of justice and power was based on the civilizing mission thrust upon the United States and, according to Roosevelt, justified American occupation and control of the Philippines. After he left office, Roosevelt gave his presidency a glowing evaluation:

When I left the Presidency I finished seven and a half years of administration, during which not one shot had been fired against a foreign foe. We were at absolute peace, and there was no nation in the world with whom a war cloud threatened, no nation in the world whom we had wronged, or from whom we had anything to fear. The cruise of the battle fleet was not the least of the causes which insured so peaceful an outlook.[62]

POLITICAL RESOLVE AND NATIONAL WILL

McKinley's diplomatic maneuvering and attempts to resolve the problems in Cuba peacefully have been well documented. While his efforts failed to prevent the Spanish-American War, he must be given credit for his valiant diplomatic efforts and his composure under tremendous pressure. The Cubans had been struggling against Spanish control sporadically for a number of years. Open revolt occurred in 1868, 1878, and again in 1895. American interest in Cuba was geopolitical as well as commercial. Its nearness to the United States and American sugar interests combined to make the Spanish colonial control over Cuba troublesome for the United States. This problem had plagued most presidents since the Civil War and had periodically inflamed public opinion. With the revolt against Spain in 1895, the situation in Cuba became particularly sensitive. The role of the press, "yellow journalism" as it has been popularly labeled, was in no small measure responsible for inflaming public opinion against Spain and for American intervention in Cuba.[63] Combined with America's antipathy towards European powers, particularly when such powers were active in the Northern Hemisphere, the efforts of the press and the pressures of public opinion soon made themselves felt in the Congress.

American involvement in Cuba did not become certain until two incidents which occurred within a few days of each other. The first was the publication in American newspapers of a letter from the Spanish minister Dupuy de Lome to Don Jose Canalejas, a Spanish editor on tour in the United States and Cuba. The letter stated that McKinley was "weak and a bidder for the admiration of the crowd, besides being a would-be politician who tries to leave a door open behind himself while keeping on good terms with the jingoes of his party." It fell into the hands of some Cubans and was turned over to the *New York Journal* for publication.[64] The letter was considered an insult to McKinley and was widely publicized as such in American newspapers. Under pressure from Washington, de Lome resigned and the Spanish government reluctantly issued a formal apology. Hoping that tensions between Spain and the United States would now be eased, McKinley returned to his diplomatic maneuvering to solve the problems in Cuba. A second incident took place within a week, however. The *U.S.S. Maine* was sunk in her dock at Havana. These two incidents sealed the course of action for the United States—war was inevitable, regardless of all of McKinley's strategies for a peaceful solution: "The de Lome letter and now the Maine shattered his following and coalesced his enemies. In his heart he knew that intervention was but a matter of time."[65]

The secretary of the navy ordered the formation of an official commission to investigate the sinking of the *U.S.S. Maine*. In the meantime the press, public opinion, and even members of McKinley's own cabinet were clamoring for war with Spain over the incident. McKinley cautioned against precipitous action and waited for the report of the official commission. The newspapers blamed McKinley for inaction, and the general public reviled him: "In Virginia a raging mob burned twin effigies of McKinley and Hanna. McKinley's picture was hissed in theaters and torn from walls in some cities."[66] The Republican party was up in arms over inaction, and McKinley's followers were fearful lest his own party turn against him. Congressional pressure increased for American intervention, even though the official commission's report concluded that the sinking of the *Maine* was an accident and did not clearly place the blame on Spain. Nevertheless, the public would not be dissuaded, and Congress had had enough of McKinley's apparent inaction. Strong measures were demanded.

McKinley's last diplomatic hope rested with a reasonable Spanish response to his protest against the *Maine* incident and his recommendations of cessation of hostilities in Cuba and mediation by the United States. When Spain rejected these last two recommendations, McKinley knew war was inevitable. In preparing for this war, he had to reconcile business interests which opposed intervention and public opinion which favored intervention. Noting his previous support of business interests and his commitment to prosperity, McKinley now prevailed on the business community to support him in Cuba. He succeeded.[67]

H. Wayne Morgan concludes that McKinley's inflexibility was partly responsible for America's involvement in Cuba and the ultimate war with Spain:

The real flaw in McKinley's diplomacy was not a lack of consistency or of courage, but a lack of imagination. Desiring peace more than anything else, he sought it by threatening war and chose to continue Cleveland's policy of ever increasing pressure against Spain, gambling that in the end she would give way rather than face war. Fearful of preceding public opinion . . . he stood against the current until the fateful point where his last alternative to war disappeared, and was then swept forward with the tide. The real flaw in his diplomacy was its lack of alternatives to ultimate intervention.[68]

The quick American victory over Spain and the relatively bloodless combat proved to be a blessing to the McKinley Administration, at least at the outset. There were, of course, a number of problems with the military services, which will be examined later in this chapter. But in terms of foreign policy, the larger problem for McKinley was what to do with the Filipino independence movement and the revolution that followed American occupation of the islands. With respect to the Philippines, McKinley leaned towards holding on to the islands and therefore sought support for that position.[69]

Debate regarding the Philippines took place not only in Congress and among the people, but also within the ranks of the U.S. Peace Commission. In an attempt to clarify and reinforce the president's position on the Philippines, Secretary of State John Hay wrote instructions to William Rufus Day, head of the American Peace Commission, which advocated American intervention there: "The sentiment in the United States is almost universal that the people of the Philippines whatever else is done, must be liberated from Spanish domination. In this sentiment the President fully concurs."[70]

There was less agreement as to what form liberating the Philippines from Spanish rule would take. The Anti-Imperialist League, which included some prominent men and women such as Andrew Carnegie, labor leader Samuel Gompers, Mark Twain, and Jane Addams, argued that acquisition of colonies by the United States was unconstitutional and contrary to the principles of the Declaration of Independence. Regardless of the motives of the Anti-Imperialists and a divided popular opinion, McKinley saw no viable alternatives but to annex the Philippines. He was supported in his views by the expansionists. The Darwinist argument and the military concepts of Mahan, combined with those of the "White Man's burden," underlined the outward thrust. In addition, there were concerns over trade advantages and protection of American shipping.

In examining the United States' acquisition of Puerto Rico, Hawaii, and the Philippines, Julius W. Pratt concludes that the United States' new role as a colonial power underscored its new world status:

These acquisitions did not cause Uncle Sam's assumption of new world responsibilities; rather, they were a result and a symbol of a new attitude toward the world. Had the United States not been ready to play a part as a world power, it would hardly have insisted upon keeping the Philippines.

The policies that the United States followed during the war and after it were precisely the policies that Admiral Mahan had been preaching throughout the 1890s.[71]

In the final analysis, while the McKinley Administration faced a number of domestic and world problems and may have vacillated on occasion, it continued the groundwork for a modern-day presidency. Moreover, the outward thrust that had been developing in the United States following the Civil War culminated in establishing the United States as a world power at the minimum cost of a "splendid little war":

Exactly one year before, McKinley had learned of the destruction of the *Maine*. In those twelve months the United States had struggled for peace, had won the war with Spain, and had gained an empire. . . . He transformed the presidential office from its late nineteenth-century weakness into a recognizable prototype of its present-day form.[72]

This brief overview of the state of the nation during the Spanish-American War period would not be complete without reference to the period immediately following the end of hostilities with Spain and the first decade of the twentieth century. This has been called the Progressive Era because historians perceive it as an era of change, improvement, and a new American view of the world. There is little agreement on the precise meaning of the Progressive Era, but it is almost unanimously seen as an exciting and significant period of American history. This period coincided with the presidency of Theodore Roosevelt whose view of the powers of the president helped develop a strong foreign policy thrust and strong leadership in domestic affairs. Most historians agree that Roosevelt brought to the presidency a type of leadership not seen since the days of Abraham Lincoln and Andrew Jackson. As Roosevelt himself has written, "The course I followed, of regarding the Executive as subject only to the people, and, under the Constitution, bound to serve the people affirmatively in cases where the Constitution does not explicitly forbid him to render the service, was substantially the course followed by both Andrew Jackson and Abraham Lincoln."[73]

While increased attention was given to foreign affairs, much of the concern of the Progressive Era was on domestic matters. Corruption and inefficiency in government, regulation of business, and welfare of the urban poor were the major underpinnings of Progressive policy. Yet, it was during the same period of time that Roosevelt received the Nobel Peace Prize for his mediation in the Russo-Japanese War. It was also a time of the "Open Door" policy in the Far East, of American involvement in an isthmian canal and in aggressive Caribbean diplomacy.

Roosevelt acknowledged that the annexations brought about by the Spanish-American War were the obligations and rights of the U.S. government. He further asserted that the principles of the Monroe Doctrine were essential elements in foreign policy:

The Philippines, Cuba, and Puerto Rico came within our own sphere of governmental action. In addition to this we asserted certain rights in the western hemisphere under the Monroe Doctrine. My endeavor was not only to assert these rights, but frankly and fully to acknowledge the duties that went with the rights.

The Monroe Doctrine lays down the rule that the western hemisphere is not hereafter to be treated as subject to settlement and occupation by Old World powers. It is not international law; but it is a cardinal principle of our foreign policy.[74]

Yet, little was heard of American involvement with the Moros in the Philippines, primarily because it was low-visibility combat and involved only the Regular Army. In addition, it was presumed that America was in the Philippines in order to civilize the Filipinos and prepare them for self-government. Finally, the Moros were considered uncivilized and enemies to both the Filipinos and Americans. Perhaps the major reason for this relative unconcern with the revolution in the southern part of the Philippines was the fact that it was on the periphery of the major events of the day. There was much more going on in the world with major powers and the Monroe Doctrine (and the Roosevelt Corollary). Most important, there was too much going on within the United States to be overly concerned about "minor" troubles in an island thousands of miles away. Most of America's attention with respect to the aftermath of the Spanish-American War was on its relationships with Cuba. The problems in the Philippines faded into insignificance.

During most of the Roosevelt Administration, the struggle in the Philippines was considered a "pacification" and "law and order" issue, not a military operation—at least in Washingtonian terms. Since the Philippines were annexed as part of the United States, and the Filipino independence movement and revolution were officially ended in 1902, the troubles in the islands were considered but minor irritants of empire. For the military, however, the counterrevolutionary policy against the Moros proved to be more troublesome than the struggles against either Spain or the Filipinos. This period, therefore, has been relegated primarily to military history rather than to major policy concerns of the Roosevelt Administration.

SOCIOECONOMIC PATTERNS

The period following the Civil War has been called "The Gilded Age," a phrase taken from the title of Charles Dudley Warner's novel to describe that era's glorification of material values and the drive by many Americans for material gains. The economic and social fabric of the nation emerging from the Civil War rested on material values. The period witnessed vast industrial expansion, which some historians have called the second revolution, combined with dramatic agricultural growth and the westward movement of the population. In the process, the Plains Indians were defeated, conquered, and placed on reservations. The expansion of commerce and the westward movement of civilization allowed little toleration of Indian tribes, whom many felt were obstacles to the growth of America.

The push for material gain, the vast expansion of the economy, and the seemingly unlimited wealth of the North American continent precipitated unparalleled waste and extravagance in government and business. The underlying philosophy was laissez-faire (the less government interferes, the better it is for the economy and for the people). This view was based partly on the assumption that economic success was linked with political and military success. The capacity of the North's industrial base to provide the implements of war that overwhelmed the South was not lost on Americans or foreigners. This capability generated its own logic and provided the basis for the Industrial Revolution which followed the Civil War. This industrial success was linked with the idea of democracy, love of country, and hatred of slavery. These nonmaterial values took on a messianic quality which was later manifested in foreign policy.

Table 4
Federal Expenditures and Gross National Product, 1890, 1900, 1910

Year	Total Expenditures (in millions of dollars)	Defense Expenditures (in millions of dollars)	Gross National Product (in billions of dollars)
1890	318	67	13.1
1900	521	191	18.7
1910	694	313	35.3

Source: U.S. Bureau of the Census, Bicentennial
        Statistics (Washington, D.C.: Government
        Printing Office, 1976).

The 1880s emerged as the highpoint of the new economic style in America. The population had expanded dramatically, and the shift from rural to urban areas continued. Big business, railroads, and trusts had become major issues in domestic affairs and economic policy. The drive to get a bigger piece of the economic pie became the most prevalent characteristic of the American economic environment. The political system reflected the nation's economic activities, as cynicism and corruption within the party ranks became commonplace.

As the socio-economic, demographic, and political character of America changed, the government expanded. Not only did the federal bureaucracy increase in size, but government expenditures increased (see Tables 4 and 5). And although America became increasingly involved in world affairs following the Spanish-American War, its military establishment remained small relative to the population. Immediately after the Spanish-American War, the military establishment was significantly reduced, particularly the Army (see Table 6). Yet, some of the most

Table 5
Federal Civilian Employment, 1890, 1900, 1910 (in thousands)

Year	Total	Executive Branch	Legislative/ Judicial
1890	157	151	7
1900	240	231	8
1910	389	380	8

Source: U.S. Bureau of the Census, Bicentennial
        Statistics (Washington, D.C.: Government
        Printing Office, 1976).

Table 6
U.S. Military Personnel on Active Duty, 1898-1914

Year	Grand Total	Army	U.S. Population
1898	235,785	209,714	73,000,000 (approx.)
1899	100,166	80,670	
1900	125,923	101,713	76,000,000
1901	112,322	85,557	
1902	111,145	81,275	
1903	106,043	69,595	81,000,000
1904	110,129	70,387	
1905	108,301	67,526	84,000,000
1906	112,216	68,945	
1907	108,375	64,170	87,000,000
1908	128,500	76,942	
1909	142,200	84,971	
1910	139,344	81,251	92,000,000
1911	144,846	84,006	
1912	153,174	92,121	95,000,000
1913	154,914	92,756	
1914	165,919	98,544	99,000,000

Source: U.S. Bureau of the Census, Historical Statistics of the
       United States: Colonial Times to 1970, Part 2.
       (Washington, D.C.: Government Printing Office, 1971),
       pp. Y 904-916.

intense fighting took place in the Philippines after 1899. Even the increasing tensions in Europe in the decade preceding World War I did not cause a growth in the American military establishment. It must be noted however, that any attention given to the American military was primarily to the Navy.

Regarding the "Gilded Age," Richard Hofstadter writes in a chapter aptly titled, "The Spoilsmen: An Age of Cynicism": "Standards of success in politics changed. It was not merely self-expression or public service or glory that the typical politician sought—it was money. Lord Bryce found that the cohesive force in American politics was 'the desire for office and for office as a means of gain.' "[75] The "Gilded Age" was spurred by the apparent economic successes of the American system. As John A. Garrity notes, "By the late 1880s the country was producing enormous amounts of agriculture and industrial goods and exporting an even larger share of this production. Exports rose in value from $450 million in 1870 to $852 million in 1880 and passed the billion dollar mark early in the 1890s."[76] Yet, behind this economic upsurge was the increasing conflict between business and workingmen. Inflationary pressures and decline in the price of agricultural goods also created economic hardships and uncertainty for farmers. Finally, the laissez-faire domestic policy of the Cleveland Administration did little to ease the situation.

It was during this period of social and economic unrest that protest movements surfaced; these were the harbingers of the Progressive Era. The farmers of the South and Prairie West reacted and in 1890 formed organizations for the purpose of electing officials who could correct economic inequities. These organizations eventually formed the Populist party and were successful in electing legislatures in a number of states and in influencing the Democratic party.

A decline in government gold reserves and the continuing decline in the economic fortunes of farmers were directly responsible for the Panic of 1893. The depression that followed created a host of economic and social problems. Banks and railroads went into bankruptcy, business floundered, and the general state of the economy changed significantly from the heyday of the 1880s. In terms of economic struggles, Williams notes that the election of 1896 was the "last full-throated attempt of the agrarian sections to regain control of the national government, the final stand of agriculture against a devouring nationalism, and the climactic defeat of the farmers in their long battle with the forces of business and finance."[77]

The Progressive Era coincided with the administration of Theodore Roosevelt. And it was Roosevelt's concern for the power of big business and trusts that led to a variety of federal regulations. In any case, it was a time of recovery from the 1890s and a time of relative prosperity; a time of upsurge in labor union power, protest movements, and concern for the common man; a time of hope and great expectations that the American system could produce well-being for all. It was in this environment that a new era in American foreign policy began—one in which Americans felt confidence in their own system and seemed to expect a major role in world affairs.

SUMMARY

The end of the Civil War ushered in a period of industrialization, accelerated westward expansion, laid the foundations for labor-business confrontation, and promoted a concern for the quality of life. The Civil War appeared to solve, once and for all, the issues of the American union and slavery. Released from the burdens of these emotional and divisive issues, Americans turned westward and towards industrialization. The demands of the Civil War had generated attention to mechanical means of energy and production. In addition, innovations demanded by four years of war had spilled over into the civilian sector following the war, stimulating industrialization. Changes were also taking place in America's political-social system. Labor unions and concern for the workingman clashed with the principles of capitalism and business expansion. Combined with serious concern with the quality of life, economic growth, and the struggles between farmers and those in industrial areas, tensions and divisiveness in the body politic increased.

Nevertheless, Americans developed a new, bold outlook. They began to show a great deal of confidence in themselves and in their country's potential. Industrialization had taken hold, and the Indian wars had come to an end. The population had increased by over 25 million in the decades from 1870–1890. Government was expanding and the wealth of America increasing. Urbanization was proceeding rapidly with the urban population more than doubling in two decades, from 14 to 30 million. America had come into its own as a world power, and it now needed to show the rest of the world that it had indeed come of age. The Spanish-American War provided that opportunity.

The debate in the United States over the perceived heavy-handed Spanish rule in Cuba was heated and emotional. Although McKinley attempted to maintain a rational and diplomatic approach to the issue, the press sparked a general public outcry against Spain. Opinion of Spanish rule was in no small measure a reflection of America's own experience of colonial rule and of the increasing domestic concern over the rights of workingmen and people in general. Americans deeply objected to an Old World power such as Spain controlling part of the New World, only a few miles from the American coast.

The actions of the Spanish government did little to ease the situation. Spanish atrocities in Cuba, widely reported by the American press, combined with a series of diplomatic blunders and the sinking of the *U.S.S. Maine* moved America into direct confrontation with Spain. In no small measure, the press exacerbated the tensions between the United States and Spain, not only in its emotional reporting of the events in Cuba, but also in its bombastic editorials about ejecting Spain from the New World.

The administration went into the Spanish-American War with broad American support. Indeed, some felt that McKinley was reluctant to challenge the Spanish and that it was public pressure that finally compelled him to declare war against Spain. The brevity of the Spanish-American War won some degree of acclaim for the McKinley Administration, although major questions were again raised regarding military leadership. Upon McKinley's death, Roosevelt took office and vigorously pursued the pacification of the Philippines and subsequently of the Moros. Although there was strong support for America's involvement in the Spanish-American War, there was increasing opposition to the acquisition of the Philippines as an American colony. The Anti-Imperialist League seriously questioned this policy and raised voices against the behavior of American troops in quelling the Filipinos and the Moros.

But the fact that the campaigns against the Filipino nationalists and the Moros became primarily a Regular Army affair did much to lessen the criticism of the Philippines venture. In addition, domestic issues and tensions in Europe shifted America's attention from the Philippines. Finally, the fact that the United States was both a political and military power allowed a reasonably coherent and aggressive policy to be pursued in pacifying the islands.

During this same period of time Americans were developing interests in foreign areas, particularly in the Far East. Trade and commerce had expanded, and many were concerned that America's foreign trade would be threatened without some show of American strength. The U.S. Navy became the primary instrument. A military strategy evolved that was based on employing the Navy to protect sea lanes and project American power outward.

The acquisition of colonies almost overnight transformed America into an imperial power. This heritage continued into the first two decades of the twentieth century. Issues of preparedness continued to crop up in national debates. The continuation of a moral posture regarding democracy and freedom also characterized the immediate World War I period (although some found it difficult to rationalize America's concern with democracy and freedom and its acquisition of the Philippines). This posture was reflected in the government's attempts not only to deal with the Filipinos, but also to reconcile itself with events taking place in Mexico. As with the Philippines, the American government found itself in a position requiring some response to the events in Mexico.

THE WILSONIAN PERIOD: IDEALISM AND REALITY

Theodore Roosevelt and the Progressives set the stage for the Wilsonian period. While the Progressive Era may not have recorded many accomplishments for the "common" man, it did raise the level of consciousness and expectations for the American political system. The visible signs of economic activity and the growth of popular movements gave the appearance of a dynamic and expanding system. Furthermore, attempts to regulate business and monopolies gave heart to the workingman's cause. Similarly, farmers became increasingly involved in politics as they tried to insure the development of a favorable market for agricultural products. But the most dramatic development of the period was the emergence of the United States as a world power.

The brash young nation of the Jacksonian era had come of age with the Spanish-American War. In the aftermath of the war, the United

States began to play an ever-increasing role on the world stage. For example, during the administration of Theodore Roosevelt, an isthmian canal was begun, and the Roosevelt Corollary to the Monroe Doctrine made it clear that the United States intended to take an active role in the Caribbean and Latin America. Thus, by the time of the European war in 1914, Americans had become accustomed (even if unwillingly) to a role in world affairs. Yet, it was also clear that most Americans did not want entangling alliances with the Old World: "Americans in general, although they deplored signs of increasing tension and growing militarism in Europe, felt little direct personal concern about them. Europeans might foolishly go to war; Americans would remain at peace."[78]

POLITICS AND POLICY ISSUES

The administration of William Howard Taft, which began as an extension of the Roosevelt period, soon ran into serious difficulties, particularly within its own party. As John A. Garrity has observed, "In nearly everything he did, however, Taft's lack of vigor and his political ineptness led to trouble. He had an uncanny ability to aggravate men whose views were substantially like his own."[79] Before long, deep splits developed within the Republican party, primarily over the tariff issue. Trouble also developed over conflicts of interest between members of Taft's cabinet and coal interests. The split became irreversible when Theodore Roosevelt came out in opposition to President Taft, his hand-picked successor. Roosevelt supporters and the Progressive party formed the "Bull Moose" party and nominated Theodore Roosevelt as their candidate for president in the 1912 elections.

The split within the Republican and Democratic parties allowed Woodrow Wilson to capture the presidency in 1912. While not receiving a popular majority, he had enough electoral votes to win. Thus, in a short span of two years, Wilson, a relative unknown, had emerged from the presidency of Princeton University to the governorship of New Jersey, and finally to the presidency of the United States.[80]

In the second decade of the twentieth century America was concerned primarily about economic equality and opportunity. While there was some public attention to world affairs, domestic issues were uppermost, at least until 1916. Wilson's "New Freedom" seemed to strike a responsive chord in the American voter:

Woodrow Wilson's "New Freedom" was based upon the idea that society should work to eliminate the institutions that had frustrated popular rule, some since the beginning of the nation. Wilson professed admiration for Jeffersonianism, but sought often the adoption of Hamiltonian programs, thereby attempting to achieve Jeffersonian ends through Hamiltonian means. . . . He favored governmental action, but only as necessary to insure the control of private power.[81]

Wilson's New Freedom was designed to appeal primarily to the American middle class, supported by rural and labor constituencies, in order to stop the exploitation of America's resources by a wealthy few.[82] It was also an attempt to galvanize these groups to fight against political manipulation by a select few within the various parties. In brief, the New Freedom was a call to restore the competitive nature of American society.[83]

The President Wilson of 1916 was quite different from the President Wilson of 1912. During his first term, he adhered to the progressive view of politics and need for reform. His moralistic views on politics and high idealism seemed to fit in with the age of reform and concern for social and economic justice. As Arthur S. Link notes, "the great majority of progressives, particularly in the South and Middle West, believed that America's unique mission was to purify herself in order to provide an example of democracy triumphant over social and economic injustice and a model of peaceful behavior."[84] Such, in fact, was Wilson's own view before 1916.

During his first term Wilson supported legislation to implement the progressive notion of government. These included the establishment of a Federal Reserve System under the Federal Reserve Act of 1913 and the Underwood Tariff Bill which reduced tariffs and established a free list. For the first time in the nation's history, a moderate income tax was enacted. This was tacked on to the tariff bill. Finally, some progress was made toward the control of monopolies. Overall, Wilson's domestic legislative accomplishments were not without importance, but his foreign policy had far greater consequences.

Although the public remained relatively isolated from foreign issues until the war in Europe began to take American lives, Wilson's energies were increasingly expended on foreign and defense policy. The role of the United States had been reasonably well established in the early years of the twentieth century. The United States had shown its ability to project its power not only into the Caribbean, but into the Far East as well. The American military was now considered an effective instrument, primarily because of the strength of the U.S. Navy, a legacy of the Roosevelt era. Finally, American involvement in international trade was important, not only in terms of America's own economy, but also with respect to the economies of a number of other countries.

During the first fifteen years of the twentieth century, the United States became deeply involved in the Caribbean, extending its influence into the various states. In addition, it showed some interest in the Far East, becoming involved in the Boxer Rebellion and the International Relief Force as well as broadening its trade in the area. The United States also became more closely associated with the politics of Europe and made a major effort to resolve disputes peacefully.[85] Its outward reach into the European and Asiatic areas, however, was not matched by its attempts to establish a sphere of influence in the Caribbean.[86]

Foreign affairs dominated Wilson's second term. This may well have been the reason behind the shift of his philosophical position from progressivism to conservatism. On the other hand, as some are quick to note, Wilson's position in 1916 may have been more the result of an opportune political posture than of higher principles. Without question, however, Wilson tried to inject a moralistic and idealistic tone in his foreign as well as domestic policy, a tone that he felt was in accord with America's history and tradition. He believed that only through such moralistic and idealistic guidelines could America hope to maintain prestige and, indeed, wield power in the world. But some scholars, notably James David Barber, believe that more politics than morals may have been involved: "Throughout his political history, Wilson displayed a remarkable ability to shift his ground, once in power, and then, when the next high opportunity for advancement offered itself, to wipe out the memory of his record by bedazzling moralistic rhetoric."[87]

In the closing days of his first term, Wilson became increasingly preoccupied with the conflict in Europe, relations with Germany, and American neutrality. Thus, after the Punitive Expedition was ordered into Mexico in 1916, he let the opportunity pass to disengage American forces without appearing to do so under threats from the Mexican government.[88]

Even issues within the domestic arena had their foreign policy impact, reflecting the concern over the European war. A major issue was preparedness. Towards the end of his first term of office, Wilson realized he would have to upgrade the American military establishment, particularly in light of the massive military instruments developed by the European powers in the course of the war. In an address to a joint session of Congress, Wilson stated, "If our citizens are ever to fight effectively...they must know how modern fighting is done.... And the government must be their servant in this matter."[89] He went on to ask Congress for approval of War Department plans to provide for an adequate defense.

Wilson presented the Garrison plan which proposed increasing the Regular Army from slightly over 108,000 to over 141,000. But the real issue was the ready reserve. At Wilson's request, Secretary of War Lindley Garrison provided an "Outline of Military Policy" as first steps in strengthening the nation's defenses. The most controversial feature was the relegation of the National Guard to local police operations and the creation of a new Continental Army of 400,000 as the first line of defense. Although there were signs that some parts of the public were aroused against the preparedness question, Wilson seemed intent on moving ahead unmindful of public opinion. He was convinced that the vast majority of Americans would support his policy of increasing the armed forces and his preparedness plans.[90] Yet, the antipreparedness forces raised a hue and cry. Among these forces was the League to Limit Armament, which was formed in December 1914, and the Woman's Peace party, organized by Carrie Chapman Catt, the woman suffrage leader. Such individuals and groups felt Wilson's support of even modest preparedness as "a shocking blow."[91]

Many Democrats, particularly those on the House Committee on Military Affairs (the chairman was James Hay of Virginia), strongly opposed the Garrison plan. The National Guard lobby was effective in its opposition and in convincing members of Congress of the plan's ineffectiveness. Prominent members of the House proposed an alternative, providing for a stronger federal role in the National Guard and making it available for federal service under a presidential call. Under pressure from Congress, Wilson switched his support to the congressional plan. Garrison was adamant, however, and resigned under protest because of the lack of presidential support for his plan. This episode made it appear that Wilson's cabinet and government were in disarray. In a period of increasing tensions, with problems both at home and abroad, some began to see Wilson's leadership as increasingly ineffective. With the election of 1916 on the horizon, the Democrats became alarmed by public opinion. Leading Eastern newspapers began to criticize Wilson's declining authority, and, more damaging, Eastern academics and upper-class people labeled his foreign and defense policies weak. The American Rights Committee was formed in December 1915 to galvanize public opinion in favor of "moral alignment with the allies and military might to enforce stern policies against Germany."[92] Wilson, always the astute politician, took his preparedness campaign to the country, not only to gather support for his foreign and defense policies but also to pave the way for the 1916 elections. After a triumphant speaking tour of the country, most agreed with one editor who wrote, "Mr. Wilson has returned to Washington, after having won the first genuine popular triumph, through personal contact with the people, in his public career. He has been rated hitherto as an austere, intellectual personality, incapable of arousing much popular interest or enthusiasm."[93]

In any case, the preparedness issue, while aimed primarily at a domestic audience, was closely linked with foreign and defense policies, and particularly with the war in Europe.

During Wilson's second term in addition to the European war, the United States became closely involved in the Caribbean and in Mexico. With all of its involvement in the Caribbean as well as in Latin America, the United States was most sensitive to its relationships with Mexico. Even before the Civil War, America had been drawn into Mexico's internal affairs. In the 1840s, the Polk Administration attempted to resolve a boundary dispute with Mexico, which had evolved from the acquisition of Texas by the United States. Desiring to annex California as well, President Polk attempted negotiations with Mexico. This attempt failed, and, according to many historians, President Polk used this as an excuse to provoke a war with Mexico. General Zachary Taylor, who had already been ordered to the Rio Grande with his army, was ordered into Mexico. The armies of Generals Taylor and Winfield Scott proved to be more than a match for the armies of General Santa Anna. Following the fall of Mexico City, the Treaty of Guadeloupe was signed in 1848, in which Mexico recognized the Rio Grande boundary and ceded New Mexico and California. The United States was to pay Mexico $15 million.

The next crisis for the young Mexican republic (independence had been gained from Spain in 1821) was the occupation of its territory by the joint forces of Britain, Spain, and France in late 1861. The purpose of the occupation was to protect their nationals in Mexico. However, the French emperor, Napoleon III, had other plans—the establishment of a French Empire in Mexico. Archduke Maximilian was placed on the Mexican throne assisted by French troops. It was only after the Civil War that the United States was in a position to act. The French government was notified that the United States could not recognize the Maximilian government in Mexico and that the United States expected the French to cease its operations there. Using the Monroe Doctrine as its principle of foreign policy, the United States successfully pressured the French out of Mexico. There were other reasons, to be sure, but the United States played the major role.

From 1877 to 1911 Mexico was ruled by dictator Porfirio Diaz. During that period of time, Americans invested heavily in Mexico, primarily in mine operations. The Mexican revolution overthrew Diaz, and Francisco Madero came to power in 1911. One result of this internal instability was the loss of American money and lives. Early in his first year of office, Wilson was confronted by the Mexican problem. In an address delivered at a Joint Session of the two Houses of Congress in August 1913, Wilson stated,

Mexico has a great and enviable future before her, if only she choose and attain the paths of honest constitutional government. The present circumstances of the Republic, I deeply regret to say do not seem to promise even the foundations of such a peace.... War and disorder, devastation and confusion, seem to threaten to become the settled fortune of the distracted country.[94]

Wilson recognized the Madero government in the hopes of bringing stability to Mexico, but Madero was assassinated not long after he came to power. His successor, Victoriano Huerta, proved to be a hindrance to Wilson's attempt to see a democratic system in Mexico. Wilson refused to recognize the Huerta regime, stating that any regime coming to power by virtue of assassination was immoral. Wilson passionately expressed his moralistic view in his address accepting renomination for the presidency in September 1916.

The unspeakable Huerta betrayed the very comrades he served, traitorously overthrew the government of which he was a trusted part, impudently spoke for the very forces that had driven his people to rebellion with which he had pretended to sympathize.... So long as the power of recognition rests with me the Government of the United States will refuse to extend the hand of welcome to anyone who obtains power in a sister republic by treachery and violence.[95]

The incident at Tampico, Mexico, in which Mexican officials temporarily held American sailors of a naval supply party, led to the occupation of Vera Cruz in 1914 by a force of 8,000 American soldiers and Marines. Although the Americans withdrew after a brief occupation, Mexican anti-American feeling was intensified. In light of President Wilson's concern to accelerate and assist the establishment of a republican form of government, the complications of this incident, followed later by the raid on Columbus by Pancho Villa, made the effort a complicated and at times an embarrassing one.

Under pressure from other Latin American countries and to avoid war with the United States, Huerta resigned and Venustiano Carranza came to power. It was during the Carranza period that banditry increased in Mexico. Raids into the United States were not uncommon, and American lives were lost in both Mexico and Texas. The border between Mexico and the United States remained tense, highlighted by the Pancho Villa raid into Columbus, which sparked the Punitive Expedition into Mexico in 1916.

PRESIDENTIAL LEADERSHIP

Most historians agree that Wilson had an idealistic and moralistic approach to politics and the presidency. His conception of politics rested on premises of the goodness of people and their relationship to God. As August Heckscher concludes, "For Wilson religion was at the heart of politics. He believed in the importance of the individual because of the individual's relationship to God; and he conceived it his task, so far as he was able, to free this individual from tyranny and oppression."[96]

Yet, Wilson was a politician: he was aware of the importance of public opinion, and he valued the powers of office. In his struggles in the latter part of his first term, his leadership ability and his sense of timing allowed him to weather severe criticism of his administration. His appointment to the Supreme Court of Louis Brandeis, the first Jew to be so honored, raised a storm of controversy, as did his struggles with the preparedness issue. But Wilson prevailed and in so doing reestablished his leadership and became his party's most prominent member, ready to challenge anyone for the presidency in 1916.[97]

Wilson's view of the presidency was in the tradition of Lincoln and Jackson. Convinced that the office could be used to correct many problems in society, Wilson felt that the powers inherent in that office had to be used with vigor, especially the power of the president in foreign affairs. "One of the greatest of the President's powers," he wrote, was "his control, which is very absolute, of the foreign relations of the nation. The initiative in foreign affairs, which the President possesses without restriction whatever, is virtually the power to control them absolutely."[98]

John G. Stoessinger gives a lucid explanation of the relationships between Woodrow Wilson's personality and character and the presidential office.

When coupled with his sense of messianic mission, Wilson's conception of the Presidency made that office into a formidable fountainhead of power. But that power was never to be used without a moral purpose. It was to become a major instrument in the struggle against evil. Three of Wilson's crucial foreign policy decisions serve to illustrate this point: the intervention in Mexico; the American entry into World War I; and the decision not to recognize the Bolshevik regime in Russia nor participate in an attempt to achieve its overthrow.[99]

The tragedy of Wilson following World War I is not directly related to our focus on the Punitive Expedition, but nevertheless, it should be noted that his final years in the presidency were years of bitter disappointment and frustration. With a deep sense of guilt about the contradiction between his ideals and purposes, involvement in World War I, and the repudiation of the League of Nations, Wilson went on an ill-conceived tour of the country. Suffering a stroke followed by rumors regarding his sanity, Wilson lost much credibility.[100]

Wilson faced a dilemma with respect to Mexico and the Punitive Expedition. On one hand, he was committed to democracy, sovereignty, and independence, and on the other, he felt there was a more pressing need to protect American lives and property, even if it meant disregarding the more idealistic notions of sovereign states. Thus, his idealistic view that America had to foster democratic systems helped him rationalize his support of Carranza. His outrage at the depredations of Pancho Villa against Americans and American territory required some action, however. Aware that the American people expected strong American action against Villa, Wilson ordered the Punitive Expedition. That this was an intervention into an independent and sovereign state was set aside under the pressure of political realities. In time, Wilson realized that Carranza's fragile support of American policies had given way to active anti-Americanism.

The dilemma created by Wilson's idealism and the realities of political life became even more pronounced with respect to American involvement in World War I. While the world war certainly overshadowed the moralistic dilemma of the Punitive Expedition, it was nevertheless an extension of the same problem faced in Mexico. World War I was, in the moralistic sense, the Punitive Expedition writ large in terms of Wilson's own values.

Involving the United States in World War I was also a fundamental contradiction in Wilson's value system. A man deeply committed to peace in the world now found himself compelled to use force to destroy what he considered was a tyrannical system, in the name of peace. Many saw Wilson's actions following World War I as an attempt to finally resolve this dilemma: he sought to justify his actions by designing a system to prevent future wars.[101] The dilemma was never resolved in Wilson's own mind, and hence it is that Wilson's career has the character of a Greek tragedy.[102] Compounding the sense of tragedy was the fact that Wilson, a religious man, hated war. Still, he led the United States into World War I, and during his presidency American forces became involved in at least fifteen armed interventions.[103]

POLITICAL RESOLVE AND NATIONAL WILL

During Wilson's presidency, particularly the last years of his first term and the beginning of his second term, the United States used both diplomacy and force to support the establishment of a democratic regime in Mexico. Eventually, the inability of the Carranza regime to control banditry, with specific references to Pancho Villa, led to American intervention. Simultaneously, Wilson was desperately trying to keep America out of the European war. In February 1916, speaking at the Gridiron Dinner in Washington, Wilson stated:

America ought to keep out of this war. She ought to keep out of this war at the sacrifice of everything except this single thing upon which her character and history are founded, her sense of humanity and justice. If she sacrifices that, she has ceased to be America; she has ceased to entertain and to love traditions which have made us proud to be Americans, and when we go about seeking safety at the expense of humanity, then I for one will believe that I have always been mistaken in what I have conceived to be the spirit of American history.[104]

Americans, in general, were more concerned with the events in Europe than with happenings on the Mexican border. While Americans tended to accept the idea that they were a peace-loving people and that the European war was not America's concern, they also felt that America was a major power and power had to be used to protect American national interests. It was in this context that Americans viewed Pancho Villa's raid on Columbus as a cowardly attack, requiring a firm response. Nonetheless, there was a deep-seated ambivalence in the American position. Few Americans were knowledgeable about American relationships with Mexico, except what was reported by the news media. There were fewer Americans who understood the implications of American intervention, beyond the fact that a bandit running around loose along the Mexican-American border had to be punished. Yet, involvement in Mexico was clouded by the Great War, which now had lasted longer than most had expected.

Nevertheless, American reaction to Villa's raid was swift...the day after the raid, the War Department telegraphed General Funston, now commanding the Southern Department, "President has directed that an armed force be sent into Mexico with the sole object of capturing Villa and preventing any further raids by his bands, and with scrupulous regard for sovereignty of Mexico."[105]

Thus, while Americans were trying to avoid entanglement in Europe, there appeared to be little hesitation about strong action against the neighbors to the South. The rationale was that Americans had an obligation to assist economic progress and democratic governments in Mexico, as well as Latin America.

Yet, there were groups in America that organized for preparedness and for intervention in the European War, for example, the American Rights Committee and National Security League. By the end of 1915, there was increasing sentiment in the United States for preparedness and an awareness of the possibility of American involvement in the European war. Nonetheless, the elections of 1916 were based primarily on the issue of war and peace. The Republicans with their candidate Charles Evans Hughes were cast as the war party, even though they tried to avoid the appearance of supporting intervention. Woodrow Wilson and the Democrats continually hammered away on the theme that electing a Republican president would mean intervention in Mexico and Europe. The antiwar sentiments and commitment to progressivism persisted, and Wilson was elected with a relatively narrow popular vote. According to T. Henry Williams, et al., the election was "a narrow mandate" for progressivism and peace.[106]

After the election, Wilson attempted to negotiate a lasting peace with the Germans. But the Germans reembarked on unrestricted submarine warfare. Combined with the increasing publicity about the atrocities of the "Huns" and the conviction that American fortunes rested primarily with Britain and France, Wilson's desires to remain out of the war became unrealistic. American sentiment for intervention increased. While there is still much debate on why America entered the European war, evidence points to the unprovoked German submarine attacks and violations of American neutrality as major reasons. It is in the context of these broader issues that American intervention in Mexico must be seen.

Most argued that American intervention in Mexico was necessary to punish a criminal, but others maintained that such intervention could not be justified since it was a fundamental violation of Mexican sovereignty. Later events were to prove that the intervention eventually faced the opposition of not only Pancho Villa, but also the established Carranza government, the peasants in the countryside, and many Americans. For Americans, this was a particularly sensitive issue, since the last thing they wanted was war with Mexico: "Aside from the Hearst press and a few jingoes who wanted war, there had been little belligerent sentiment during the first stages of high tension with Mexico. Not even news of the Carrizal incident had set off any general agitation for hostilities; on the contrary, it prompted fervent appeals for peaceful settlement."[107] (See Chapter 3 for details of the Carrizal incident. In brief, American cavalrymen conducting a reconnaissance as part of the Punitive Expedition were fired upon and defeated by Carranza forces.) Although Wilson pressed for American operations into Mexico, he made it clear to General John J. Pershing, as well as others, that extreme care had to be taken to avoid war. The purpose of the expedition was to punish Pancho Villa, ostensibly with the cooperation of the Carranza government. But Carranza had been misled:

Carranza had tolerated the Punitive Expedition's entry under protest in part because [Alvaro] Obregon had obviously counseled cooperation, and in part because Wilson's statements had led the First Chief to believe that Pershing would not stay long. Unrest and bitterness against the American violation of national dignity were spreading through Mexico in early April 1916. Public opinion would have compelled Carranza to try to force American withdrawal in any event.[108]

Throughout the course of the Punitive Expedition, Wilson and his spokesman insisted that America's involvement was to the higher good of Mexico and in accord with the traditions of American democracy. Wilson's secretary of the interior, Franklin K. Lane, made this point abundantly clear in an interview in July 1916:

President Wilson's Mexican policy is one of the things of which, as a member of his administration, I am most proud. . . . He has always sought the right solution. . . . The policy of the United States toward Mexico is a policy of hope and helpfulness; it is a policy of Mexico for the Mexicans. That, after all, is the traditional policy of this country—it is the policy that drove Maximilian out of Mexico.[109]

Table 7
U.S. Population and Military Personnel, 1915-1918

Year	Total Population (in millions)	Urban/Rural (in millions)	Total Military (in thousands)	Army Personnel (in thousands)
1915	100.5	42/50	174	106.5
1916	102	42/50	179	108
1917	103	43/51	643.8	421.5
1918	103	44/51	2,897	2,395.7

Source: U.S. Bureau of the Census, Historical Statistics of the United States, Colonial Times to 1970, Part 2 (Washington, D.C.: U.S. Government Printing Office, 1975), pp. 1114-1115.

In explaining the reasons for the Punitive Expedition, Wilson had emphasized the importance of protecting America's security: "It goes without saying that the United States must do as she is doing—she must insist upon the safety of her borders; she must, so far as order is worked out of chaos, use every instrumentality she can in friendship employ to protect the lives and property of her citizens in Mexico."[110]

As we will see later, military operations in Mexico became complicated and increasingly burdensome. The cautious military involvement in Mexico not only reflected a fear of serious entanglement in Mexico which might lead to war, but perhaps more importantly, the concern of Americans with the European war. The Wilson Administration was worried lest the United States became bogged down in Mexico while at the same time faced with war in Europe. In the final analysis, war did come to the United States in Europe. This was but a few months after the withdrawal of the Punitive Expedition and, fortunately for the United States, provided a trained and experienced cadre of officers and men. They were put to good use in developing the large armies and in serving on the Western Front in World War I.

SOCIOECONOMIC PATTERNS

During the Wilsonian period, issues of economics and social conditions in the United States evolved out of the Progressive Era and merged into Wilson's New Freedom. Concern with social and economic justice spurred efforts to give the middle classes and workingmen a fair share of the economic pie. At the same time, demographic patterns were changing radically, one of the most important being the shift of the majority of Americans from rural to urban areas (see Table 7). Moreover,

Table 8
Federal Expenditures and Gross National Product, 1915-1918

Year	Total Expenditures ($ millions)	Total Defense ($ millions)	Army ($ millions)	Gross National Product ($ billions)
1915	746	298	208	40
1916	713	305	183	48.3
1917	1,954	602	377	60.4
1918	12,662	7,110	4,869	76.4

Source: U.S. Bureau of the Census, <u>Historical Statistics of
the United States, Colonial Times to 1970, Part 2</u>
(Washington, D.C.: U.S. Government Printing Office,
1975), pp. 1114-1115.

during the first two decades of the twentieth century, the population
increased by over 30 million.

Almost from the beginning of Wilson's presidency, however, economic and social issues within the country were dominated by tensions
in Europe and the coming of World War I. The growth of the economy,
the manpower distribution in economic sectors, and federal expenditures were all distorted as a result of the European war. For example,
the gross national product jumped from slightly over $48 billion in 1916
to over $76 billion in 1918 (see Table 8). Thus, except for the first year
of the Wilson presidency, there appeared to be little concern for unemployment and social issues. Involvement in World War I demanded
the economic and political energies of most Americans. This did not
mean, of course, that social and economic issues were absent. Rather,
such issues were submerged, only to surface in the aftermath of World
War I.

Henry Ford's mass-produced automobile in 1909 set the stage for what
was later to become the age of mass production, increasing factory production and creating a large group of factory workers and urban dwell-
ers. The years immediately preceding World War I also created conditions
which would vastly expand the purchasing power of the middle and
working classes. While this change was not immediately apparent in
the pre-World War I period, the groundwork had clearly been provided.
For example, Daniel J. Boorstin has commented on the impact of the
automobile:

When Henry Ford's assembly line began turning out automobiles by the thousands, it was not hard to awaken the American's desire to own a car. But
democratizing the automobile was not merely a question of engineering or of
automotive and production design.... Even after improved production tech-

niques and widening demand reduced the 1916 Model T Runabout to $345, the price strained the budget of the American millions.... To put the automobile in the hands of the American people required other social inventions no less novel than the assembly line.[111]

The acquisition of automobiles by the average American had been made possible by new financial institutions and new marketing and merchandizing techniques that had outdistanced automotive production.[112] In any case, domestic social and economic issues were submerged beneath the greater demands of the war, a war that required the greatest degree of mobilization of industry, the military, and the population since the Civil War.

SUMMARY

The extension of American power continued through the first decade of the twentieth century. Ultimately, Americans came to accept their role as guardians of the Western Hemisphere. They were particularly sensitive to developments in Mexico. While welcoming the overthrow of the Dictator Porfirio Diaz and the Mexicans' attempt to establish a republican form of government, most Americans became incensed by the depredations against Americans and American property committed within Mexico and along the Mexican-American border. Throughout the Mexican revolutionary period beginning in 1910, American presidents tried to influence the course of events there, particularly President Wilson after his election in 1912 and following his reelection in 1916. Thus, at the time of Pancho Villa's raid on Columbus in 1916, most Americans were prepared for strong actions against Mexican raiders. While most had little hesitation about supporting strong measures against Villa, they did caution against any precipitous action that might involve America in the European war. With the presumed permission of the Carranza government in Mexico, the Punitive Expedition was undertaken with the blessings of the American people. However, as the American involvement became more serious and it became apparent that Villa was not going to be captured easily, American opinion began to call for a withdrawal. The increasing threat of American involvement in Europe and threats by the Carranza government against the United States were also responsible for changing American attitudes about continual involvement in Mexico. Recognition by responsible leaders that the Mexican involvement was but a side show to the greater issue of the world war sparked the timely withdrawal of the Punitive Expedition.

At the time of the Mexican intervention, President Woodrow Wilson was making a valiant attempt to keep the United States out of war, both in Mexico and in Europe. Indeed, Wilson was reelected in 1916 by a narrow margin on the basis of peace and progressivism. However, there was a strong undercurrent of opinion supporting preparedness and intervention in Europe.

Wilson's leadership, although sometimes vacillating and based on misjudgment of events in Mexico, was positive and showed little hesitation in trying to influence events in that country. The Wilson Administration used many methods to set the direction of Mexican development, ranging from diplomatic maneuvers, temporary occupation of a Mexican port, arms embargoes, outright assistance to forces in Mexico, to military intervention in northern Mexico. Within one day of the raid on Columbus by Villa in 1916, for example, General Frederick Funston was ordered to organize an expeditionary force to enter Mexico and capture Villa.

The events in Mexico and the Punitive Expedition cannot be understood separately from the events leading to American involvement in World War I. Events in Europe affected not only American political-military policy, but domestic socioeconomic issues as well. The years immediately preceding World War I saw significant changes in the socioeconomic system. There was growth of the middle class and working class, much of it stimulated by the new methods of mass production reinforced by the egalitarian impulses stemming from the Progressive Era. While the population almost stabilized, the gross national product grew by $10 billion in two decades. Although the American people were becoming increasingly concerned about events in Europe, the need for war material by the belligerents spurred American production, which continued throughout the war.

Following World War I, many Americans were convinced that the war to end all wars had succeeded. The United States again tried to isolate itself from the Old World and entered a long period of isolationism. Even the agreement establishing the League of Nations was ignored. In the twenty-year period following World War I, a series of events unfolded in Europe and elsewhere that set the stage for another world war. For the most part, American attention was on domestic economic growth and prosperity (that is, the Roaring Twenties), followed by the Great Depression and attempts at recovery which lasted until the beginning of World War II.

VIETNAM: THE MORAL CRUSADE

The twentieth century opened with the United States embarking on world empire. A "splendid little war" lasting less than six months and almost bloodless allowed the United States to expand dramatically into the Pacific and Far East. The successful use of military power to achieve far-reaching political goals established the United States as an imperial power, allowing the country to take its place among the ranks of the Old World powers. In the second half of the twentieth century, after securing its world status in two world wars, the United States reached the end of empire. Indeed, it was compelled to retreat from empire, not by a major power but by the resistance and tenacity of a small, industrially backward country of about fourteen million people.

The purposes and policy of American involvement in Vietnam remain clouded even after more than a decade following the American withdrawal. There are a variety of explanations and a great deal of literature, published and unpublished, examining the American involvement in Vietnam, ranging from the ideological to the issues of military tactics. Yet there remain questions on the reasons for the involvement, the stakes involved, matters of strategy and tactics, and the relationship between Vietnam and American domestic politics.

It is not the intention here to reassess the events and the problems or to provide another explanation of the war even if it could be done in a brief review. Rather, the intent is to focus on the problems of counterrevolution from the American perspective in order to draw conclusions regarding policy. But to understand the character of the counterrevolutionary conflict and the complexities of American involvement we need to go back to the period immediately following World War II.

POLITICS AND POLICY ISSUES

The Cold War, the Atomic Age, and a series of lesser conflicts throughout the world dispelled any notion that victory in World War II would bring a long period of peace. Almost from the end of World War II, American presidents were faced with serious foreign policy issues. While Americans continually tried to focus primarily on domestic issues of inflation, unemployment, equal rights, and prosperity in general, external political forces and crises continually demanded public attention. Thus, from the Truman Administration through that of Ronald Reagan, presidential politics have necessitated a great deal of attention to foreign affairs and security issues.

The world in the two decades following World War II was quite a different place for America than in previous decades. As most historians are quick to note, the mantle of leadership of the West was thrust upon the United States whether it liked it or not. The Cold War with all of its tensions and confrontations, combined with a series of smaller wars in Greece, Korea, and the Dominican Republic and confrontations as in Cuba and Berlin, kept the American people in a constant state of concern about world developments. Yet, until the Kennedy presidency, there was a general feeling of satisfaction that the United States and its policy of containment had been reasonably effective, even with the "loss" of China to the Communists. However, the French defeat in Indochina and the wars of national liberation in various parts of Southeast Asia seemed to signal the end of the relative success of containment policies.

Up to the 1960s, the U.S. view of the world was conditioned by perceptions of a monolithic Communist structure encompassing Eastern Europe and China with central control emanating from Moscow. With few exceptions, this led to the belief that there was a continuing struggle against communism at all levels and across the entire range of world politics. Every thrust of the Communist monolith was to be countered by the forces of anticommunism spearheaded by the United States. This global view was provided a moralistic and universalistic content by Secretary of State John Foster Dulles whose pronouncements and policy approaches in the 1950s were tantamount to an anti-Communist crusade. The legacy of this period in U.S. history carried over into the Kennedy and Johnson eras. Although many recognized that changes were taking place in the world, it appeared that very little of this recognition was reflected in the foreign policy of the United States. The Sino-Soviet split and its impact on the Communist nations in general, the development of a stable and strong Western Europe, the emergence of a modern Japan, the potential of China, the increasing frequency of revolutions, the increasing irrelevance of nuclear power—these factors, among others, changed the rules of the game in world politics. The United States was slow in adjusting to these changes.

U.S. global strategy, in the main, reflected the perceptions of the world environment. From the Truman Doctrine, Eisenhower's "New Look," to Kennedy's flexible and graduated response, which was continued by Lyndon Johnson, the basic premise of strategy still seemed to rest on a universalistic approach in the idea of countering Communists anywhere, anytime. This inevitably led to the view that revolutions occurring in any part of the world were basically a Communist plot for the overthrow of the established governments. This view was reinforced by the Soviet Union, when Premier Nikita Khrushchev in 1961 gave his now famous speech on support of wars of national liberation. U.S. policy in Southeast Asia reflected these assumptions and were further magnified by the "domino theory," which assumed that a takeover of one country by the Communists would inevitably lead to the takeover of all of Southeast Asia.[113]

But the real causes for the coming apart of American policy of containment as well as its benign policies in the Third World stem from a number of consequences of World War II, three in particular: the collapse of colonial empires, the success of Mao's revolution in China, and the evolution of a bipolar world. In a short period of time the political-military dominance of Western powers over much of the world collapsed. The European-prescribed and -controlled world order collapsed, and in its place arose a seemingly chaotic one with the appearance of many new nation-states primarily in Asia and Africa. Not only did this change bring with it a new international system, but it also created a variety of states whose internal security and stability were fragile, thereby producing a volatile and inherently unstable environment. The success of Mao's revolution in China demonstrated the feasibility of war against an established system and proved that revolution against industrial colonial powers could succeed. The rise of a bipolar world system, buttressed by atomic technology—one camp led by the United States and the other by the Soviet Union—made all regions of the world potential battlegrounds.

The world was in transition, and no one was quite sure where it would lead. Particularly challenging was the groundswell of nationalism in Asia and Africa. This nationalism, combined with the demonstration of a successful form of unconventional warfare (wars of national liberation), created a volatile international security situation. Concepts of limited war and wars of national liberation began to appear in the vocabulary of warfare. Unfortunately, only a few members of the political-military establishment of the United States recognized the wide-ranging implications of this development.

The unsettled world environment and the erosion of containment made it appear to many in the West, particularly the United States, that communism was beginning to succeed in various parts of the world. The anti-Communist crusade had to be joined in earnest both at home and abroad. By the end of the Eisenhower Administration, most of the political actors were in place and the conditions had been created for American involvement in Southeast Asia, specifically Vietnam. Moreover, the containment policy had begun to unravel.

This had repercussions in domestic politics. One result was the searching out of Communists under the inspiration of Senator Joe McCarthy. While McCarthyism faded from view quickly, it did damage many prominent Americans and left a legacy of unbridled anticommunism that lingers in America today. Its impact in the 1950s created a psychology of anticommunism which fostered a "hard-line" approach, precluding flexibility in foreign policy, and reduced the discretion of officials to respond to the subtle nuances of political-military challenges within the developing world.

The confluence of these events—the collapse of colonialism, the bipolar world order, and the rise of Communist China—created forces that propelled American foreign policy toward Vietnam and influenced domestic views of communism and the world, initially supporting (and even demanding) the Vietnam adventure.

The Korean War coming almost on the heels of World War II made it clear that American victory only a half decade earlier could not prevent American involvement in shooting wars. While, on the one hand, this was disturbing to Americans in the 1950s, on the other hand, they were being conditioned to conflict with the continuous tensions brought on by the Cold War and the horrors of nuclear war. Nagging domestic problems had to share the spotlight with troublesome foreign and defense matters. Therefore, when the presidential campaign began in 1952, there was little question in most people's minds that the Korean War would be the focal point of campaign politics.

Following the Truman-MacArthur controversy over the prosecution of the Korean War, some elements in the Republican party pushed for General Douglas MacArthur as their candidate. But the majority of Republican party delegates favored Dwight Eisenhower. He not only attracted a number of conservative Republicans but also appealed to the liberal wing of the party, many of whom favored parts of the Democratic party's domestic and foreign policies. The fact that in 1948 liberal Democrats had tried to draft Eisenhower as their Democratic party candidate was not lost on the liberal wing of the Republican party. Thus, the momentary popularity of MacArthur was soon lost in the appeal of General Dwight Eisenhower, whom most Americans remembered as the leader of the "Great Crusade" against the Axis powers. Untainted by "politics" and versed in diplomacy and leadership, General Eisenhower was thought to be the best candidate for the Republican party.

Eisenhower, running against Adlai Stevenson of Illinois, the Democratic party candidate, completely swamped his opponent. The electoral vote was 442 for Eisenhower and 89 for Stevenson. The Republican candidate also won a sizable majority of the popular vote, almost 34 million to his opponent's 27.5 million. In the final analysis, the Korean War gave the Republican party control of the presidency as well as both houses of Congress. In troubled times, the American people had turned to a popular general and experienced leader.

The first term of the Eisenhower Administration proved to be one of relative tranquility and stability in domestic affairs. Even today, a number of Americans recall the first Eisenhower years with nostalgia and longing for the "good old days." During the latter years of Eisenhower's second term, however, many domestic issues surfaced. An increasing number of Americans felt that the character of the Eisenhower Administration prevented it from effectively responding to compelling issues. Eisenhower's perception of office and his style of leadership reflected a stewardship role of the presidency. Eisenhower felt that the president should stand above "politics," and, when it became necessary to make a decision, this should be done in the name of the whole people. His political philosophy rested on stability and trust, with cautious government involvement in areas that were traditionally viewed as the private sector. This philosophy of governmental restraint placed the government against socialized medicine, large welfare policies, or an expanded role in local and state matters. At the most, the Eisenhower Administration would join in a partnership arrangement with local or private enterprises. Eisenhower's cabinet of businessmen reflected this approach.[114]

Nonetheless, Eisenhower's administration did provide the groundwork for what was to be a massive social and economic change in the American political system. While it may not have been recognized at the time, at least two events during the Eisenhower period were harbingers of things to come. First was the Warren Court decision in the case of *Brown v. the Board of Education*, in which segregated schools were declared unconstitutional. Second was the passage of the Civil Rights Act of 1957, the first civil rights act passed since Reconstruction. This act provided federal protection for blacks who wanted to vote. While the court decision opened the way for equal treatment in all public facilities, the Civil Rights Act provided an opportunity for black people to gain voting power.

During the same period of time, major issues emerged in foreign affairs, ranging from the Korean Armistice in 1954, the Suez Crisis in 1956, to the declaration of the Eisenhower Doctrine in 1957 (providing American economic and military involvement in the Middle East if necessary). It was during Eisenhower's first term that the door was opened for American involvement in Southeast Asia. Not only was the Geneva Conference concluded, temporarily dividing North and South Vietnam after the defeat of the French at Dien Bien Phu, but Eisenhower offered assistance to South Vietnam. Few people at that time were aware of the implications of the French defeat or of the opening presented to the United States in Southeast Asia. The primacy of other issues left little time for what was seen as a tangential problem.

The presidency of John F. Kennedy in 1960 was the beginning of a new era in American politics. Although John Kennedy had served in the Senate, he was a relative newcomer in national politics. Yet he was from a very political family, where politics, competition, and winning were bywords.

After he declared his presidential candidacy for the Democratic party, most felt that Kennedy would be lost in a field of nationally prominent contenders. Kennedy knew that his only hope was to win state primaries if he was to attract the party bosses and party support. And with a methodical plan designed to show his effectiveness, he ran in eight state primaries. He won in Wisconsin, but this victory was expected since there was a heavy Catholic vote. Most observers felt that West Virginia was the key. Here where there were few Catholics, Kennedy would have to show his appeal to the non-Catholic majority. Proclaiming that voting on religious beliefs was tantamount to bigotry, Kennedy rose beyond religious issues and managed to win West Virginia, thus assuring him the candidacy of his party.

The election battle between Kennedy and Nixon provided a clear choice between a new and an Eisenhower-type president. The highlight of the campaign was the first televised presidential debate in which there is general agreement that Kennedy was the winner. Subsequently, he won the presidential election by a small margin.

From the outset, the administration of John F. Kennedy was buffeted by foreign policy crises ranging from the Bay of Pigs debacle, the Berlin Crisis, and the Missile Crisis in Cuba. Most public attention was turned to these issues. Yet, the problem in Southeast Asia, specifically Laos and Vietnam, was beginning to develop into a major one. Few Americans were aware of the issues—the Soviet Union and Cuba captured most of the attention. Moreover, civil rights issues began to surface dramatically. In such an environment, the primacy of Europe, the Caribbean, and civil rights overshadowed the dramatic events unfolding in Southeast Asia.

What Kennedy had started was left for others to finish. His assassination in November 1963 was an American tragedy in the deepest sense, and it left undone many of the domestic policies aimed at social justice and equality. For many Americans the assassination was the end of hope and inspiration; the Kennedy presidency had only begun to open the door to what many had hoped would be a better society and a higher level of politics. It was left for Lyndon Johnson to carry on. He did to a great extent in domestic politics, but he left the nation bitter, divided, and sunk in the Vietnam debacle.

Domestic issues surfacing during the Eisenhower era began to develop into full blown policy issues in the short period of the Kennedy Administration. Yet, because of the continuing crises in foreign policy these could not develop or hold the attention of the majority of either the public or policymakers. These crises as well as the increasing complexity of domestic issues during the Kennedy Administration effectively precluded serious attention to the long-range consequences of American policy in Southeast Asia, at least initially. Kennedy's New Frontier never fully developed and it was left to Johnson's "Great Society" to address major social and economic issues.[115]

Yet, the Kennedy presidency was not without its accomplishments in both domestic and foreign affairs. His handling of the Cuban Missile Crisis and the Berlin Crisis are well documented. Less well known is the Kennedy Administration's efforts to expand the economy. The federal government's policies were in no small measure responsible for preventing expected recession and unemployment. But most important of all was Kennedy's legacy of civil rights and social justice. While his efforts were primarily symbolic, since the conservative Congress prevented much of Kennedy's legislation from becoming law, his pronouncements did spark what most considered a civil rights revolution. To be sure, these had begun in the Eisenhower era, but it was Kennedy who provided the inspirational and symbolic thrust that caught the imagination of the American people.

With the president's death, Lyndon Johnson embarked on his Great Society. He soon pushed through massive civil rights legislation, which in no small measure was made possible by the impact of the Kennedy assassination. Johnson, stating that this legislation was what Kennedy would have wanted, skillfully played upon the emotions of the American people, as well as Congress, to pass such measures as the Civil Rights Bill of 1964 and Medicare:

The death of Kennedy had robbed the civil rights opposition of much of its sting. The emotional reaction to Dallas changed the climate of opinion, both in Congress and the country, and intangibly brought it into far more sympathetic response to the Negro revolution. Nor did Johnson feel any embarrassment in appealing to the country and to the Congress to pass this bill out of respect for John Kennedy.[116]

The election of 1964 and his overwhelming defeat of the Republican party's Conservative candidate, Barry Goldwater, gave Johnson the mandate he sought to carry out his own programs. The consensus of 1963–64 upon which he based most of his presidential politics provided Johnson a continuing base upon which to advance his programs during his full term. Combined with his intimate knowledge of Congress and his long-time friends and acquaintances on Capitol Hill, Johnson had well-established informal alliances and coalitions upon which he could call for support. One of his major accomplishments during 1964 was the reassertion of presidential dominance over the Congress—something Kennedy was unable to do.

Unfortunately, the Great Society was soon overshadowed by Vietnam. And what Johnson hoped would be a presidential administration known for its great domestic accomplishments turned out to be a war presidency known for its Vietnam debacle. President Johnson tried desperately to separate domestic programs from American involvement in Vietnam. But increasingly the public and critics associated all of the Johnson presidency with Vietnam, virtually nullifying any good that might have been part of the Great Society.

Simultaneously, waiting in the wings were those whose lack of confidence in the political system and dissatisfaction with the quality of American politics were growing, first with the dramatic loss of John F. Kennedy and second with the unfulfilled expectations of the Great Society. What made matters worse was that Johnson's leadership style and view of the presidency did not provide the necessary political-psychological symbols to cement a consensus within society.

Nothing that President Johnson could say or do, nothing that the Great Society was to accomplish, could fill the inspirational and psychological vacuum left by the death of Kennedy. This prepared the way for the loss of confidence in America's ability to prosecute the Vietnam War. It also planted the seeds of emotional distress and reaction against American institutions and politics, which for many Americans were accomplices of the destruction of "Camelot."

The coming together of these two great waves—the one from the external world and the other from deep within American society—propelled America into Vietnam and finally doomed its venture there. While the external wave eroded the basic premises of American political-military policy, the internal wave gave vent to the frustrations of society in an outburst of moral indignation, not only against the Vietnam War, but also American institutions and leaders, and the ills of American society. Within a short period of time, many Americans saw the crusade to save South Vietnam as an immoral undertaking wrought with unethical relationships and behavior—and a symbol of all that was wrong with America. While the fragile consensus on American involvement in Vietnam was in the process of disintegrating, the military commitment was growing. When the consensus finally collapsed, there were over 500,000 American servicemen in Vietnam fighting a war many Americans did not want to fight.

Spurred by the Kennedy charisma, Americans had come to believe in the search for perfection in themselves and the political system. By the time of America's deep involvement in Vietnam in 1966–67, the American people had still not reconciled themselves to the imperfections of either the political system or those who led it. This became particularly damaging to the military effort in Vietnam.

The divisiveness over Vietnam led to President Lyndon Johnson's decision not to seek reelection in 1968. Hubert Humphrey, Johnson's vice-president, became the Democratic candidate, and Richard Nixon reemerged as the Republican candidate for president. The campaign was fought primarily over America's involvement in Vietnam. Although Humphrey made a strong showing, he could not completely shed his image as Johnson's man, and thus he was tarnished with Johnson's Vietnam policies. Nixon won the election, and many hoped that he could do something about getting America out of Vietnam.

Richard Nixon became president in 1968 on a platform of "Vietnamization," among other things. According to this policy, the South Vietnamese military would be given the primary task of carrying the war to the North Vietnamese and the Vietcong. Simultaneously, American forces would gradually withdraw from active combat, and would eventually be reduced in numbers. The policy did not work as intended. It was difficult for America to withdraw from active combat without incurring heavy casualties, and the South Vietnamese military was hard pressed to maintain a momentum against the enemy.

During President Nixon's first term, the Vietnamization policy was established, and serious efforts were made to implement it. This was accompanied by the American incursion into Cambodia in an attempt to destroy the enemy's bases and prevent their use against American forces withdrawing from combat. In addition, serious efforts were made to arrange a peace treaty. The American people were given some hope, not only because of the peace efforts, but also because steps were being taken to shift the basis of military manpower from selective service to a volunteer system. To the mild surprise of high-level American officials, the Cambodia incursion created a storm in the United States and was quickly ended, regardless of the efforts to justify it as a measure to protect American forces.

In any case, when Richard Nixon moved into the Oval Office, American policy and involvement in Vietnam were set, perhaps beyond the ability of any one president to change without a total collapse of the South Vietnamese effort and the appearance of an American retreat. The Vietnamization policy did provide a basis for American withdrawal and, most of all, reduced the number of American casualties. In the end, however, regardless of American efforts, the American withdrawal was quickly followed by the South Vietnamese collapse.

If there had been no Watergate, America's foreign policy effort and the Vietnamization policy may have resulted in a different Southeast Asia. But Watergate seriously damaged President Nixon's credibility and eroded his efforts in Vietnam. Nixon's foreign policy achievements were totally lost in the deception of Watergate.

PRESIDENTIAL LEADERSHIP

Three presidents were deeply involved in directing American policy in Vietnam. Kennedy, expanding from the groundwork laid by Eisenhower, increased American involvement, committing over 16,000 American advisors by the time of his death. Johnson dramatically broadened the scope, committing combat troops (eventually numbering over 500,000) to South Vietnam. Nixon came into office committed to Vietnamization and winding down the American role. All three presidents provided a continuity to the Vietnam War and viewed American involvement in almost identical terms.

The Kennedy presidency has been well documented in a number of publications.[117] Most of these works are sympathetic and provide insights into the Kennedy personality, character, and style of leadership. These accounts also hint of greater things for American politics had Kennedy lived. According to Theodore Sorenson, Kennedy "was a happy president. Happiness, he often said, paraphrasing Aristotle, is the full sense of one's faculties along lines of excellence, and to him the Presidency offered the ideal opportunity to pursue excellence."[118] Sorenson describes Kennedy's concept of government as follows:

His philosophy of government was keyed to power, not as a matter of personal ambition but of national obligation: the primacy of the White House within the Executive Branch and of the Executive Branch within the Federal Government, the leadership of the Federal Government within the United States and of the United States within the community of nations.[119]

Kennedy's view of power had no moral implications, except in terms of the purposes for which it was used. "Power was not a goal he sought for its own sake. It was there in the White House, to be used, without any sense of guilt or greed, as a means of getting things done."[120]

John Kennedy provided a degree of hope and optimism that the problems of mankind could be solved by commitment to the ideals of America. His now famous "passing the torch" inaugural address set the tone of his administration. The youth in America were particularly affected by this young president who seemed to reflect all that was "good" in the United States. His assassination created a myth, and, indeed, a legend, although his political accomplishments were not noteworthy and his programs in Congress were in deep trouble. His appeal to get the country moving again was particularly attractive after two terms of what many felt was a status quo administration. Eisenhower's stewardship approach to the presidency seemed uninspiring and unimaginative. John Kennedy's political and prerogative view of the presidency, in stark contrast, appeared to be a dynamic and promising approach.

Kennedy was not a slave to ideology, however. He was committed to what has been described as the New Frontier. Although he was at first criticized for lack of direction, he soon provided a sense of purpose to the nation. This was generally under the rubric of democratic ideology—the idea of justice, civil rights, and liberty. These became the philosophical underpinnings of "Camelot."

Kennedy's general slant on the world maintained itself in the White House. He found earth an exciting place to live, and said so. Emphasis on arousing democracy to action is obvious, from "Ask not..." on. The toughness theme was also there, perhaps exacerbating a tendency to see the communists in the role of Hitler in World War II.... He had come along into politics immediately after a war in which the good guys and the bad guys were clearly distinguishable. Some of that had climbed up into his brain again.[121]

The Bay of Pigs, the Cuban Missile Crisis, the Berlin Crisis, and Vietnam reveal Kennedy's firm anti-Communist perspective. Yet his view of the Third World was relatively simplistic, as is reflected in his policies towards Cuba and Vietnam. While some would argue that Kennedy had few options open to him in these policy areas, given the Eisenhower policies, others like Richard J. Walton point to his lack of understanding of the process of revolution in the Third World and his failure to separate U.S.-Soviet conflicts from the Third World. Some critics argue that these failings led to a number of serious miscalculations on Kennedy's part.

Kennedy. . .was a counterrevolutionary. For it is only as counterrevolutionary that his policies in Cuba and Vietnam, and even the insignificant British Guiana, make sense. The great buildup in conventional war-making capacity, his passion for the Green Berets, the "counterinsurgency" programs—all these make sense only as preparation for counterrevolution. Perhaps he did not even know it himself; perhaps he genuinely believed in change and simply did not understand that the gradual, slow evolution he wanted was no longer possible under modern circumstances. Nor did Kennedy understand that the Soviet-American rivalry was essentially a distinct phenomenon.[122]

Kennedy's policies toward Cuba reflected his views on democracy and communism and were consistent with his views on the role of the United States: "we must attempt to strengthen the non-Batista democratic anti-Castro forces in exile, and in Cuba itself, who offer eventual hope of overthrowing Castro. Thus far these fighters for freedom have had virtually no support from our government."[123]

Kennedy emerges as an individual who was sincerely concerned about doing "good" not only in the United States but also in the world. Yet there was a naivete about his approach which presumed that inspirational leadership and symbolic policy positions could achieve almost idealistic goals. The realities of politics, particularly in dealing with Congress and with allies and protagonists in the world arena, limited what could be accomplished. This was particularly troubling with respect to Vietnam policy. In earlier speeches, Kennedy expressed the view that South Vietnam was a cornerstone of democracy and that America was morally committed to its defense. But after entering the Oval Office, Kennedy found that the situation in Vietnam was such that it did not necessarily respond to American policy goals or efforts. He became convinced that President Diem was an obstruction to the achievement of democracy in the South. That Kennedy was troubled about America's policy in Vietnam seems clear. What was less clear was America's policy direction. Raising the number of advisors from 1,500 to 16,000 by November 1963, Kennedy increased American involvement dramatically. Whether he would have withdrawn or continued with this commitment is pure speculation. Given Kennedy's anti-Communist perspective and his view that South Vietnam was an important link in containing communism, it is conceivable that little would have changed in respect to American policy had Kennedy lived.

Although some argue that Kennedy's Vietnam policy would have differed considerably from that pursued by Lyndon Johnson, there is compelling evidence to the contrary. Even the most sympathetic accounts reveal that Kennedy's approach reflected a determination and commitment to the defense of Vietnam. Arthur Schlesinger, for example, states that "the President unquestionably felt that an American retreat in Asia might upset the whole world balance. In December he ordered the American build-up to begin."[124] Moreover, in his 1963 State of the Union Address, Kennedy "summed up the mood at the turn of the year: 'The spearpoint of aggression has been blunted in South Vietnam.' "[125]

The Pentagon Papers also provide evidence that the American commitment to South Vietnam had changed fundamentally under the presidency of John F. Kennedy. According to Hedrick Smith, "The limited risk gamble undertaken by Eisenhower had been transformed into an unlimited commitment under Kennedy.... President Kennedy and his senior advisors are described in this study as considering defeat unthinkable."[126] (The study referred to was the Pentagon study commissioned in 1967 by Secretary of Defense Robert McNamara, commonly known as the Pentagon Papers. The study covers American involvement in Indochina from World War II to May 1968.)

Johnson's handling of the Vietnam War, while an expansion of the policy established by Kennedy, also reflected Johnson's own particular character and personality. His commitment to the Great Society and to the civil rights legislation of Kennedy projected an image of a sensitive public figure sincerely concerned for justice and fair play at home. Johnson's views on America's role in Vietnam, however, projected an image of a determined, tough, anti-Communist committed to fighting aggression.

Amidst the chaos of Johnson's verbal productions, two themes persisted, sometimes alternating in the same speech: a tough, hard, militaristic theme and a dedicated humanitarianism—Johnson mean and Johnson nice. Together they add up to a view of the world in which the strong-weak dimension is paramount. Never fully consistent in any philosophic sense, Johnson found a way to let these themes live together by separating the arenas in which they were operative. To the outerworld of foreign policy, Johnson presented his hard soldierly visage; to the deprived at home, he showed a kindlier face.[127]

The major difference between the Kennedy and Johnson presidencies is in the style of leadership—a reflection of character and personality.

For Johnson, personal relationships and loyalties were the key to the power of the presidency. He used these as an administrative tool. For example, stressing his personal contacts in the Congress, Johnson played upon the weaknesses and loyalties of members of Congress, encouraging, cajoling, and threatening them in order to gain support for his viewpoint and policies. He did not hesitate to intimidate and to play upon obligations and political reciprocity. Some critics maintain that Johnson's style of leadership was not only cruel and intimidating, but also crude and blatant in the exercise of power. Thus, instead of being encouraged to provide objective assessments, Johnson's advisors tended to be dominated by his personality and exercise of power, and many hesitated to provide anything but optimistic reports which tended to perpetuate existing policy.

Both Kennedy and Johnson saw communism as monolithic. As a senator, Johnson advocated treating all aggression by Communist forces anywhere in the world as acts of the Soviet Union.[128] Johnson felt that the military might of the United States was the major pillar of American democracy. As a representative and later as a senator, he sat on and chaired various committees and subcommittees overseeing various aspects of the armed forces. From these positions he generally felt that the use of force against Communist aggression was the best policy.

Johnson viewed with envy the rapport Kennedy had with the press and the American public. Try as he did, Johnson could not achieve the broad consensus he needed to sustain the war effort in Vietnam. Much of this can be traced to Johnson's personality and the image he projected in the mass media.[129] Never understanding how to deal with the press, he continually complained about it and threatened those in the press who were opposed to him with "excommunication."[130]

Regardless of changing conditions, Johnson was determined not to lose Vietnam as he felt America had lost China. He did not want to be noted in history as the president who lost the Vietnam War. He was determined to push the military effort, but he also sought to end the conflict peacefully as long as it did not mean the loss of South Vietnam. In the end, unable to convince the American people of the continuing need to aggressively pursue a military solution in Vietnam, haunted by the specter of domestic disorders, and disturbed by the serious erosion of Great Society programs, Johnson declined to run for reelection in 1968. His withdrawal from the 1968 presidential race was not a decision based solely on Vietnam. A number of other political factors entered into the equation, notably, political gamesmanship and party disenchantment. But the fact remains that Vietnam had become an albatross tarnishing virtually everything that the Johnson Administration touched. For all of the great dreams that Johnson had inherited from Kennedy and had expanded with his own vision of the future, Johnson had become known as the war president with the millstone of Vietnam around his neck.

The pledge to get America out of Vietnam contributed a great deal to Richard Nixon's election in 1968 and reelection in 1972. By 1968 American society was torn by Vietnam, and while many Americans did not necessarily want to see a withdrawal without a clear victory, all wanted relief from the internal agony of Vietnam. Nixon pledged that, in addition to restoring law and order within the United States, he would achieve a peace with honor.

The Nixon character and personality remain somewhat of a mystery. He was a man difficult to understand and to know. Even some of his closest associates never really knew him in a way that associates knew Kennedy. Whereas Kennedy, and to some extent Johnson, projected sensitivity and sincerity, Nixon was seen as a relatively cold and calculating politician. Nixon's view of his duty as president included a sense of martyrdom. As president, he felt that he would perform his duties as best he could. Yet he also felt that no one could really know the difficulties of the office or the burdens placed upon the incumbent. He alone had to face the threats and challenges of the world. In the end, Nixon felt that history would see him as an individual who did his best for his country, in one of the toughest jobs in the world. As Nixon was fond of quoting, "When the going gets tough, the tough get going."

Aware of historical patterns in which lesser civilizations dominated greater ones, Nixon was fearful of the dangers this posed to America. He perceived that the United States was faced with serious threats, particularly from Communist-aligned nations and the Soviet Union. In this respect, like his predecessors, he saw communism as a monolith, at least initially. Later, following the break between China and the Soviet Union, and the evolution of Titoism, he adopted the view that communism was as much a state of mind and an ideological tool as a foreign policy tool.

Thus, he implemented his policy of Vietnamization and American withdrawal with great caution. Nixon wanted to insure that America's withdrawal would not be taken as an ideological retreat or as a sign of moral weakness. "The trick was to withdraw from the war without having it appear that the United States was giving up. This policy had two essential features: 'Vietnamization' and a negotiated settlement with Hanoi."[131]

While the propriety of Nixon's policies may be questioned, the perceptions of the American people and the image projected by the media invariably reflected a degree of skepticism and suspicion. Nixon never did reconcile himself to this situation, convinced that the media and certain groups in society were against him, regardless of his efforts in bringing peace and tranquility at home. According to some historians, this persistent antagonistic relationship between the president and important groups in society developed into a political-psychological adversarial relationship that influenced policy and the perceptions of the president. In the long run, Nixon may well have been affected psychologically by what he considered constant and unrelenting pressures brought to bear against him by the media and anti-establishment groups.[132]

Nixon's involvement in Watergate and the pressures forcing him to continually defend his position, publicly and privately, left him with little time and energy to devote to the issues in Vietnam. Moreover, as foreign governments began to understand the full implications of Watergate for the American presidency, they became wary of Nixon's foreign policy initiatives. America's policy in Vietnam became more of a holding action than anything else. And most felt that holding action could accomplish little but prepare the way for American withdrawal, regardless of the consequences to South Vietnam.

High officials in Nixon's administration recognized the linkage between Vietnam and Watergate:

Indochina would be the first Watergate casualty, Kissinger predicted bitterly. The Congress, the press and the people would never permit the administration to demonstrate the resolve that it needed to save it. When Vietnam fell, American foreign policy would be reduced to a myth. What is strength without the will to use it? Kissinger asked rhetorically.[133]

For Nixon, all of the efforts in foreign affairs, including the reestablishment of relations with China, Vietnamization, and withdrawal from Vietnam, were lost in the disaster of the Watergate affair. Interestingly, all three presidents failed in one way or another in their Vietnam involvement. One met an untimely death, while Vietnam was being expanded into a major policy problem. Another was virtually driven from office as a result of America's involvement. The last was prevented from exploiting his Vietnam policies, by the linkages between America's involvement in Vietnam and Watergate; this ultimately led to American withdrawal and the defeat of South Vietnam.

While Kennedy's personality, character, and style of leadership could have provided the leadership and inspiration to develop realistic policies on Vietnam and receive the support of the American people, his untimely death makes this historical speculation. Johnson and Nixon possessed neither the style of leadership nor the character and personality that inspire. Thus, the American people were confronted by an ambiguous and complex situation in Vietnam, which those in and around the Oval Office were unable to clarify. In the long run, those who had supported American policy in Vietnam turned against the president in an implicit alliance with the war resisters. According to the supporters, if America did not want to "win" in Vietnam, they must get out. The war resisters were against American involvement regardless of the policies.

All three presidents shared common misperceptions. None fully understood the nature of revolutionary or counterrevolutionary war, nor grasped the significance of the colonial impact and the culture, which was so alien to Western democracy. Although each attempted to respond with what he presumed was reasonable policy, none was able to appreciate the totality of revolutionary war. Kennedy's preoccupation with the military dimension of counterinsurgency war and the expansion of the Green Berets, Johnson's advocacy of the economic development of the Mekong Delta, or Nixon's view of Vietnamization—all focused on a "piece" of revolution or counterrevolution, without getting at the essence of the issue: who should rule and the exercise of power.[134]

Could things have been different? Probably not. By 1968 domestic disenchantment had gone too far, and the character of military operations in Vietnam was well established and precluded major changes. While military units could still win local battles, as was the case in the 1968 Tet Offensive, the political-psychological consequences worked against American policy. National will and political resolve continued to erode. Presidential leadership was not up to the task, while the military attempted to carry out operations with declining morale and a vacillating sense of purpose. A fundamental tenet of Maoist revolutionary strategy was confirmed. Battles could be lost, but the war could be won in the political-psychological arena. In brief, consciously or not, Mao's political-psychological principle played the major role in determining America's role in Vietnam. America's national will and political resolve eroded to such a point that continuation of the Vietnam War could have only led to disaster for America's military and collapse of the moral and ethical tenets of American democracy.

POLITICAL RESOLVE AND NATIONAL WILL

Most Americans and their leaders initially supported America's role in Vietnam. Even at the time of the Gulf of Tonkin Resolution and the first commitment of American combat troops in 1965, there was considerable support for Lyndon Johnson's policies. By 1966, however, questions were being raised about American policy, first by newspaper correspondents and then gradually and increasingly by members of Congress. Optimistic reports by the American Military Assistance Command in Vietnam (MACV) were countered by pessimistic reports by correspondents in the field with American troops. The crescendo of criticism that culminated in the 1968 demonstrations in Chicago reflected the erosion of consensus on Vietnam and the collapse of America's national will and political resolve to continue the war.

The end of the Johnson presidency came rather dramatically, although throughout 1966 and 1967 it became apparent that Vietnam had become the key issue in American politics. Johnson has stated in his own work on the presidency that he had already decided in 1965 not to seek a second term. This decision was based on his health and his concern about the policies and programs associated with the Great Society. It seems clear, however, that the major reason for Johnson's decision not to seek reelection in 1968 was Vietnam.

In those final months, as the announcement of my decision neared, I believe only one thing could have changed my mind—an indication that the men in Vietnam would regard it as unfair or unwise. I asked General Westmoreland to come home in November 1967, and I put the question to him. As we sat in the family living room on the second floor of the White House one evening after dinner, I asked him what the effect on troop morale would be if I announced that I would not run for another term. Would the men think the Commander in Chief who had sent them to the battlefield had let them down?

General Westmoreland looked for a few moments at the windows facing out to the rose garden. Then he turned to me. "Mr. President," he said, "I do not believe so."[135]

Johnson knew that the continuation of the Vietnam involvement and his attempt at a second term of office were inseparable. To a number of observers Johnson's withdrawal from the presidential race in 1968 was simply a way to keep whatever reputation he had remaining—it was simply a case of "necessary" politics. But undoubtedly, this was an agonizing decision.

The election of 1968 turned on the issue of Vietnam. Richard Nixon ran against Hubert Humphrey, the vice-president under Johnson. Nixon, running essentially a noncampaign, began with a tremendous advantage. Humphrey was tarnished as a "Johnson man" and by Vietnam. Yet he ran a vigorous campaign against Nixon, who simply told the American people that he had a plan to end the war in Vietnam. No one knew what the plan entailed, and Nixon did not reveal what his plan was. Regardless of how hard Humphrey tried to disassociate himself from the Vietnam War, many still viewed him as a spokesman for the Johnson Administration and its war policies.

The 1968 campaign saw candidates for both parties, including Eugene McCarthy and Robert Kennedy (both of whom served as rallying points for antiwar forces), trying to become spokesmen for peace in Vietnam:

candidates from both parties fell over themselves in their eagerness to abandon both anti-Communist slogans and the war, offering instead hopes for an "honorable peace" in Vietnam and for "Law and order" at home. Halting Communist aggression was abandoned as an issue; stopping further costly foreign adventures—"No More Vietnams"—became the issue.[136]

With prominent individuals campaigning hard for the presidency on a platform that included withdrawal from Vietnam, the change in national will and political resolve was consummated. Support for the continuation of American involvement had become political suicide. Most candidates tried to outdo each other in advocating policies to bring American involvement to an end. The 1968 campaign seemed to be a clear signal that the Vietnam conflict had turned decidedly in favor of the Vietcong and North Vietnam.

The general theme of withdrawal from Vietnam was not limited to national politics. At the grass roots level, disenchantment with the war and continued American casualties for a cause now lost merged with the withdrawal theme at the national level. This political environment was not lost on military professionals. It had its impact on military effectiveness. As one high-ranking military professional, General Fred Weyand, observed:

Vietnam was a reaffirmation of the peculiar relationship between the American Army and the American people. The American Army really is a people's Army in the sense that it belongs to the American people who take a jealous and proprietary interest in its involvement. When the Army is committed the American people are committed, when the American people lose their commitment it is futile to try to keep the Army committed. In the final analysis, the American Army is not so much an arm of the Executive Branch as it is an arm of the American people. The Army, therefore, cannot be committed lightly.[137]

President Nixon took office in 1968 on a platform that included peace in Vietnam. The basis for this policy was a program of Vietnamization, which was based on the premise that by supplying modern weapons, intensifying training, and expanding the combat role of the South Vietnamese Army, that army would eventually assume all of the combat actions in South Vietnam. At the same time, this would lead to a parallel withdrawal of U.S. combat forces. Simultaneously, the capacity of the South Vietnamese government and administration would be expanded and made more effective. In essence, the purpose of Vietnamization was to improve the effectiveness of the South Vietnamese military to allow U.S. ground troops to disengage and withdraw from Vietnam. Before this could be accomplished, there would be many more American casualties in Vietnam and more domestic conflict. And when America did withdraw from Vietnam, it was under the cloud of Watergate and the smell of defeat.

Meanwhile, the administration was faced with an increasing dilemma regarding the prosecution of the war. Pressures increased for withdrawal, while others cautioned against any precipitous pullout. Sir Robert Thompson, a noted British counterinsurgency expert, assessed the call for immediate withdrawal and concluded that it was tantamount to retreat.

The option of intentionally ending the war by a sell-out was also not one that could be undertaken lightly. Plenty of hopeful reasons have been produced on economic and political grounds to justify the United States getting out of Vietnam at any cost. It is interesting to note that very few have been prepared to spell out the likely consequences of such an eventuality.[138]

Vietnamization had its proponents as well as opponents. Senator William Fulbright, an outspoken critic of U.S. policy in Vietnam, stated:

But I welcome it [Vietnamization] only in the sense that I would rather be riding in a car heading for a precipice at 30 miles an hour than at 80 miles an hour. Granting the new policy that is its due, I am still unwilling to adorn the lesser folly with the name of wisdom. [It is a policy to keep] our proteges in Saigon staggering around the ring for a few years longer.[139]

Robert Shaplen commented on the importance of the manner of withdrawal:

By 1969, while we could not simply write off Vietnam and withdraw precipitously, I came to feel, along with many others, that we had no alternative but to diminish our commitment as best we could keeping in mind that the manner and method of our withdrawal were not only vital to Vietnam but even more vital to the rest of Southeast Asia. . . . the American people were disposed to end the war as soon as possible but most in such a way that the Vietnamese would not be abandoned and that American willingness to lend support to the rest of Southeast Asia would be sustained, if restricted.[140]

On April 30, 1970, the president announced the U.S. military campaign in Cambodia for the purpose of destroying Vietcong sanctuaries, to ease the pressures within South Vietnam and lessen the dangers for withdrawing U.S. troops. This action, although completed on June 30, did raise speculation as to the possibilities of an expanded war and created doubts about the efficiency of Vietnamization. In addition, the Cambodian incursion provided an impetus to antiwar groups, which had lately staged fewer public protestations.

The war sparked massive campus protests in the United States and became the focal point for the coalescing of protests regarding a variety of ills in American society. This amalgam of issues led to an almost continual series of college disturbances, some producing violent confrontations between students and police. Berkeley and Columbia University were cases in point. Following America's invasion of Cambodia, a confrontation took place at Kent State in Ohio in May 1970 in which four students were killed by National Guardsmen while protesting the U.S. campaign in Cambodia, a tragic result of what was supposed to be the beginning of American withdrawal.

The Kent State affair also illustrated one of the most significant phenomena associated with the Vietnam War; the politicization of youth groups. Among the presidential candidates for the 1968 elections were a number who stood on a platform of opposition to the Vietnam War. One of these was Senator Eugene McCarthy whose campaign was surprisingly effective, although unsuccessful. McCarthy's campaign caught the imagination of the youth who were opposed to the war and resulted in a vocal "Youth for McCarthy" movement.

Frustrations with the war, alienation from the "establishment," and questions over the right to dissent culminated in the Democratic convention disorders in Chicago in 1968. The result of these confrontations further polarized the anti-establishment and establishment forces into an uncompromising position regarding the Vietnam War. Demonstrations against the war had precipitated counterreactions by various groups. One of the most publicized was the violent reaction of construction workers against peace demonstrators in New York in 1970.

On the heels of the Cambodian excursion (1970) and the Vietnamization policy, American air and sea forces provided maximum support for the South Vietnamese forces. In the hopes of withdrawing gracefully, the Nixon Administration promised total support for the Vietnamese government. Thus, by the beginning of 1973, American ground forces had for all practical purposes withdrawn from South Vietnam. But by 1975 the North Vietnamese had overwhelmed the South and acquired what they had sought since World War II. Symbolic of the tragedy of the South was the picture of the last American helicopter out of Saigon before the takeover by the North Vietnamese. South Vietnamese desperately clinging to the helicopter were beaten off by Americans as the helicopter lightened its load to leave. For many it seemed a sad but appropriate symbol of American involvement in Vietnam.

When the Vietnamization policy was first being put into effect, the Nixon Administration sought peace negotiations with the Hanoi regime. Earlier peace efforts by the Johnson Administration had been unsuccessful. Although peace negotiations were still in progress when Nixon took office, the new administration brought with it high hopes for success. By late 1969 the optimism had changed to pessimism. Efforts continued, however, and by October 1972 Hanoi and the Nixon Administration tentatively agreed to a draft cease-fire. While several items remained unclarified, President Nixon ordered bombing of the

North in December. By early January 1973 heavy bombing of North Vietnam had apparently persuaded the Hanoi regime to seek an end to hostilities. By the end of January a cease-fire went into effect in all of Vietnam.

The most important provision of the agreement was that all Americans involved in military combat would be withdrawn from Vietnam within 60 days and the American prisoners of war would be released to American authorities within the same period of time. Although the Paris negotiations with the Communists of Hanoi seemed paralyzed, American troops were coming home—115,000 had already come back by April 5, with another 150,000 going home over the next twelve months. In early February, as the television cameras whirred away, Americans saw most of their prisoners of war returning. Esteem of Nixon among his countrymen rose to its peak, surpassing in every public opinion poll the approval he had won in the official count of the election votes in November 1968.

Watergate was soon to turn triumph into tragedy, however.

SOCIOECONOMIC PATTERNS

The 1960s, as we have already noted, were years of change and transition. The Kennedy Administration marked the beginning of this change; the Nixon Administration marked the end of this period and the beginning of another. The 1960s saw great domestic disturbances, coupled with expanded political awareness and political participation by a variety of minority groups. Supported by Supreme Court decisions and legislation as well as executive action, social programs increased dramatically, individual rights, both civil and criminal, were expanded, and a great deal of effort went into a war on poverty. In the aftermath of the decade, with the Watergate affair and the resignation of President Nixon, the Democratic party seemed to have all but captured the national government and with it many state governments.

During the 1960s, however, the Democrats were identified as the war party; it was by exploiting this issue that the Republican candidate Richard Nixon captured the White House. For the greater part of the decade, the Vietnam War was the focal point of national politics. The costs of the Vietnam War in terms of American lives and dollars, and its impact on domestic programs were crucial issues in politics. Although Vietnam was a limited war, in dollars it was the most expensive war ever fought by the United States with the exception of World War II. At its height in 1968, over 14,000 servicemen lost their lives in combat and over 46,000 more were wounded. This was the same year that violent demonstrations against the war disrupted the Democratic National Convention in Chicago.

Table 9
Federal Expenditures and Gross National Product, 1960-1970

Year	Total Expenditures ($ billions)	Defense Expenditures ($ billions)	Gross National Product ($ billions)
1960	92.2	45.2	506.5
1962	106.8	49.0	548.2
1965	118.4	47.5	659.5
1966	134.7	54.9	724.1
1967	158.3	68.2	777.3
1968	178.8	78.8	831.3
1969	184.6	79.4	910.6
1970	196.6	78.6	968.8

Source: U.S. Bureau of the Census, Statistical Abstracts of the United States, 1981, 102d ed. (Washington, D.C.: U.S. Government Printing Office, 1981), p. 354; and U.S. General Accounting Office, Defense Spending and Its Relationship to the Federal Budget (Washington, D.C.: U.S. General Accounting Office, June 9, 1983), p. 114.

The Vietnam involvement may well have precipitated the turmoil of the 1960s, but profound social changes had already been brewing. The use of drugs reached epidemic proportions in the population, particularly among the youth. Use of drugs in the armed forces became a major problem in Vietnam. Combined with a search for "the free life" and cultural channels for uninhibited expression, the 1960s took on a psychedelic veneer, affecting education, business, attitudes, and, of course, the idea of service to the country. Alienation and disenchantment with American society were commonplace, gathering steam following the assassination of John F. Kennedy and culminating in the massive emotional protestations against the Vietnam War in Chicago during the summer of 1968. Some observers have stated that the 1960s represented a particular kind of American revolution.[141] America had apparently lost control of its own destiny and had developed a serious crisis of confidence.[142]

The decade was not without socioeconomic advances, although a number of groups did not perceive them as such. The gross national product increased from $506 billion in 1960 to over $968 billion in 1970 (see Table 9). The per capita income also showed a marked increase, from $3,620 in 1960 to over $4,958 in 1970. Even with inflation, there

Table 10
U.S. Population and Military Personnel, 1960-1970 (in millions)

Year	Total Population	Total Military	Army	Navy	Air Force	Marines
1960	180.7	2.5	0.87	0.617	0.814	0.170
1962	186.5	2.8	1.10	0.666	0.884	0.190
1964	191.9	2.7	0.973	0.667	0.856	0.189
1966	196.6	3.1	1.20	0.745	0.887	0.261
1968	200.7	3.5	1.57	0.765	0.904	0.307
1970	204.9	3.1	1.32	0.692	0.791	0.259

Source: U.S. Bureau of the Census, Statistical Abstracts of the
United States, 1981, 102d ed. (Washington, D.C.: U.S.
Government Printing Office, 1981), pp. 5, 362.

was improvement. At the same time, the median income between white
and black families narrowed, with the black family's median income
reaching over 60 percent of that for white families. In black families
where both husband and wife were in the labor force, the median income
reached 85 percent of that for comparable white families. Although expenditures for national defense in the 1960s increased, they were considerably less than the dramatic increases in expenditures for social
welfare. In 1960, expenditures for national defense and social welfare
(human resources) were $45.2 and $25.5 billion, respectively. In 1965
these figures had increased to $47.5 and $35.4 billion, respectively, and
by 1970 the amount of money spent on national defense reached $78.6
billion, but on social welfare (human resources) $73.4 billion. By 1973
the national defense budget had dropped to $74.5 billion, while social
welfare (human resources) jumped to over $116 billion annually.

Even with the heavy commitment to Vietnam, the total number of
servicemen and women in the American military represented only 1.75
percent of the total population (see Table 10). The South Vietnamese
military, on the other hand, represented over 7 percent of their population.

While much remained to be done, the opportunity for minority groups
expanded in both the political and economic spheres. Educational opportunities in colleges and universities broadened, sparked by increased
government aid. Social relationships and political power among various
minorities and between minorities and the vast majority of the populace
also underwent change. Increased opportunities and expanded power
eventually led to confrontations, with some accommodation between
groups, even more entrenchment by some groups, and a drive for power
by others.

In sum, the decade of the 1960s was marked by serious domestic turmoil; at the same time, the economic system had improved the general lot of the people, as well as the human resources and social welfare commitment of the country. But the specter of Vietnam tarnished all of the social and economic gains. Some argue that rising expectations, socioeconomic gains, and the Vietnam War all worked together to increase demands for social justice and an individual self-interest. This combination did much to erode the national will and weaken the political resolve to continue involvement in Vietnam. Thus, despite the social and economic gains, the 1960s ended on a note of pessimism and disenchantment.

SUMMARY

American involvement in Vietnam began slowly, arousing little public attention at first. By the time of President Kennedy's assassination, about 16,000 Americans were in Vietnam. Shortly thereafter, President Lyndon Johnson changed the role of Americans from advisory to combat, thereby changing the complexion of the war. But even then, there was little appreciation of the implications. Most Americans felt the need to stop "Communist" aggression.

During the Kennedy period and the first years of the Johnson Administration, most Americans focused on the dramatic events taking place within America. The passage of the Civil Rights Bill, demonstrations and marches for equality, and the political conflicts that developed over these issues seemed to take most of the time and energy of politicians, political groups, as well as the American people as a whole. In the meantime, decisions were being made that deepened America's involvement in Vietnam. In this respect, the initial involvement, and, indeed, the shift from an advisory to an active ground combat role, were only tangential public concerns and minor debate issues. Only after American forces engaged in bloody battles and casualties began to rise did the American people become more aware of the depth of the American commitment and the difficulties of the war. To many it appeared that overnight America had taken on a tremendous burden in Vietnam.

At the same time, a number of domestic trends came together, creating a politically volatile environment and gradually producing mass demonstrations and political divisiveness. The period of turmoil began with the assassination of Kennedy and the dashing of expectations about the "goodness" of America. The expanding civil rights issues coincided with these developments and eventually found their way into antiwar protests. These protests were aimed at the "establishment," and the military was made a key target. The eventual commitment of over 500,000 American servicemen in Vietnam, the relatively high casualty rates, and the perceptions of the war perpetuated by the media and antiwar groups in the United States made it appear that the United States was morally wrong in its involvement. These antiwar dissenters were later joined by those who felt America should withdraw because it was not prepared to win.

Presidential leadership was at best vacillating and at worst based on false assumptions about America's ability and the nature of the war in Vietnam. The temper of the times and the lack of effective presidential leadership considerably eroded the national will and political resolve to continue the American involvement in Vietnam. The military institution soon reflected these characteristics. Following the Tet Offensive in 1968 and Lyndon Johnson's decision not to seek reelection in 1968, most military men were convinced of eventual American withdrawal. The withdrawal began under President Nixon and eventually led to the total defeat of South Vietnam.

All of the internal American developments must be viewed in the proper context. The assassination of John F. Kennedy had a long-range impact on the American psyche and the political system. The loss of confidence, the sense of personal loss, and dashed expectations lingered on throughout the 1960s. This political-psychological context was the handmaiden of events in the latter part of the decade.

The coming together of these forces during the 1960s made that decade a most traumatic one for America. Whether the results would have been the same without the Vietnam War or the assassination is pure speculation. Even without these two factors, the forces for change had already emerged. Given the nature of the American political system and the character of its leadership in the political-military realm, one can be justified in concluding that things would probably not have been greatly different, even if less costly.

CONCLUSIONS

Traditionally, American public response to counterrevolutionary conflict has begun from one of two positions: Either the people are convinced of the necessity for military action, or they are preoccupied with domestic issues and are unaware or unconcerned about the conflict or the implications of military involvement. In the cases of the Spanish-American War and the Punitive Expedition, most Americans felt (and indeed demanded) that some kind of military action be taken against what they considered aggression and injustice. In both cases, the visible involvement of American forces lasted but a short period of time. Only in the latter phases of the Philippine revolution did the conflict become protracted, and then, the war was fought almost exclusively by Regular

American troops. Only then did serious questions arise regarding American policy and the conduct of American troops.

The Anti-Imperialist League provided the focal point of opposition to American foreign policy and its counterrevolutionary effort in the Philippines. Many Americans, however, supported America's power projection into the foreign area. Most were convinced of the justice of America's role in Cuba and the Philippines and the stand against the Spanish rule in those areas.

Tensions in Europe, fear of involvement in the European war, and attention to the promises of the Progressive Era were the primary political-social patterns during the first decade of the twentieth century. Although Mexican depredations against Americans in Mexico and along the border convinced Americans that action had to be taken, this issue was overshadowed by the larger one of the war in Europe and its domestic implications.

In the cases of the Second Seminole War period and the years immediately preceding the Vietnam War, most Americans were concerned about specific domestic issues. In the 1830s American attention was on westward expansion, commercialization, and industrialization. Little concern was expressed about the plight of the Seminoles, who in any case were viewed as savages and obstructionists. The Kennedy period of the early 1960s was highlighted by attention to civil rights, equality, and the perceived aggressiveness of the Soviet Union. Few Americans were concerned or aware of the events unfolding in Southeast Asia. Indeed, few had ever heard of Indochina.

In all four cases, the president's leadership style and skill as a politician set the tone and direction of counterrevolutionary policy. Furthermore, the way the president articulated policy and the means he used to develop support and consensus among various political actors created certain expectations about the nature of American involvement. In turn, these expectations served as a criteria to assess the performance of the president and to judge the progress and credibility of American involvement. Once set, policy had to appear reasonably firm and effective, if the American people were to remain committed to that particular course of action. This was the case in all but the Vietnam War. During that war, even though American policy remained steadfast in its commitment to defend South Vietnam, the differing leadership styles of the presidents most directly involved in policy direction gave the impression that American policy was ineffective and based on a no-win scenario. While presidential leadership may have been constrained and affected by political and military pressures beyond direct American influence, it was the presidential posture and overall leadership capability that shaped the nature of America's commitment and determined the vigor with which policy was pursued.

National will and political resolve were closely related to the effectiveness of presidential leadership and the policy directions of the periods in question. In the Seminole War period, most Americans took their cue from President Jackson and supported the Indian removal policy. Jackson's populist appeal and his skill as a politician allowed him to assert his policy vigorously with minimum opposition. The brevity of the Punitive Expedition in Mexico and the Spanish-American War precluded the possibility of erosion of national will and political resolve, particularly in light of the public demands for involvement in both instances. However, as the Philippine-American War progressed and evolved into the conflict with the Moros, domestic opposition increased. Anti-imperialist sentiments coalesced and increased as the war progressed. But the war had a minimum impact on the American people, demanding little sacrifice in either material or human resources.

The Vietnam issue was more complex. Initially, there was a general consensus that American troops had to defend South Vietnam if necessary. It was only later in the war, when American casualties increased and Americans became convinced that the war had developed into a no-win situation, that the national will and political resolve to continue the war eroded considerably. Influential groups in American society, a host of political leaders, and the media reflected these attitudes. Ultimately, these attitudes found their way into the ranks of the military.

In every period of American counterrevolutionary involvement, important changes have taken place in domestic political and socioeconomic structures. The growth of American nationalism and expansionism as well as the broadening of the political base characterized the Jacksonian era, not to mention the great Panic of 1837 and attempts at recovery. The Spanish-American War period brought with it a vast expansion of the industrial base, the evolution of workingman versus business groups, and major concern with the quality of life. At the same time, America was projected into the world as a major power. The pre-World War I period was a continuation of the Progressive Era of the Spanish-American War period, and the New Freedom concept again focused on the workingman. It was also a period in which dramatic events were unfolding in Europe. The Vietnam War coincided with monumental breakthroughs in the American domestic order. The emphasis on civil rights and justice, perpetuated by a leader whose charisma and style touched most Americans, seemed to usher in a new age of Americanism. The assassination of Kennedy was a blow to American expectations and damaging to the American psyche, which only a generation later seemed to be recovering. Nonetheless, in each period of the counterrevolutionary period, the quality of life had improved.

What does all this mean with respect to American counterrevolutionary policy? First, the American people and their leaders had little understanding of the meaning of revolution and counterrevolution. As a result, the costs and consequences of counterrevolutionary policy were rarely anticipated with any degree of accuracy, nor were these weighed and balanced with respect to other policy requirements. Second, involvement in these conflicts either had the support of the American people, or was tangential to the major issues of the day. If the issue was tangential, either it had to stay that way, or a consensus had to be developed in support of American policy. Third, socioeconomic patterns were in the process of change, establishing new relationships and providing opportunities for bold policy initiatives. However, in all of the cases, American political-military policy remained rooted in its traditional orientation. Fourth, the key political actor in linking all of the elements of the state of the nation was the president. What he did, how he did it, and his personality and character, determined the coherency and acceptability of the counterrevolutionary policy. Finally, each element making up the state of the nation had an impact on the shaping of counterrevolutionary policy. It established the boundaries within which policy was designed and created political, psychological, moral, and legal limits to presidential actions taken in the pursuit of counterrevolutionary policy. As the American domestic environment changed, it reshaped the boundaries and limits of presidential action and policy direction.

In sum, there was a close linkage between domestic socioeconomic issues, political forces, national will, and political resolve. Each of these affected the environment within which presidential policy was designed and implemented. This state of the nation was also affected by American perceptions of the war. The perceptions were initially formed by the manner in which issues were presented and pursued by the president. The quality and effectiveness of this presentation and pursuit, in turn, were determined by the quality of presidential leadership, style, and skill as a politician. Combined with the nature of the war, these shaped national will and political resolve. Presidents who were sensitive to the state of the nation and who understood its relationship to the power of the presidency and to the nature of the conflict were those who usually succeeded in carrying out their policies.

NOTES

1. Robert V. Remini (ed.), *The Age of Jackson* (Columbia, S.C.: University of South Carolina Press, 1972), p. xxvii. T. Harry Williams, *Americans at War: The Development of the American Military System* (Baton Rouge: Louisiana State University Press, 1960), p. 22, states:

If most of the war's lessons are negative, showing what should not be done, and if its conduct exhibits the dangers of prosecuting a war with weak administrators and a faulty administrative structure, it should be noted that some of the lessons were learned and that attempts were made to improve the sy⌒tem—too late to affect the course of the war but carrying promise for the future.

2. Richard Hofstadter, *The American Political Tradition and the Men Who Made It* (New York: Vintage Books, 1974), p. 64.

3. Ibid., pp. 63–64.

4. Richard B. Latner, *The Presidency of Andrew Jackson: White House Politics, 1829–1837* (Athens: University of Georgia Press, 1979), p. 24.

5. Ibid., p. 8. One of the best studies of the Jacksonian period is Arthur M. Schlesinger, Jr., *The Age of Jackson* (Boston: Little, Brown, 1945). The politics and policy issues of the period as well as Jackson's performance as president are particularly well presented and analyzed.

6. Hofstadter, *American Political Tradition*, p. 68.

7. Robert Remini, *Andrew Jackson and the Course of American Freedom, 1822–1832*, Vol. 2 (New York: Harper and Row, 1981), p. 147.

8. T. Harry Williams, Richard N. Current, and Frank Freidel, *A History of the United States to 1877*, 3d ed. (New York: Alfred A. Knopf, 1969), pp. 381–382. The death of Jackson's wife and its impact on Jackson are described in Robert Remini, *Andrew Jackson*, pp. 149–155.

9. John A. Garrity, *The American Nation: A History of the United States* (New York: Harper and Row, 1966), pp. 275–276.

10. See Daniel J. Boorstin, *The Americans: The Democratic Experience* (New York: Vintage Books, 1973), p. 323.

11. Garrity, *American Nation*, p. 259.

12. Remini, *Age of Jackson*, p. xix.

13. J. P. Mayer (ed.), *Alexis De Tocqueville, Democracy in America* (New York: Anchor Books, 1969), p. 393.

14. Garrity, *American Nation*, p. 273.

15. Latner, *Presidency of Andrew Jackson*, pp. 3 and 5.

16. Marcus Cunliffe, *American Presidents and the Presidency* (London: Eyre and Spottiswoode, 1968), p. 276.

17. Williams, et al., *History of the United States*, p. 392. See also Schlesinger, *Age of Jackson*, pp. 47–52.

18. Julius W. Muller (ed.), *Presidential Messages and State Papers*, Vol. 4 (New York: Review of Reviews Co., 1917), p. 1249.

19. Mayer, *Alexis De Tocqueville*, p. 387.

20. Remini, *Age of Jackson*, pp. xxv–xxvi.

21. See Latner, *Presidency of Andrew Jackson*, pp. 101–103.

22. Ibid., p. 90.

23. Remini, *Age of Jackson*, pp. 63–64.

24. Latner, *Presidency of Andrew Jackson*, p. 90.

25. Ibid., p. 89.

26. Williams, et al., *History of the United States*, p. 398. There is some question whether Jackson actually made such a statement. There is general agreement, however, that the Supreme Court decision was not enforceable. See, for example, Remini, *Andrew Jackson and the Course of American Freedom*, pp. 276–277.

27. Latner, *Presidency of Andrew Jackson*, p. 98.

28. Ibid., p. 97.

29. Muller, *Presidential Messages*, pp. 1334–1335.

30. Ibid., p. 1367.

31. Hofstadter, *American Political Tradition*, p. 71.

32. Remini, *Age of Jackson*, pp. xxvii–xxviii.

33. Garrity, *American Nation*, pp. 260–261.

34. Ibid., p. 261.

35. Williams, et al., *History of the United States*, p. 252.

36. Julius W. Pratt, *A History of United States Foreign Policy* (Englewood Cliffs, N.J.: Prentice-Hall, 1960), p. 382.

37. Hofstadter, *American Political Tradition*, p. 218.

38. Ibid., pp. 231–232.

39. Williams, et al., *History of the United States*, p. 194.

40. Lewis L. Gould, *The Presidency of William McKinley* (Lawrence: Regents Press of Kansas, 1980), p. 2.

41. Ibid., p. 3.

42. Ibid., p. 4.

43. Williams, et al., *History of the United States*, p. 228.

44. Gould, *Presidency of William McKinley*, pp. 12–13. For a brief study of the election, see William Carl Spielman, *William McKinley: Stalwart Republican, A Biographical Study* (New York: Exposition Press, 1954), Chapter XI.

45. Gould, *Presidency of William McKinley*, p. 153.

46. Pratt, *History of United States Foreign Policy*, pp. 367–368.

47. Garrity, *American Nation*, p. 622.

48. Pratt, *History of United States Foreign Policy*, p. 164.

49. As quoted in Henry F. Graff (ed.), *American Imperialism and the Philippine Insurrection* (Boston: Little Brown, 1969), p. vii.

50. Frank Freidel, "Dissent in the Spanish-American War and the Philippine Insurrection," in Samuel Eliot Morrison, Frederick Merk, and Frank Freidel (eds.), *Dissent in Three American Wars* (Cambridge, Mass.: Harvard University Press, 1970), pp. 65–95.

51. Graff, *American Imperialism*, pp. 171–172.

52. Gould, *Presidency of William McKinley*, p. 59.

53. Ibid.

54. Ibid., p. 8. See also Spielman, *William McKinley*, particularly Chapter III.

55. Gould, *Presidency of William McKinley*, p. 9. For a useful insight into the personality and character of McKinley and an overview of his presidency, see Lewis L. Gould, *The Spanish-American War and President McKinley* (Lawrence: University Press of Kansas, 1982), especially pp. 1–18. The author states:

McKinley emphasized formal procedures in the conduct of domestic and foreign policy that enhanced the role and power of the federal government. Imperceptibly but inexorably, the power of the presidency expanded under McKinley's deft direction. He left no overt statement that he intended to restore the prestige and authority to his office, but his actions during the first year reveal a president with an instinct for power and a clear purpose of augmenting it (p. 17).

56. William H. Harbaugh (ed.), *The Writings of Theodore Roosevelt* (Indianapolis, Ind.: Bobbs-Merrill, 1967), pp. 52–53.

57. Wayne Andrews (ed.), *The Autobiography of Theodore Roosevelt* (New York: Scribner's, 1958), pp. 197–198.

58. Harbaugh, *Writings of Theodore Roosevelt*, p. 31.

59. Ibid., p. xxiii.

60. Andrews, *Autobiography of Theodore Roosevelt*, p. 26.

61. Harbaugh, *Writings of Theodore Roosevelt*, p. xxxiii.

62. Andrews, *Autobiography of Theodore Roosevelt*, p. 294.

63. Marcus M. Wilkerson, *Public Opinion and the Spanish-American War: A Study in War Propaganda* (New York: Russell and Russell, 1967), p. 132. See also Morgan, *William McKinley*, p. 329.

64. As quoted in Gould, *Spanish-American War*, p. 34. See also Morgan, *William McKinley*, p. 356.

65. Morgan, *William McKinley*, p. 361.

66. Ibid., p. 367.

67. Ibid., p. 332.

68. Ibid., p. 375.

69. Ibid., p. 388. U.S. motivation for taking the Philippines remains a matter of debate; a variety of views have been offered, ranging from American ambition to America's economic needs and concern with the Chinese trade. See, for example, Richard E. Welch, Jr., *Response to Imperialism: The United States and the Philippine-American War, 1899–1902* (Chapel Hill: University of North Carolina Press, 1979), pp. 3–10. See also Teodoro A. Agoncillo, *A Short History of the Philippines* (New York: New American Library, 1969), p. 221.

70. Arthur S. Link and William M. Leary, Jr. (eds.), *The Diplomacy of World Power: The United States, 1889–1920* (New York: St. Martin's Press, 1970), p. 37.

71. Pratt, *History of United States Foreign Policy*, p. 395.

72. Gould, *Presidency of William McKinley*, pp. 151–152.

73. Andrews, *Autobiography of Theodore Roosevelt*, p. 148.

74. Ibid., pp. 270–271.

75. Hofstadter, *American Political Tradition*, pp. 217–218.

76. Garrity, *American Nation*, p. 623.

77. Williams, et al., *History of the United States*, p. 213.

78. Pratt, *History of United States Foreign Policy*, pp. 462–463.

79. Garrity, *American Nation*, p. 662.

80. James David Barber, *The Pulse of Politics: Electing Presidents in the Media Age* (New York: Norton, 1980), p. 111.

81. Max J. Skidmore, *American Political Thought* (New York: St. Martin's Press, 1978), pp. 189–190.

82. Hofstadter, *American Political Tradition*, p. 331.

83. Ibid., p. 337.

84. Link and Leary, *Diplomacy of World Power*, p. 24.

85. Pratt, *History of United States Policy*, p. 451.

86. Ibid., p. 412.

87. Barber, *Pulse of Politics*, p. 128.

88. Link and Leary, *Diplomacy of World Power*, p. 282.

89. James Brown Scott (ed.), *President Wilson's Foreign Policy: Messages, Addresses, Papers* (New York: Oxford University Press, 1918), pp. 132–133.

90. Link and Leary, *Diplomacy of World Power*, pp. 19–20.

91. Ibid., pp. 24–25.

92. Ibid., pp. 42–43.

93. Ibid., pp. 49–50.

94. Scott, *President Wilson's Foreign Policy*, p. 3.

95. Ibid., p. 231.

96. August Heckscher (ed.), *The Politics of Woodrow Wilson: Selections from His Speeches and Writings* (New York: Harper & Brothers, 1956), xvii.

97. Link and Leary, *Diplomacy of World Power*, p. 362.

98. Woodrow Wilson, *Constitutional Government in the United States* (New York: Macmillan, 1908), p. 138.

99. John G. Stoessinger, *Crusaders and Pragmatists: Movers of Modern American Foreign Policy* (New York: Norton, 1979), pp. 11–12.

100. Hofstadter, *American Political Tradition*, pp. 365–367.

101. Ibid., p. 353.

102. Heckscher, *Politics of Woodrow Wilson*, p. ix.

103. Thomas A. Bailey, *The Pugnacious Presidents: White House Warriors on Parade* (New York: Free Press, 1980), p. 350.

104. Heckscher, *Politics of Woodrow Wilson*, p. 257.

105. Richard O'Connor, *Black Jack Pershing* (Garden City, N.Y.: Doubleday, 1961), p. 117.

106. Williams, et al., *History of the United States*, p. 391.

107. Link and Leary, *Diplomacy of World Power*, p. 315.

108. Ibid., p. 281.

109. Scott, *President Wilson's Foreign Policy*, p. 392.

110. Ibid., p. 409.

111. Boorstin, *Americans*, p. 422.

112. Ibid., p. 422.

113. Paul M. Kattenburg, *The Vietnam Trauma in American Foreign Policy, 1945–1975* (New Brunswick, N.J.: Transaction Books, 1980), p. 84.

114. Very recently, a different view of the Eisenhower presidency has emerged—one that pictures Eisenhower as a strong-willed politician, exercising aggressive leadership behind the scenes. See, for example, Fred I. Greenstein, *The Hidden-Hand Presidency: Eisenhower as Leader* (New York: Basic Books, 1982).

115. Barber, *Pulse of Politics*, pp. 85–86.

116. Rowland Evans and Robert Novak, *Lyndon B. Johnson: The Exercise of Power: A Political Biography* (New York: New American Library, 1966), p. 379.

117. See, for example, Sorenson and also Arthur Schlesinger, Jr., *A Thousand Days: John F. Kennedy in the White House* (Boston: Houghton Mifflin, 1965).

118. Sorenson, *Kennedy*, p. 436.

119. Ibid.

120. Ibid.

121. James David Barber, *The Presidential Character*, 2d ed. (Englewood Cliffs, N.J.: Prentice-Hall, 1977), pp. 316–317.

122. Richard J. Walton, *Cold War and Counterrevolution: The Foreign Policy of John F. Kennedy* (New York: Viking Press, 1972), p. 166.

123. Ibid., p. 38.

124. Schlesinger, *A Thousand Days*, p. 548.

125. Ibid., p. 550.

126. Hedrick Smith, "The Kennedy Years, 1961–63," in Neil Sheehan, Hedrick

Smith, E. W. Kenworthy, and Fox Butterfield (eds.), *The Pentagon Papers* (New York: Bantam Books, 1971), p. 84.

127. Walton, *Cold War and Counterrevolution*, p. 87.

128. Barber, *Presidential Character*, p. 88.

129. Ibid., p. 84. See also George Reedy, *Lyndon B. Johnson: A Memoir* (New York: Andrews and McMeel, 1982), especially pp. 11–19.

130. Ibid., p. 84.

131. Seyom Brown, *The Crisis of Power: An Interpretation of United States Foreign Policy During the Kissinger Years* (New York: Columbia University Press, 1979), p. 51.

132. Henry Kissinger, *The White House Years* (Boston: Little, Brown, 1979), p. 298.

133. Bob Woodward and Carl Bernstein, *The Final Days* (New York: Simon and Schuster, 1976), p. 200.

134. John Stoessinger, *Why Nations Go to War* (New York: St. Martin's Press, 1981), p. 84. See also Bernard Brodie, *War and Politics* (New York: Macmillan, 1973), especially Chapters 4 and 5. Among the reasons for America's involvement in Vietnam the author cites American traditions and perceptions of leadership. He completely rejects the view that the U.S. system worked and that involvement was a consequence of a rational policy process based on anticipated policy goals. For example, he writes, "The implication that in 1965 Lyndon B. Johnson foresaw anything like 1968 is on the face of it an absurdity" (p. 129). My own analysis supports Brodie's view.

135. Lyndon Baines Johnson, *The Vantage Point: Perspectives of the Presidency, 1963–1969* (New York: Holt, Rinehart and Winston, 1971), p. 429.

136. John Spanier, *American Foreign Policy Since World War II*, 8th ed. (New York: Holt, Rinehart and Winston, 1980), p. 150.

137. General Fred C. Weyand, Chief of Staff, U.S. Army, "Vietnam Myths and American Realities," *Cdrs Call* (July-August 1976), also reprinted in *Armor* (September-October 1976). General Weyand was the last commander of the Military Assistance Command Vietnam (MACV) and supervised the withdrawal of U.S. Military Forces in 1973. As quoted and printed in Harry G. Summers, Jr., Colonel, Infantry, *On Strategy: The Vietnam War in Context* (Carlisle Barracks, Pa.: U.S. Army War College, 1981), p. 7.

138. Sir Robert Thompson, *No Exit from Vietnam* (New York: David McKay, 1969), p. 194.

139. *New York Times*, April 5, 1970, p. 1.

140. Robert Shaplen, *Time Out of Hand: Revolution and Reaction in Southeast Asia*, revised ed. (New York: Harper Colophon Books, 1970), pp. 377–378.

141. Charles A. Reich, *The Greening of America* (New York: Bantam Books, 1971), pp. 2–3.

142. Arthur M. Schlesinger, Jr., *The Crisis of Confidence* (New York: Bantam Books, 1969), p. 41.

3

Military Posture

AMERICA'S MILITARY ESTABLISHMENT: THE BEGINNINGS

America's attitude toward standing armies was generally set in the aftermath of the Seven Years' War. In order to help pay for the great expenses of that war, the British government established policies to insure that the American colonists contributed their share. This contribution was to be used not only for payment of war debts, but also for future defense, including the support of a British standing army in the colonies. The imposition of a variety of taxes and trade restrictions were in no small measure responsible for the ill-feelings which the colonists felt toward standing armies. These feelings carried over into the Revolution and the formation period of the American Republic.

The debate over standing armies centered on two positions: complete abolition of standing armies or the integration of a small standing army with militia. Arguments for one or the other position generated a great deal of emotion, presaging similar arguments and emotions regarding the present-day volunteer military and selective service systems. For example, Samuel Adams writing to the *Boston Gazette* in 1768 stated:

It is a very improbable supposition, that any people can long remain free, with a strong military power in the very heart of their country: Unless that military power is under the direction of the people, and even then it is dangerous.... Even when there is a necessity of the military power, within the land, which by the way but rarely happens, a wise and prudent people will always have a watchful and a jealous eye over it; for the maxims and rules of the army, are essentially different from the genius of a free people, and the laws of a free government.[1]

Similarly, de Tocqueville wrote over sixty years later: "After all, whatever one does, a large army in a democracy will always be a serious danger, and the best way to lessen this danger will be to reduce the army. But that is not a remedy which every nation can apply."[2]

Alexander Hamilton clearly articulated the argument for a standing army in *Federalist 25*:

The American militia, in the course of the late war, have, by their valor on numerous occasions erected monuments to their fame; but the bravest of them feel and know that the liberty of their country could not have been established by their efforts alone, however great and valuable they were. War, like most other things, is a science to be acquired and perfected by diligence, by perseverence, by time, and by practice.[3]

James Madison, writing in the *Federalist No. 41*, also commented on the standing army:

The means of security can only be regulated by the means and the danger of attack.... A standing force, therefore, is a dangerous, at the same time that it may be a necessary provision. On the extensive scale its consequences may be fatal. On any scale it is an object of laudable circumspection and precaution. A wise nation will combine all these considerations; and whilst it does not rashly preclude itself from any resource which may become essential to its safety, will exert all its prudence in diminishing both the necessity and the danger of resorting to one which may be inauspicious to its liberties.[4]

The Founding Fathers apparently had a fear that went much deeper than their fear of standing armies: they feared the power of the central government. Therefore, in order to control the potential for arbitrary power, they established a system of checks and balances and also placed important powers regarding control and regulation of standing armies in a popularly elected assembly. As Hamilton argued in *Federalist 23*,

A government, the constitution of which renders it unfit to be trusted with all the powers which a free people ought to delegate to any government, would be an unsafe and improper depository of the national interests. Wherever these can with propriety be confided, the coincident powers may safely accompany this.[5]

Not only was a standing army viewed as necessary to the federal government, but it was also to be restrained and limited as part of the total concept of the limited powers of the federal government.[6] Although the fear of standing armies was natural for a democracy, it was held that a democratic "standing army" could be developed—one whose values and goals paralleled those of the democratic political system. This was to be done by intermixing Regulars with civilian militia, by instilling the army with democratic values, and by providing a proper balance between society and the military. Josiah Quincy expressed this concept at the time of the Coercive Acts.

No free government was ever founded or ever preserved its liberty without uniting the characters of citizens and soldier in those destined for defense of the state. The sword should never be in the hands of any, but those who have an interest in the safety of the community.... Such are a well regulated militia composed of the freeholders, citizen and husbandman, who take up arms to preserve their property as individuals, and their rights as freemen.[7]

While many Americans looked to Europe for a model for their standing army, a uniquely American formulation developed based on the experience in the Revolution and the attitude of the Americans toward the British Regulars. According to the American model, in times of crisis America would transform itself into a nation of free men under arms and develop a citizen army; hence there was little need for a large standing army (indeed, according to some, there was little need of any army). The only requirement was a small cadre of professionals whose sole responsibility was to guard the military stores and man fortifications, and to provide teachers and leaders for the citizen armies.

Some argued that Americans had been victorious against the British without a standing army, notably at the battles of Lexington and Bunker Hill. A militia was not only sufficient, but it could also stand against any foreign invasion.[8] But as Hamilton argued, the militia itself was inefficient and "War, like most other things is a science to be acquired and perfected by diligence, by perseverance, by time, and by practice."[9]

The experiences in the Revolutionary War reflect these contending views. For example, at the Battle of Guilford Court House in 1781, General Nathanael Greene's Regulars saved the day, as they fought the British Regulars to a standstill. This occurred after the American militia broke and left the field in disarray. On the other hand, Lord Burgoyne's invasion through Lake Champlain and the Hudson River route was stymied by American irregulars. Vermont farmers rushed to arms and, using what we would now call unconventional tactics, harassed the invading column to such an extent that the invasion failed. At the Battle of Cowpens in 1781, General David Morgan with 1,500 Continental Regulars and 3,000 militia was attacked by 1,900 British Regulars under Lord Tarleton. The efficient use of the militia in conjunction with the American Regulars routed Tarleton's forces.

These experiences gave rise to the concept of democratic intermix: a

nation of free men under arms, a citizen army, and a regular establishment. If used correctly and employed according to their capabilities, the
militia could give a good account of themselves. Yet, it was understood
that in a face-to-face struggle with the British Regulars, only American
Regulars could hope to achieve victory. While there are proponents of
one or the other way, the two themes of a citizen army and Regular
Army became intermixed in our political-military philosophy.

The end of America's revolutionary period was ushered in by the
Jacksonian presidency. While the signs of change appeared in the immediate aftermath of the War of 1812, it was the Jackson Administration
that reflected a new direction in American politics and economy, one
that was not wedded to the past revolutionary period. This had its
parallel in the military system.

The difficulties of the American military in conducting operations
against the British in the War of 1812 generated considerable debate
about the shape of the postwar American military establishment. The
first decade of the 1800s had been one of relative quiet, as the new nation
began its independence, and relations with France and England, at times
acrimonious, seemed to be nonthreatening. However, the War of 1812
showed Americans that some effort had to be made in establishing a
political-military policy that was relevant to the challenges inherent in
independence and sovereignty. Moreover, the War of 1812 had revealed
a number of problems in political-military policy that were to persist
throughout the century.

Conflicting experiences from the war added fuel to the controversy
regarding citizen-soldiers versus a standing army. On the one hand, the
Battle of New Orleans provided ample evidence that citizen-soldiers
could perform well against British Regulars. On the other hand, the
battles of Chippewa and Lundy's Lane showed that American Regulars
were needed to stand up against British Regulars. The exploits of General
Jackson and his mixed bag of militia and privateers at the Battle of New
Orleans captured the popular imagination and provided the basis for
attacks on the regular military establishment.

In military affairs, not Chippewa and Lundy's Lane but Andrew Jackson's victory
at New Orleans came to symbolize the new egalitarian attitudes. New Orleans
was interpreted as a triumph of the natural American—strong precisely because
he was unschooled and therefore natural—over the trained and disciplined and
therefore artificial and even effete European.[10]

But what left a marked impression on the emerging regular military
establishment was not the role of militia, but of trained Regulars.

The battles of Chippewa and Lundy's Lane in upper New York in
July 1814 were to become the guideposts for American military profes-

sionals until the Civil War. Taking a cue from the British, General Winfield Scott established a camp of instruction for the training of American Regulars. Over a period of four months, approximately 3,000 American troops were trained in musketry, deployment, and tactics. In addition, Scott established a rigorous regimen of sanitation and discipline. Scott relied on his own skills and the tactics of the British to train officers who in turn trained their men, first in individual soldiery and then in squad, company, and battalion tactics. The British linear deployment and disciplined musketry were made part of American training.

On July 5, Scott's Brigade, part of Major General Jacob Brown's force, made contact with parts of three British regiments of regular infantry, dragoons, and artillery, and some Canadian militia and Indians. Before this contact elements of American and Canadian militia had been skirmishing throughout the previous day. British General Phineas Raill attacked Brown with a force of 2,000, after routing the American militia and before Brown could conduct a flanking movement. At this juncture Brown ordered Scott's Brigade to attack.

The British forces were deployed in two columns. Scott deployed his men in extended formation forming a concave line extending beyond the British columns. Both forces pressed in on each other firing volley after volley. And in the best tradition of Regulars, Scott's Brigade advanced surely and steadily, finally routing the British by a bayonet charge. Raill's surprise at the effectiveness of the American force was expressed in what is now a classic comment and has become a part of American military tradition, "Those are Regulars, by God!"[11]

The British retreated and regrouped at Lundy's Lane at the end of July. British forces occupied a small rise overlooking open fields. Scott's advance caught the British by surprise. Outnumbered, the British began to retire. Reinforcements sent by Lieutenant General Gordon Drummond from Fort Schlosser arrived on the field, reoccupied the rise, and prepared for Scott's assault. Late in the afternoon, Scott's Brigade attacked with three regiments against the hill and one in a flanking movement. Although the British general was wounded and captured, Scott's troops met a withering fire from the British and were turned back each time they neared the British position.

By nightfall, one of Scott's regiments was decimated, but each side still held its ground. The remainder of Brown's army reached the field at about the same time that the remainder of Drummond's army appeared. The Americans attacked again, and the battle continued into the night. The hill was taken only after a night attack in which the Americans fought with fixed bayonets against British batteries. Although the British retreated from the hill, they counterattacked three times, taking heavy casualties in each instance. As Harry L. Coles writes, "Volleys were exchanged muzzle to muzzle. Both Brown and Scott were hit and both evacuated."[12] Eventually, the American Army withdrew from the hill, primarily because of low supplies of ammunition and lack of water. By the next morning the armies remained facing each other in the same positions they had occupied a day earlier. Casualties were about equal on both sides—approximately 900 men were killed or wounded on each side.

The Americans eventually withdrew from the field, and the British won a strategic victory, although the battle was a tactical standoff. For the American Army, however, Lundy's Lane and Chippewa proved that American Regulars could fight it out man for man with the best in the British Army. The British, involved in two battles against American Regulars within a month, found them as steadfast and disciplined as their own Regulars.

In the annals of American military tradition, Chippewa and Lundy's Lane epitomized the best of American arms. These battles became classic examples of what American military professionals could accomplish and became standards by which the regular American Army was judged, at least through the Civil War period.

The battle of Chippewa was the only occasion during the war when equal bodies of regular troops met face to face, in extended lines on an open plain in broad daylight, without advantage of position; and never again after that combat was an army of American regulars beaten by British troops. Small as the affair was, and unimportant in military results, it gave to the United States army a character and pride it had never before possessed.[13]

A major step towards establishing a permanent military establishment was the founding of a military academy at West Point. Following its establishment as an engineering school in 1802, it quickly became a center for studying military science and training officers. By 1812, there were 89 graduates. Sixty-five still serving in the Army played an important role in the conduct of the War of 1812.[14] Later, under Sylvanus Thayer, the academy became more than an engineering school; it became a school for the serious study of war, embracing military history and leadership, as well as a range of academic subjects.

But there were more pressing issues, as the president and Congress struggled over the best means to secure the Western frontier against the Indians, the defense of the United States along the seacoast, the size and composition of the regular military establishment, and the relationship between the militia, volunteers, and the regular establishment. Among other things, the War of 1812 revealed that the permanent defense of the nation could not rest mainly on citizen-soldiers, regardless of the victory at the Battle of New Orleans. Yet, political-military realities did not lessen the fear of standing armies.

Combinations of Regulars and citizen-soldiers were employed in the Indian wars following the War of 1812. Jackson's exploits during the First Seminole War (Creek War) were cases in point. Using a force of Regulars, militia, and volunteers, he defeated the Creeks, invaded Spanish territory, occupied Spanish forts, and eventually captured and hanged two British subjects. Jackson had opened the door to the eventual cession of Florida to America and the Second Seminole War.

The results of this foray into Florida proved worthwhile. It ruined the prestige of the British among the Creeks and Seminoles. Deserted by their allies the Indians disappeared into the wilderness. Further, the victory thrilled the West, that section of the country which most actively supported the war. It gave Jackson confidence in his men and in turn gave them confidence in him. This feeling of mutual respect coupled with British ineptness played no small part in the American victory in the Battle of New Orleans two months later. Jackson's invasion of Florida also whetted his appetite to wrench this region permanently from Spain's grasp. But that objective was seven years distant.[15]

The widespread popular involvement in the election of President Jackson in 1828, as we noted earlier, was the beginning of a populist political system replacing the "gentlemanly" selection and election of previous presidents. For the first time, grass roots political structures had an important impact on the election of a president. Jacksonian democracy, noted for its populist philosophy, reflected not only a concern for the average American, but also a distaste for the professional soldier. While there was always an egalitarian opposition to a regular military system, it was only in the Jacksonian era that such opposition became widespread and took on a political character. There were a number of indicators preceding the Jacksonian era.

Following the War of 1812, the regular military establishment was allowed to deteriorate. With the onset of the Jacksonian era, the military as an institution—West Point in particular—was attacked as incompatible with republican institutions. In 1821 Congress passed legislation reducing the Regular Army to 6,000 enlisted men. The memories of the war and wartime nationalism had faded, with the Congress and the people turning towards the expanding business and commercial arena and the extension of the nation westward. Even though the new Regular Army was reduced in strength, the military establishment was saved from complete decimation by the efforts of John C. Calhoun. As secretary of war from 1817 to 1825, he had a major impact in developing the basis for a professional military establishment in the pre-Civil War years. His defense of a regular military establishment kept critics from gaining any major political leverage.

Calhoun's major contribution may well have been the concept of an expandable Regular Army—an idea that the Congress of the time could not accept. Nonetheless, this concept became a part of American polit-ical-military philosophy that would surface again at the end of the nine-teenth century and carry through the twentieth century. While Calhoun was repudiating the military tradition, he strengthened the arguments for a professional military force and was instrumental in reviving the Military Academy, which had earlier been the target of the first egali-tarian critics and of economy moves by Congress.

By the end of the 1830s, some major improvements had taken place in America's military posture. Aside from West Point, specialist schools of artillery had been established at Fortress Monroe, and seacoast for-tifications had improved. Attention was also being given to the quality of the soldier's life; Army regulations were published regarding certain standards for Army life; the first surgeon general was appointed; some effort was made to develop a more efficient system of recruiting with the establishment of recruiting depots in major cities; and finally, a system of command was established, including a commanding general of the Army, in name if not in fact.

From the first beginnings of a professional military system and a po-litical-military policy following the War of 1812, there developed a system based on European models. While the actual organization of the Regular Army was based on the British model, the French and Prussian expe-riences were major influences in the training and education of military professionals. This European orientation developed despite the expe-rience of American Regular forces against the Seminoles in Florida and the unconventional campaigns earlier against British Regulars.[16]

The greatest threats were thought to be from European powers. In-deed, those involved in professional military education were likely to use the battles of Chippewa and Lundy's Lane as examples of the ca-pability of American Regulars, using European tactics, to stand against the British Regulars. As Russell Weigley notes, "Few incidents contrib-uted so much to the prestige of the Regular Army and its acceptance as the necessary axis of American defense as Chippewa and Lundy's Lane."[17] Thus, from the outset the education of professional officers was rooted in conventional tactics of a European mold, and, for all practical pur-poses, concern with unconventional tactics of the Revolutionary War period was forgotten.[18]

The European tradition was also reflected in training manuals that were first published in the third decade of the 1800s. For example, the procedure for arms drill was detailed in the manual *Infantry Tactics* by Winfield Scott. Issued in 1835, this manual, according to John K. Mahon, "was actually a translation of the best French drill guides."[19] Its execution depended on regular line drill.

Regardless of the presumed organizational and training advances made in the regular military establishment, however, criticism of the military had surfaced by the end of President Monroe's administration in the early 1820s. Initially sparked by the depression of 1819 and fostered by the populist surge in the 1820s, the egalitarian criticism of the military took on a new life. While concern and fear of standing armies were part of the Revolutionary period, the criticism later broadened to include what some thought would be the military's opposition to democracy coupled with a threat to the liberty of a new nation.

The fundamental philosophy behind this criticism was based on the idea that the citizen-soldier was sufficiently motivated and skilled in warfare to defend the United States against all enemies. As C. Robert Kemble points out:

Fundamental to this attitude was America's growing faith in the common man. War, the Democrats reasoned, was an occasional and short-lived emergency that could be met by nonprofessionals. Any good white Anglo-Saxon American male could, on short notice, be a successful general—or, for that matter, president of the United States.[20]

Fear of privilege and aristocratic power was another important part of this underlying philosophy. This feeling was reflected in the deep suspicion of regular soldiers as well as in the desire of the Jacksonians to abolish the U.S. Military Academy. Many Jacksonians also charged that officers trained at the academy were ineffective in fights against Indians. They argued that the incompetence of conventionally trained officers who were placed in command of line units usually cost lives in Indian fights.[21] Such charges were to surface frequently during the conduct of the Second Seminole War.

This criticism of the regular establishment and of West Point did not mean a loss of faith in the use of military force. Indeed, Jacksonian democracy was characterized, among other things, by its strident posture towards Europe and, as we noted earlier, by its Indian removal policy. The concern was not about the utility of military force, but about its composition and size. Any military force controlled by citizen-soldiers was thought to be more democratic and certainly more capable against the Indians, at least in the minds of many Jacksonians.

There appears to be little question that it was the nation's experience with standing armies that influenced the civil-military relations during the first decades. Rooted in the struggles against the British during the Revolution and later confirmed by the incident at Newburgh, where Washington's army was on the verge of mutiny, many congressmen felt that the only control that could be exerted over a standing military establishment was to keep it exceedingly small, while insuring that the state militia remained a basic part of America's defenses. It was no wonder that West Point became the focus of antimilitary criticism. A standing army smacked too much of an Old World social order and an Old World aristocracy bent on subduing democracy. And West Point seemed to reflect the aristocratic social hierarchy as well as the authoritarian environment of the Old World military.

Within the military, the attitude of Jacksonians was well known. With the expansion of economic opportunity and the growing trust in the common man, few could justify selection of the military as a profession. The nationalistic fervor of 1815 and 1816 was aimed primarily at the concept of a free independent America that could now get on with its work as a nation-state.

The Regular Army of the 1820s and 1830s was divided into three distinct classes of individuals: academy graduates, non-academy officers, and enlisted men. West Point graduates were found mainly in the middle and junior officer grades. They were only then beginning to make an impact on the military establishment. Thus, they were separated from the top leaders of the Army by education and training, and by degree of professionalism. Both the generals and civilian leaders had evolved from the same mold. Most had grown up in the early years of the nation and had been through the War of 1812, and some had Indian-fighting experience. Only four generals held actual commissions in that rank. According to Mahon, "The other generals, fourteen in all, held their grades by brevet only. None of them, whether by commission or brevet, was a graduate of the Military Academy, but most of the rest of the officers corps were."[22] In this environment many professional officers felt separate from society, with a professional value system that many officers considered increasingly incompatible with the economic and populist orientation of society.[23]

The quality and composition of the enlisted structure reinforced the civilian-military separateness. Opportunities that abounded in civilian life attracted the motivated and skilled American. However, most enlisted men were usually from the lowest socioeconomic groups in society. Most were ignorant and foreigners. Almost half of those killed in the Dade Massacre signaling the start of the Second Seminole War were foreigners.[24] Not only was the enlisted structure separate from society, but it also reflected a wide gap between officer and enlisted man.

The officers were separated from society not only in education and training, but also in terms of economic status. The professional values evolving from such a separate and closed military system placed little trust in citizen-soldiers or in the efficiency and effectiveness of "democratically" composed armies. What compounded the separation from society and the perpetuation of a distinctly professional value system was the separation between the enlisted system and the officer corps.[25]

By the Second Seminole War, the regular establishment had been reduced to about 6,000 officers and enlisted men.[26] At the same time the militias of various states continued to see themselves as important parts of the nation's defense. Thus, at the outbreak of the Second Seminole War, the Regular Army was small in size, had little experience in large-scale maneuvers, had virtually no training in unconventional warfare, and was organized and trained according to European standards. West Point had turned out officers who reflected this European orientation.

In the aftermath of the War of 1812, Secretary of War Lewis Cass was preoccupied with defending the United States against invasion by European powers, mainly evolving from Jackson's brinksmanship diplomacy. The Seminoles were considered a minor nuisance and could be contained, it was thought, by building a series of forts supported by active military patrols.[27]

Aside from the actual combat front, the Seminole War had various political arenas. One was in Congress. The resolution of the Seminole War became increasingly a Washington concern, as slavery and the war became closely associated as time progressed. The issue of the role of citizen-soldiers in the regular establishment also surfaced in Congress. There remained a strong element in Congress who felt that the militia was the key to winning against Indians. Some went so far as to say that the Regulars should be cleared out of Florida so that the militia could do the job. Congressional activity was also marked by acrimonious politics which had consequences on the command of military forces—another political battlefront. Jacksonians accused Whigs of supporting Whig generals such as Winfield Scott to the denigration of generals such as Thomas S. Jessup, who was a Jacksonian. Not only did the politics of command over forces in Florida lead to the removal of various generals, but it also had an impact on the strategy and tactics of the war.

Another arena was in Georgia, where Georgians took issue with any conciliatory presidential policy in Florida and the role of Regulars in the war. Georgians were most vociferous in supporting a policy of total subjugation and removal of all Seminoles. This aggressive policy reflected the desire for land occupied by Seminoles, and it also stemmed from the efforts of owners to capture runaway slaves hiding out with the Seminoles. The Georgians were supported by several other states that supplied militia, such as Tennessee and Missouri. All of these states supported an aggressive policy towards the Indians. They also felt that Regulars were antagonistic towards the militia and that at times regular officers deliberately placed the militia in difficult combat situations.

The Seminole War was hardly a partisan affair, though its operations occasionally became one. A good deal more debate was stimulated, however, regarding the volunteer militia. By April, 1838, after nearly two and a half years of war with no end in sight, East Florida settlers were not only berating the regular army for its inability to capture a small band of marauding Seminoles, but also demanding to know why no local volunteers were being mustered into service.[28]

The impact of the Seminole War thus went beyond the battlefield and became enmeshed in Washington politics, reflecting continuing concern about the organization and shape of the military establishment and its political consequences. The conduct of the war became the subject of some debate in Congress, and between the executive and Congress, which was not without impact on battlefield operations. Yet, little concern was expressed about the purpose of the war itself.

The end of the Second Seminole war did not end the Indian problem. The Third Seminole War followed some years later and was primarily a mopping up military operation as far as the United States was concerned. Most of the public's attention was on the events taking place in Mexico and on the issues separating the North from the South. With regard to the American military, however, there were few changes (mostly in ordinance) in its military posture until the Civil War.

The Mexican War in 1845–48 brought some change in the composition of the Regular Army officer corps. Over four-fifths of the officers were trained at West Point or had fought in the Seminole wars. The level of professionalism had increased dramatically with such officers as Irvin McDowell, U.S. Grant, George B. McClellan, George Meade, William T. Sherman, Robert E. Lee, James B. Longstreet, and Thomas ("Stonewall") Jackson seeing service in the Mexican War. Later, each of these officers played a major role in the Civil War.

When Americans entered the Mexican War, the Regular Army stood at only 5,300. Congress belatedly granted the Army authorization to expand. A regular force of 18,000 and a volunteer force of 50,000 were authorized. No militia were used in the Mexican War.

By 1850 the slavery issue dominated American politics: "so deeply, in this decade, was the nation divided over the slavery question, that any proposal of expansion put forward by the pro-Southern administration of either Franklin Pierce or James Buchanan was sure to be viewed with suspicion by the anti-slavery forces of the North."[29] In fact, Julius W. Pratt calls this the decade of "manifest destiny" frustrated.[30]

While the debate over slavery became increasingly heated, with the country becoming more and more polarized, American expansion brought it into conflict with Great Britain and Mexico. The conflict with Great Britain over the Northeastern Boundary and Oregon was eventually resolved peacefully. The conflict with Mexico over American annexation of Texas by America led to the war with Mexico. Part of the dispute was over the actual boundary between Texas and Mexico and claims by American citizens against Mexico that were unpaid. Moreover, some argued that the major basis of the dispute was President James K. Polk's desire to acquire California and make it part of U.S. territory.[31] Summing up the expansion of the United States in the first part of the century, Pratt writes, "In three years, 1845–1848, the area of the United States had grown by over 1,200,000 square miles, an increase of more than 66 percent. It was no wonder that expansionist-minded Americans proclaimed their faith in Manifest Destiny."[32]

Regardless of the American experience in the Mexican War, most thoughtful Americans and military officers remained fixed on European military systems and the conflicts there. The Crimean War (1835–55) and the character of the military systems involved became the subject for serious study.[33] The American military, as was the case with European military systems, ignored the technological developments and their potential in warfare. Military formations were still massed, even though weapons development suggested that such formations had outlived their usefulness. Similarly, the possibilities of new transportation and communications systems for warfare were ignored. Thus, on the eve of the Civil War, the American military posture had changed little from the 1820s and 1830s. What had changed in a very important way, however, was the composition of the officer corps. As the Civil War was to prove, West Pointers determined the outcomes of battles and the general conduct of the war. The officer corps had developed a professional dimension which established the guidepost for the military system and traditions that persist to the present day.

The Civil War dominated the next decades. This war is frequently characterized as the first modern war. The concepts of total war and strategic maneuvering were relatively new concepts and, combined with modern transportation systems, weapons technology, and joint operations between land and sea forces, ushered in an era of warfare that is more characteristic of modern war than of the classic wars in Europe. In this respect, the grand battles of the Civil War became the primary teaching vehicles for military professionals.

The Civil War also provides a convenient dividing line between post-Revolutionary and industrial America. Having settled for all time the issue of slavery, America's energies turned to other matters, which had an important impact on the development of America's military system.[34]

SUMMARY

At the time of the War of 1812, the American military establishment was just beginning to emerge from its revolutionary past. In the aftermath of the war the military system now had a combination of Regulars and militia, with many, including Jackson, arguing that the militia remained the key to American military strength. The American military, adapting to the European style of warfare, was not prepared for the unconventional warfare waged by the Seminoles. Only after several years of experience did the America military adopt tactics (search-and-destroy operations) focusing on the Seminoles' food sources and on area control. While this did reduce the Seminole threat, the Indians were never totally conquered.

Questions of military leadership and tactics became major issues, with a succession of generals trying their hands at conquering the Seminoles. Clearly, European-style tactics and conventional warfare had little chance of success in Florida. Although Americans had engaged in unconventional war during the Revolution, they quickly forgot the lessons of such warfare and presumed that military effectiveness rested with European-type formations. Indeed, Chippewa and Lundy's Lane became the foundations of the professional American establishment. The Battle of New Orleans, however, supported the view that well-led militia were as good as any regular troops. The controversy regarding Regulars or militia was to continue throughout the century.

Following the end of the Second Seminole War, the military again forgot its experiences in the ensuing years. Slowly but surely, the American military was being organized around European-style warfare with professional officers, and the U.S. Military Academy following the French system of military instruction.

The Civil War, viewed by many as the first modern war, confirmed the views of those who had held that Chippewa and Lundy's Lane were the guidelines for military professionalism. The battles of the Civil War proved the worth and need for professionals, and they also became the basis for instruction at the U.S. Military Academy at West Point. The professional perspective became well established on grand battles of the Civil War. These developments were to set the pattern for the next involvement in counterrevolutionary war.

AN ARMY FOR EMPIRE

The period following the Civil War marked great change in American society and in the American military system as well. While the country moved into a period of industrial and urban growth and westward migration, the military (now considerably reduced in strength) was faced with a number of missions ranging from Reconstruction in the South to maintaining peace on the frontier.

To defense of the frontier were added military occupation of the southern states, neutralization of the Mexican border during Napoleon's colonial enterprise under Maximilian, elimination of a Fenian (Irish Brotherhood) threat to Canada in the Northeast and dispersion of white marauders in the border states. But these and other later involvements were passing concerns. The conflict with the red man was the overriding consideration in the next twenty-five years until Indian power was broken.[35]

In carrying out the Reconstruction policies of Congress, the Regular Army became involved in police duties and responsibilities normally entrusted to civilian leaders and bureaucrats. One result was that military officers became deeply involved in a wide range of political, social, and economic activities.[36] Fortunately for the American Army, its involvement in Reconstruction was relatively shortlived, freeing it from a variety of nontraditional military activities and consequences that may have been damaging to its professional posture.

The Army's task of making the frontier safe was made considerably more difficult by the westward migration of Americans and a policy that was aimed at defeating the Indians and placing them on reservations. To successfully carry out these policies required involvement in unconventional warfare against the Indians who were well versed in this style of fighting. As Robert M. Utley points out, "the frontier army was a conventional military force trying to control by conventional military methods, a people that did not behave like a conventional enemy, and indeed, quite often was not an enemy at all."[37]

Thus from the period 1866 to 1890, the American Army found itself engaging in a variety of skirmishes and battles against the Indians, and for part of that time it was also involved in forcing Reconstruction in the South. Many veteran officers of the Civil War faced these unorthodox operations with the mind set of Civil War conventional battles: "In truth, the Civil War had made at least one important difference in the Army's handling of the Indian wars; it had accustomed leaders and soldiers to conventional war fought according to white men's rules, and readjustment to guerrilla-style war was not easy."[38]

William Ganoe has concluded that the period from 1865 to 1880 was "The Army's Dark Ages" and that the period from 1881 to 1898 was the first phase of "The Army's Renaissance."[39] These conclusions are based on the difficult and varied missions that had to be performed with minimum resources. Ganoe states that the renaissance began with the establishment of the School of Application for Infantry and Cavalry at Fort Leavenworth, Kansas.[40] In the main, the renaissance had more to do with the Army's own internal awakening than with presidential or congressional initiatives.[41]

By the time of the Philippine revolution, American military forces had undergone a series of developments aimed at instilling a higher sense of professionalism. While the armies of the Civil War were quickly disbanded, the core of the regular establishment had begun to develop a system of officers schools for the training and educating of officers in the skills of command.

Following the Civil War various command and staff schools were established. The Military Service Institution, a voluntary association for the study of and discussion of military matters, was founded in 1897. It was open to Regular Army and National Guard officers and produced studies and proposals for Army reform. In addition, there was a great deal of improvement in the state militia system. The names of many of the state militias were changed to National Guard, budgets were increased, and subsidies from the federal government were provided on a systematic basis. A minimum number of drills were required of state militias, and a systematic procedure was established to maintain a minimum level of proficiency. Nevertheless, many problems remained, since the organizational structure of the National Guard varied from state to state; there was no established procedure to incorporate the state militias into federal service, and the level of competency varied considerably. The National Guard was not ready for war duty.

The regular establishment faced similar problems; even with many improvements, officers became bogged down in fighting Indian wars, with units scattered throughout the frontier. The expertise and experience of commanding large units with all of the logistical and administrative problems these posed were soon lost.

The Army's manned companies and battalions, scattered across the continent in over seventy small posts, functioned mainly in police actions against rebellious Indians or striking laborers. It had no permanent troop formations larger than regiments—seldom were entire regiments assembled at a single post—and neither detailed war plans nor a staff for making them existed.[42]

To be sure, a small number of officers worked with Navy officers to seek reform and improvement. Moreover, the Army had been equipped with the new Krag-Jorgenson rifle that used smokeless powder. It was as good as, if not better than, the weaponry used by European armies. But even with improvements in officer education and in ordinance, in 1898 the United States did not have a truly operational army: "It possessed instead a large collection of companies, battalions, regiments, and batteries—those of the Regular establishment well equipped, trained, and commanded, those of the state militia indifferently or poorly outfitted and led."[43]

The organization at the War Department level also reflected an uncoordinated and fragmented establishment. There was a conflict of authority between the secretary of war and the commanding general, as well as an institutionalized conflict between the various bureaus and the commanders in the field: "The lines of authority and responsibility within the department were poorly defined, so that the making of military decisions required much negotiation among independent centers of power.... The lack of articulation in the department began at the top and penetrated down through all levels of the Army."[44] The Army's inadequate central command system provided ample opportunity for the staff departments to expand and extend their own power.[45] Indeed, after years of virtual autonomy, it would have been difficult to regroup these departments into a cohesive command structure.

The Battle of Wounded Knee ended not only the Indian wars, but also the era of the Frontier Army. By 1890 the frontier had disappeared. The Indians had been placed in reservations, and the westward expansion of America had been completed. This expansion was a result not simply of the defeat of the Indians and the occupation of their lands, but also of the expansion of transportation, commerce, and population:

In the year of Wounded Knee four transcontinental railroads spanned the West, where in 1866 there had been one. In 1890, 8.5 million settlers occupied the Indian's former hunting grounds, where in 1866 there had been less than 2 million. The buffalo herds that blackened the Great Plains with perhaps 13 million animals in 1866 had vanished by 1880 before the rifles of professional hide hunters. These figures tell more about the means by which the Indian was subjugated than do battle statistics.[46]

At the same time, Army life changed from frontier campaigning to peacetime garrison duty. The quality of life improved, allowing a more settled family environment. Transportation and communications provided better access to the outside world and between Army posts and garrisons. The end of the Indian wars also shifted the focus of the Army to external matters.

More importantly from the professional perspective, the Battle of Wounded Knee saw the passing of the Frontier Army leadership. While a few of the higher ranks were to remain through the Spanish-American War, generals such as Sherman, Sheridan, McDowell, and Crook had departed the scene. A new generation of officers had come to the forefront at a time when America moved into a new era—one that was to look outwards, freed from the role of internal security. Frontier wars against Geronimo, Sitting Bull, Crazy Horse, Chief Joseph, and other Indian leaders taxed the Regular Army to its limits. For over two decades, the frontier had been torn by combat between the Regulars and a variety of Indian tribes and leaders. But this combat was hardly the conventional kind of the Civil War era; it was unconventional combat in which the Indian was well versed. Nevertheless, the expansion of American society westward and the ability of the Regular Army to use the expanding network of railroads allowed a degree of mobility and superior firepower to be brought to bear against the Indians. In only twenty years the westward expansion had destroyed the Western tribes' way of life: "Their territory appropriated, their traditional food sources destroyed, they had yielded to military coercion and diplomatic persuasion and accepted the proffered substitute—reservations and government dole."[47]

Civil-military relations following the Civil War also underwent changes. The Jacksonian distrust of the Regular Army remained, although in modified form. In rapidly developing urban centers in the East, there developed increasing antagonisms between the urban workers and the military. Spokesmen for urban workers using the Jacksonian critique of the military as their basis argued that the aristocratic military system had become a tool of capital and the business elite. This reached dangerous heights during the 1870s as the Regular Army was called in to suppress labor riots.[48]

Another strand of opinion held military officers in relatively high esteem. According to this view, strong nations needed a committed and strong military force, and those serving in the officer classes were honorable gentlemen. Such a view coincided with opinions within the professional officer class regarding their own role. Most military professionals saw themselves as the guardians of American values and defenders of American democracy. These opinions were generally associated with the upper classes of American society.

The more practical elements in American society perceived the military in still different terms. Accepting the fact that wars were a part of history, and not likely to disappear, these groups maintained that military officers were servants of the state and that their duty was to defend the state. All that was needed was a reasonably effective regular military establishment. Such views were found in intellectual circles, and in religious and middle-class groups as well.

Regardless of these views, by the closing years of the nineteenth century, nearly everyone acknowledged that the Regular Army was at least a necessary evil. The professional officer class, by years of isolated frontier duty, slow promotions, and internal conflicts and politics, with its own ethics and values, had become isolated from the mainstream of American society. Similar attitudes emanated from the professional officer corps regarding society.[49] The general opinion of society was that "The regular officer—whether bureaucrat, aristocrat, or mercenary—was no longer a leader of, but a misfit in, American society."[50]

During the same period of time, changes taking place in American society were having an impact on the military establishment. In one sense these changes broadened the military professional perspective, and in another it isolated the profession from the mainstream of American political and social life. The ultimate result was a military profession that entered the twentieth century with a higher level of professional capability than it previously had achieved, but limited in its intellectual and political horizons: "It is true that the origins of military professionalism are found in this period. But it is also true that the parade ground of a two-or-three company post in the West defined the intellectual and professional horizons of most line officers in the postwar decades."[51]

Professional officers turned on themselves, engaging in internal politics and political maneuvering to secure better positions or to seek promotion. Thus, while some may argue that the isolation led to an increased professionalism, military professionals were increasingly becoming intellectually isolated. The emerging professional values and attitudes were to affect the military profession for decades. The idea that a truly professional military officer was not political, or at least apolitical, emerged. Moreover, a professional view developed that isolation from society brought benefits to the military, enabling it to concentrate on military skills and military matters with no interference by civilians and unblemished by political considerations.

Prior to the Civil War, military instruction at West Point was rooted in the European military system. The French and later the Prussian military system was used as a model, and the great battles engaged in by European armies were the basis for military history. Following the Civil War, instruction at the U.S. Military Academy shifted to the great battles of that war, and to the strategic and tactical operations that brought victory. Thus, total victory and the need to commit overwhelming force to win became an entrenched view in American military thought.[52]

The American military professional's view of war was shaped by the great battle concept and the view that victory was based on bringing maximum firepower to bear at the point of decision. Thus, regardless of the experiences in the American Revolution and the frontier environment, the pre-Civil War European tradition continued in the postwar period with a distinct American flavor. This tradition, now well established, stressed the need for a disciplined Regular Army as the basis for America's defense. This tradition, institutionalized in the training and education at West Point, stressed the maneuvering of disciplined troops, the use of cavalry and artillery, and outmaneuvering and overwhelming the enemy with men and firepower. Disciplined troops advancing on a wide front, even against the devastating fire of entrenched enemy, appeared to epitomize the "dash and elan" of the "great leader." By now the experience in the Revolution and of the Seminole Wars had been long forgotten.

By the end of the nineteenth century, the American Army had reached the end of one era and was entering another. Russell Weigley labels this period the "Twilight of the Old Army: 1865–1898," and Maurice Matloff calls it "Darkness and Light: The Interwar Years."[53] In this state of transition, the American Army was thrust into a foreign war, like none it had experienced in the past. Its previous focus on coastal defense, internal disorders, and marauding Indians did not provide a strategic perspective for conducting offensive operations against foreign powers outside the confines of the North American continent.

The post-Civil War period, as we have seen, provided little motivation or inclination for Army professionals to develop a broad political-military view that gave attention to foreign military issues and broad American national security concerns. Indeed, professionalism was concerned primarily with tactical skills and gave little attention to broader intellectual and strategic considerations.

The Navy, however, stimulated by the writings of Admiral Alfred Thayer Mahan, developed an outward perspective and a strategic philosophy. The very character of the Navy, with its mobility and access to world sea lanes, required an intellectual and strategic perspective beyond the confines of the North American continent. In the latter part of the nineteenth century increasing attention had turned to the protection of American markets overseas and the expansion of trade. This required an effective Navy and the projection of American power into foreign areas, a mission that many considered solely within the capability and responsibility of the U.S. Navy.

During the latter part of the decade Brevet Major General Emory Upton returned from abroad after studying the armies of Europe and Asia. Using his research as the basis, he submitted a report that provided an assessment of American armies in the past. Unfortunately, he was able to complete the study only up to the Civil War period before he died. Only in the next century was his work revived and made part of Army doctrine.[54] But even from his first report, it was clear that Upton was convinced that there had been no coherent U.S. military policy.

Aside from intellectual and strategic weaknesses, the Army also suffered from an absence of an historical "sense." With all of its experiences in nonmilitary and unconventional operations, the American Army failed to incorporate these lessons into its professional and institutional structure. The traditional mind set with its focus on the conventional and grand battles of the Civil War remained the distinguishing military characteristic. One hundred years later, with a wealth of experience in unconventional operations and nontraditional military operations, the U.S. military (particularly the Army) retained its traditional and conventional characteristics.

The American Army entered the Spanish-American War with the same organizational and command structure it had had during the frontier wars. The bureau structure, combined with eight geographical military departments and the unclear lines of authority of the commanding General, kept the Army from becoming a unified entity: it was "a collection of disconnected agencies—fairly efficient—rather than a unified institution animated by common plans and purposes."[55] Moreover, by 1897 the Army had been reduced to a strength of 25,000 officers and men, which still operated mainly in less than regiment size. Although concentration of Army units had begun in the 1880s, the Army was still oriented toward frontier security and a frontier organizational structure.

More significantly, American military professionalism remained wedded to a concept of war that was to prove irrelevant to the unconventional and revolutionary conflict in the latter phases of the Spanish-American War. The same type of professionalism which was to carry into the Punitive Expedition and into Vietnam remains characteristic of today's American military system.

The gathering currents of military professionalism, centering on conventional wars of the future, left almost wholly untouched the unconventional wars of the present. Neither West Point nor the postgraduate schools addressed themselves more than incidentally to the special conditions and requirements of Indian warfare. Indian campaigns found their way into professional literature as interesting history rather than as case studies from which lessons of immediate relevance might be drawn.[56]

SUMMARY

Following the Civil War the military establishment became a frontier Indian-fighting Army. During the period from the end of that war to the turn of the century, the U.S. Army was relegated not only to Indian fighting, but also to coastal defense and an instrument of home defense. The Navy meanwhile became an instrument for projecting American power overseas.

The Army was scattered throughout the West in small detachments which were rarely larger than company size. One result was that it became isolated from the political and social mainstream of America. To be sure, the Army was in close contact with frontier settlements and helped spearhead the movement westward. But this remained outside of the main centers of political and economic power in the East.

By the end of the century, the small detachments were being consolidated into larger garrisons. This change provided more realistic training and command experience, and made social life more pleasant. In addition, improvements were being made in the quality of life such as a better system of personnel management and logistics, and better pay and allowances. An improved professional education system emerged, stressing battlefield skills for officers and making the study of war a part of the professional system. A number of specialist military schools were established with a strong commitment to professional development.

Eventually, the Command and Staff School emerged at Fort Leaven-worth, Kansas.

In its fight against the frontier Indians, the Army again learned about unconventional warfare. Eventually, the extension of railroads, the expansion of American civilization, and the establishment of law and order throughout the West became the basis for the defeat and pacification of the frontier tribes. By the end of the century, fighting had all but ended, and the Army searched for a new posture and purpose.

After concluding its Indian-fighting days the American Army was left in an anomalous position. It was involved in putting down labor strife, but it did not seem to have a doctrine for guiding its future force posture. Ground wars with foreign powers seemed improbable. Coastal defense and internal law and order appeared to be the most likely missions. Yet, Army professionals studied war in the fashion of European professionals and struggled over the proper force posturing. Army operational doctrine did not realistically envision an outward projection. Nonetheless, it rested on conventional tactics combining the experiences in the Civil War with European developments.

The Navy became the recognized arm for the projection of American power. It improved technologically, and it had support in the Congress and the executive branch. Moreover, the Mahan strategy provided an operational doctrine which most Navy professionals and many civilian leaders understood and accepted.

Thus, when the American military became involved in the Spanish-American War, the Navy was reasonably prepared, while the Army wrestled with its burdensome command system and lack of training and experience in moving large bodies of men, not to mention the technological and logistical weaknesses. Moreover, its conventional posture, although serving well in the first and shortest phase of the war, made it difficult to adapt to the latter phases.

Going into the Spanish-American War, the American military again used the regular-militia-volunteer system to organize its armies. For better or for worse, this system was initially used in Cuba and in the Philippines. The brevity of the war and the relatively light American casualties indeed made the war a "splendid little war." However, in the Philippines, the struggle against the Filipino nationalists, and later the Moros, was transformed into unconventional war and a war against a revolutionary system. This was a different type of war, more bitter than the conventional phase against the Filipino nationalist Army. The American military was to learn again that conventional tactics and posturing did not necessarily bring success in the conduct of military operations. Conventionally trained troops had difficulty adjusting to the character of revolutionary war. Even veteran troops that had served in China during the Boxer Campaign found it difficult to adapt. However, the momentous events taking place in the rest of the world in the first decade of the twentieth century, and American pride in its "White Fleet," the U.S. Navy, diverted attention from the kind of struggle going on in the Philippines. The attention of the American Army was on developing the kind of professionalism that was seen in European armies. The battles of the American Civil War and the organization and structure of European military establishments became the guiding principles of American military professionalism.

PRELUDE TO THE GREAT WAR AND ITS AFTERMATH

The Spanish-American War revealed a number of deficiencies in the American Army and military capability. Rapid technological changes in weaponry and new forms of military organization in Europe made the American system appear obsolete. The stimulus for modernization and change in the Army was the appointment of Elihu Root as secretary of war. Although initially reluctant, Root accepted the appointment and began to lay the groundwork for what was to become a reasonably efficient military system.

Historically, there had existed a conflict in authority between the secretary of war and the commanding general, and between the commanding general and the Army staff bureaus. Secretary of War Root proposed the reorganization of this structure and the appointment of a chief of staff who would head a General Staff. The chief of staff would be the directing brain of the Army, reporting directly to the secretary of war. Staff bureaus would function directly under the chief of staff. Root's proposal faced stiff opposition from traditionalists, both civilian and military, particularly from the adjutant general who traditionally played the most important role in Army policy. Nevertheless, Root prevailed, and Congress approved the creation of the General Staff in 1903. Of all the reforms, this probably was the most notable during this period of time.[57]

Proper functioning of the new organization required the reeducation of Army officers. The War College Board established in 1901 for this purpose was supplanted by the Army War College in 1903. A number of other schools of instruction had been reorganized in response to the new General Staff system, including those at the five service schools: the Artillery School, Engineer School of Application, School of Submarine Defense (mines and torpedoes), School of Application of Cavalry and Field Artillery, and Army Medical School. In addition, the General Staff and Service College at Leavenworth and a War College were established.[58] To stimulate strategic thought within the Army, Secretary Root published Emory Upton's *The Military Policy of the United States*.[59] Thus, twenty-five years after his report, Colonel Upton's work finally received the attention many thought it deserved.

Following on the heels of Secretary Root's reforms, the chief of staff of the Army, General Leonard Wood, taking office in 1910 moved to make the General Staff more efficient and to regroup Army units into larger maneuvering forces following the European pattern. Through his insistence, the training focus of the Army shifted to European-type wars. In these efforts, he cut through a great deal of staff bureau red tape and attempted to place Army training and policy in the hands of commanders. General Wood faced a great deal of resistance from staff bureaus, especially the adjutant general, as Secretary Root had earlier. Nevertheless, through internal management reform Wood did make the General Staff more efficient, and he centralized Army command and control, placing them under the chief of staff's supervision. Perhaps more important, Wood was able to concentrate a large number of small army units into maneuver units, even if for only a short period of time.

The extent of the problem for the Army was reflected in the attempt to garrison troops along the Mexican-American border at the outbreak of the Mexican Revolution in 1911. Because the average Army garrison consisted of less than a battalion, it took almost ninety days to "concentrate fewer than 13,000 troops, to make a division that was both understrength in terms of the latest tables of organization and an organizational hodgepodge at that."[60]

Many members of the regular American military establishment looked with envy at European armies. The armies of Europe at the turn of the century proved to be imposing military machines, disturbing and threatening to even the most optimistic American military man. The apparently disciplined, trained, and well-led armies of Germany and France were thought to be the epitome of military capability and a model for the American Army. The traditions of the European military reinforced the professional educational basis of the American military. The battles of the Civil War became the cornerstone of military education. Conventional in orientation, concerned with administration and logistical factors in the support of large conventionally postured armies, the leadership and battles of the Civil War instilled a sense of grand strategy in which masses of men were maneuvered in order to overpower the enemy.

This professional education reinforced the view of many members of the regular military establishment that only a well-trained regular establishment could defend America. Thus, the heated debates regarding the Uptonian principles of military policy were reopened. Emory Upton advocated a system based on the German model. This not only envisioned the establishment of a general staff, but also placed the primary reliance on professional soldiers and a regular establishment. Arguing that it required at least two years to train a soldier, Upton had little use for the citizen-soldier concept. The Uptonian premise was "that only soldiers as thoroughly trained as the Europeans, with their two years or more of active duty and their long hitches in the reserves, could fight effectively against a European army."[61] Upton's thesis stressed that military institutions and the military profession stood above and separate from the political system.[62] Not only did this tend to be antidemocratic in tone, but also it was received sympathetically by a number of younger officers in the early twentieth century.[63]

General Wood, although supporting many Uptonian ideas, rejected the idea that two years were required to train effective soldiers. Convinced that citizen-soldiers could be effective and useful in the regular establishment, Wood stated that six months was all that was required to train citizen-soldiers.

Major General John Pope, speaking to the Army of the Tennessee a few years following the Civil War, spoke of an even more citizen-oriented Army. He argued that soldiers had to remain a basic part of the people if the Army was to retain the respect of the people. Without sharing the people's desires and maintaining its roots in the people, Pope argued that the Army would "become an object of suspicion and dislike."[64]

Captain John McAuley Palmer, a 1910 graduate of the Staff College at Fort Leavenworth, echoing General Pope, provided an alternative to the Uptonian idea and partially reflected the views of General Wood. He authored the War Department report, "The Organization of the Land Forces of the United States" whose main thesis was that the Regular Army should be trained and organized to fight immediately. It should not be a Regular Army skeletonized and based on the expansible concept. Palmer argued that the Regular Army needed a standard organizational structure such as divisions and lower units. Moreover, he felt that the Army had to retain a combat readiness for immediate commitment. Such availability and effectiveness could not be achieved with citizen-soldiers, especially during the initial period of wars in which a great deal of time was necessary for organization and mobilization.[65] Palmer felt that the citizen army was essential: "A free state cannot continue to be democratic in peace and autocratic in war. . . . An enduring government by the people must include an army of the people among its institutions."[66]

As captain and later as colonel, Palmer felt that citizen-soldiers could be part of the regular establishment, as advocated by General Wood. A citizen army, he said, could be mobilized and effectively trained in a reasonable period of time. Palmer's concepts transferred the reliance from a regular establishment to a citizen army in times of national emergency. In the main, however, views such as those held by Pope and Palmer had only a tangential impact on civil-military reforms.

From the end of the Spanish-American War until the entry of the United States into World War I, the American military was still struggling over the issues of a citizen army or the Uptonian concept of a professional Regular Army. The regular-state militia concept was still in effect during the Spanish-American War and the first phase of the Philippine revolution. In the later part of the Filipino nationalist revolution and during the Moro revolution, the American forces consisted mainly of Regular Army troops. With the tensions in Europe, particularly on the heels of the Russo-Japanese war, American military thought focused on a military posture capable of extending American military power and fighting a European-type ground war.

By the time of the Punitive Expedition and involvement in World War I, the American Army had clearly established a sense of professionalism and an organizational structure that reached back to Chippewa and Lundy's Lane. In light of the major events in Europe and the professional levels of European armies, it was to be expected that the American Army would follow suit. Nonetheless, it is also true that much of the Army's experience was in unconventional war. Yet this experience was neither institutionalized within the profession nor systematically studied in the military educational system. Reinforcing this view was the lack of appreciation of political leaders regarding unconventional wars. Indeed, the main element of power was seen to be a strong navy to project power overseas and an army primarily for internal defense and to deter foreign invasions.

In an apparent anomaly, nearly a third of the Regular Army troops served overseas during the period 1902–11. Although most of them were in the Philippines, others served in Alaska, Hawaii, China, and elsewhere. During this period of time, the average strength of the Regular Army was 75,000 officers and men. Because of the thin manpower resources, increasing concern was turned to the reserve forces. In this respect, some of the most heated debates concerned the reorganization of the state militia.

In 1903 the Dick Act was passed which "retained the principle of universal military obligation, inherited from England by the first colonies. But it discarded the general enrollment and personal weapons of the old militia laws. . . . All the able-bodied manpower of the states was declared to constitute the 'Reserve Militia.' "[67] In addition, the organized militia was to include National Guard companies and regiments. In an attempt at uniformity and to upgrade effectiveness, the federal government was to issue arms and equipment to the National Guard without charge. Criteria were established to insure that a certain number of drills were held and field instruction occurred, with a system of inspections by regular officers.

In another effort, Army Chief of Staff Leonard Wood established summer camps at Plattsburg, New York, as a way of providing military training for college students during the summer months. The students had to pay their own way. As part of the preparedness movement, the "Plattsburg Idea" began to spread after World War I began.

In 1916 Representative James Hay, chairman of the House Military Affairs Committee, proposed a plan by which federal authority over the National Guard would be increased, as a means of insuring available forces, but also as a counterproposal to the Continental Army idea. This was a proposal to relegate the National Guard to a minor role, with a ready reserve under federal control in direct support of the Regular Army.

Although Congress did not accept Hay's bill, most of its elements were incorporated into the National Defense Act of 1916 which Congress approved after much debate. Essentially, the debates reflected a struggle between the Uptonians pushing for an expansible regular establishment and those committed to a citizen army role in which the Regular Army would be augmented by National Guard units in case of war. The Hay's bill was a compromise. It provided for a larger Regular Army to be augmented by the National Guard. However, the National Guard would be increasingly responsible to the federal government for its equipment and training.

Under the National Defense Act of 1916, the strength of the Regular Army was increased to 175,000 over five years while providing for an expansible Regular Army to 286,000 during war. Inasmuch as the French alone suffered 120,000 casualties in the Nivelle Offensive during the month of America's entrance into the European war, the National Defense Act in retrospect hardly appears adequate. Yet, it did provide the basis for a systematic approach to the issue of military manpower. Even in its inadequacy, it proved that manpower for modern-day armies would require national conscription.

Aside from improving the organizational structure and manpower levels, the Army upgraded its weaponry. It adopted the Springfield rifle with its bolt action and magazine-loading features, a weapon so effective that even in World War II and the Korean War they were sought after as sniper weapons. The .38–caliber revolver was replaced by the heavier, more lethal .45-caliber Colt automatic pistol. In addition, the Army eventually adopted machine guns, which were modern versions of the Gatling gun used throughout the Army since 1866. Finally, although European armies had moved considerably ahead of the United States in artillery, the Army did adopt a new 3–inch gun, which was a vast improvement over artillery pieces used in the Spanish-American War. Thus, on the eve of the Great War, the United States had a military that had greatly improved since 1900:

The changes which had been inaugurated since the war with Spain had resulted in an improved officers corps, a greater professional competence in both staff and line, and a more effective co-ordination at some of the higher levels of command. But it was not clear that the system created by Root was capable of successfully waging a major war.[68]

Even greater modernization was taking place within the Navy, which was still considered the first line of defense.

The modernization had begun in the 1880s, primarily as a result of Alfred Mahan's *The Influence of Sea Power Upon History, 1660–1783*, which "urged his fellow-countrymen to build up their sea power in order that the United States might be enduringly prosperous and influential. Widely read and respected at home and abroad, friend and confidant of Theodore Roosevelt and Senator Henry Cabot Lodge, Mahan exerted a potent influence upon the current of affairs."[69] The thinking of the day was that a strong navy was needed not only to protect American power abroad, but also to harness the strength of American trade, particularly in the Pacific.

During the years from 1800 to World War I, the United States Navy replaced its outmoded wooden cruisers and coastal defense monitors with modern battleships. The change from wood to steel, adoption of modern weaponry, and the increase in tonnage soon made the navy one of the most effective navies in the world. This new navy was to become a formidable instrument of American foreign policy.

The Navy's success in the Spanish-American War provided the impetus to continue its modernization and expansion. By the time the United States entered World War I, the Navy was more powerful than that of any Great Power, with the exception of Great Britain and Germany.

In the aftermath of World War I, three major characteristics of American military policy emerged. First, Congress and the American people were convinced that the Great War had once and for all solved the problems of wars. They felt that there was little need for a large standing army or for commitment of major resources to defense. Second, the Navy assumed a major role in projecting American military power. America's concern was not with the possibility of major land warfare, but with conflict with sea powers such as Japan. But equally important was the need to protect American trade. Reliance on the Navy as the first line of defense was a continuation of the tradition established earlier in American history. Third, the American Army reflected these views, was relegated to internal defense, and was tangentially involved in American domestic issues. Moreover, the American Army, as in the 1870s, turned back into itself and passed through another "dark ages."

The difficulty of establishing a realistic military policy for the United States was clear to most military leaders. As expected, Congress established a committee to inquire into the conduct of the war and to devise proper legislation for military policy. After much deliberation, particularly over the Uptonian concepts, Congress passed the National Defense Act of 1920. Some important provisions of the act were based on Colonel John Macauley Palmer's testimony about the need for a citizen army rather than one based on Uptonian principles. Cutting the War Department's request for a 500,000 man Regular Army, Congress established a ceiling of 280,000, with the main reliance on citizen-soldiers.[70] The roles of the chief of staff and the General Staff were strengthened and enlarged, primarily in developing plans for the conduct of future wars.

The military education system also received a great deal of attention:

The United States Military Academy and the Reserve Officers Training Corps program furnished most of the basic schooling for new officers. Thirty-one special service schools provided branch training. Three general service schools provided the capstone of the Army educational system. The oldest, located at Fort Leavenworth, Kansas, and known after 1928 as the Command and General Staff School, provided officers with the requisite training for divisional command and General Staff positions. In Washington the Army War College and, after 1924, the Army Industrial College trained senior officers of demonstrated ability for the most responsible command and staff positions. In establishing the Industrial College the Army recognized the high importance of logistical training for the conduct of modern warfare.[71]

Passage of the National Defense Act of 1920 was initially presumed to be the basis for a new modern American Army: "It looked as though the United States at last had learned its lesson—that we were going to acquit ourselves like men and be strong. The army took on new hope of sufficiency and progress. It also took on the labor and responsibility of modernization."[72] A more immediate consequence of the act was the establishment of air, chemical warfare, and tank services. New pay scales were established for officers and men, and attempts were made to upgrade the quality of life within the services. Enlisted life was particularly upgraded, making soldiers feel they were part of an effective organization.[73]

But America reverted to its historical posture. Following victory in war and a return to internal domestic issues, trade and commerce, the military was allowed to languish.

So unpopular did military strength and training become that government action on defense was pushed from the back porch into the dog house. Many persons and organizations, who after the World War had savagely demanded a protection for our country, grew absorbed in other pursuits and were lulled by general prosperity. In degree we resembled our decadence between the Revolution and 1812, with, of course, advanced intelligence.[74]

The 1930s brought with it economic disaster in the United States and the rest of the world, which seemed to open the way for the resurgence of militarism in Japan, Germany, and Italy. With increasing military activity in these countries and the Japanese activities in China, some attention was again focused on the American military. As a result, in 1935 the military received a relatively large appropriation which allowed increased combat effectiveness. Moreover, the General Staff undertook realistic planning, and with it came a modest increase in the size of the military and its state of readiness.

During the early 1930s the Army was again involved in domestic issues, most notably in dispersing the Bonus Marchers who gathered in the nation's capital in the summer of 1932 and in nonmilitary tasks such as the development of the Civilian Conservation Corps (CCC) in 1933. By 1935 a number of reserve officers were called to active duty to replace Regulars who had been serving in the CCC.

Beginning in the 1930s, the Army emerged from its second dark age and began to rebuild. Attention was given to mobile warfare rather than to the static warfare of World War I. Nevertheless, World War I weapons were still the mainstay of the Army. The air arm and tank warfare also received some attention. The Germans, French, and British were far advanced, however, and it would take a massive national effort several years later for the United States to match and then to outdistance these countries in military weaponry.

The story of America's role as the "Arsenal of Democracy" and the struggle of the Allies in World War II is well told in a variety of sources and need not be repeated here, except in the context of our concern for lessons not learned. Throughout the 1920s and 1930s the main task of the Army seemed to be survival under the pressure of economics and antiwar attitudes. The Navy fared better, mostly because it remained relatively isolated from public view and because it appeared to be supported by those concerned with commerce. Moreover, this was a continuation of the traditional preference for the Navy as the first line of defense. The Army training remained fixed on European wars, resting primarily on America's experience in World War I. Again this was an extension of the tradition established early in our history. Involvement against the Indians, the Filipinos, and the Moros, and operations during the Punitive Expedition became historical curiosities. But the grand battles on the plains of Europe, combined with the traditions of Chippewa, Lundy's Lane, and the battles of the Civil War, had established a solid basis for the professional education and training of armies.

Isolated from meaningful civilian contact and for years scorned as an unproductive element in society, the Army again turned inward during the 1920s and early 1930s. While increased attention was paid to education and training, the Army's involvement in nonmilitary tasks and its minimum resources required constant supervision of day-to-day operations. Its professional dimensions increasingly focused on purely military skills. Although the Army performed nonmilitary tasks with a great deal of efficiency, most military men considered these tasks tangential to the precepts of military professionalism. Politics were likewise shunned. Yet, internal politics went unabated. Within the military competitiveness and a drive for promotion and for good assignments encouraged internal political maneuvering. Thus, on the one hand, professionalism was reinforced, while on the other, a political dimension emerged and with it a narrow view of the meaning of professionalism. Nevertheless, by the outbreak of World War II, the Army had already established the basis for a modern military system. It had gone through two decades of uneven development and at times decay, but because of the efforts of its chiefs of staff such as General Douglas MacArthur and Malin Craig, the Army now had a system designed to mobilize manpower and prepare it for major wars. The Army had also been able to instill a sense of professionalism in its officer corps which was to be the basis for the massive military machine in World War II.

Fortunately for the United States, the American Army had come a long way since World War I in planning and in mobilizing industry. Efforts in the 1930s based on contingency planning, directly related to the realities of international politics, provided a basis for expansion that would help prepare for World War II.[75]

SUMMARY

Throughout our history, America's basic military attitudes and perceptions have been formed by the experiences of the military during the fallow periods, that is, between the wars, and isolated from the main streams of society and from non-American sources.[76] During the nineteenth century, the primary source was Germany. Yet, American military professionalism differed from that of Europe.

The drive for professionalism emerged from within the American military; civilians contributed little, if anything. And in contrast to Europe, the concept of American military professionalism was tempered by a conservative military trying to function within a liberal society.[77] One result was that American military professionalism was heavily influenced by the perceptions of military officers of their own society and the detached nature of their relationships to their civilian counterparts. Professionalism became equated, in part, to the nonpolitical, while focusing primarily on the military skills and competence required in the conduct of war. The more detached from society and its political influences, the more professional the military could become. Such a view served as the guide to professionalism well into the post-World War II period. In terms of our concern here, such a view nurtured the conventional and traditional concept of military competence and of war in terms of grand battles. The concept of a military professional involved in the political-social system of our society, much less foreign societies, was totally incompatible with professionalism. The notion of military education and professional competence therefore became associated with a semi-isolated military system, whose autonomy and effectiveness were linked to traditions that reached back to Chippewa and Lundy's Lane.

Long forgotten were the Seminole Wars in Florida, where conventional military maneuvering and traditional professional perspectives proved inadequate. Forgotten too were the unconventional and bitter struggles in the Philippines, against the nationalists and the Moros. The lessons of the Punitive Expedition into Mexico, while not forgotten, had been distorted and translated into a rehearsal for World War I; and the political-social implications of the kind of war fought by Pancho Villa, the Carranzistas, and the Mexican people against Pershing's forces were completely ignored. Faced with similar situations in the post-World War II period, the American military responded as it had in all unconventional wars: it relied on its experience in conventional wars detaching itself from the more crucial political-social issues which, in the final analysis, always determined the outcome of such wars.

THE WRONG WAR

The United States emerged from World War II as the world's leading military and industrial power. Europe was in shambles, the Soviet Union was economically and socially devastated, and China was trying to recover from a war that had lasted over a decade. Although the United States had a monopoly on nuclear weapons, the Soviet Union remained militarily powerful and had large contingents of troops in over half of Europe and parts of the Mideast and Japan.

Not many Americans recognized the crucial and overpowering position of the United States. The American people thought that a return to the pre-World War II period was the first priority. The American military was demobilized almost overnight. For those who lived through that period, who can forget the sight of General Dwight Eisenhower, the commander of American forces, being cornered in his office by a distraught group of wives demanding that their soldier husbands be returned to the United States immediately. In Europe, some American soldiers staged marches and demonstrations demanding their return home now that the war was over. The political-military naivete with which most Americans viewed their world role was matched by the Soviets' intent to use their newfound military power as a weapon to expand their country's influence in Europe and in other parts of the globe. So convinced were some of our leaders that peace could be attained without further involvement that the military draft was ended and the military returned to a volunteer system, albeit for only a short period of time.

The Cold War, sparked by the Soviet Union's destruction of Czechoslovakian democracy, awakened most Americans to the need for a long-range political-military strategy. The Marshall Plan and the reinstatement of the selective service system were two notable efforts. For the American military, the period immediately following World War II was characterized by changing organizational structures formed around nuclear weapons.

Several other political-military events added to the changed nature of international security and to the challenges to American security. The United States and the Soviet Union emerged from the war as superpowers, both militarily and politically. Their incompatible ideologies and the goals of the Soviet Union in Europe and around its periphery were major threats to the West. With Europe in no position to challenge the Soviet Union, the United States became the focal point of Western strength. Thus, whether or not it wanted to, the United States emerged as a superpower and defender of the democratic West with the Soviet Union as its main protagonist. Russia was seen as the center of a monolithic communism which had control over Eastern Europe and China, with an ideology based on communizing the world.

The demise of colonialism planted the seeds for future conflicts in non-European areas, although few anticipated the challenges that would follow the breakup of Europe's colonial empire. Signs had appeared early—the British struggles in Malaya, the French in Indochina, and the Huks in the Philippines. Moreover, Americans had become involved in Greece and experienced revolution and counterrevolution early in the post-World War II period. As early as 1948, it had become clear that revolutions and colonial conflict were to become endemic.

Most Americans at the time were more concerned about domestic matters and about the dislocations of the war. Many presumed that the newly established United Nations would solve the problems of the world. America's nuclear monopoly gave a sense of security: surely, this would force proper behavior on the part of the Russians. Understandably, Americans turned their attention to the 1948 presidential elections and the economic and domestic issues in a transition to peace.

Not all military matters were ignored, of course. Indeed, one of the most far-reaching military reorganizations took place with the passage of the National Security Act of 1947, which corrected a number of organizational weaknesses revealed in World War II. This act established a separate Air Force, the Central Intelligence Agency, and a Department of Defense; the departments of the Army, Navy, and Air Force were subordinated to the Defense Department. For the first time in American military history, there was a centralized structure over all the armed services, under the control of a civilian secretary of defense. While there have been some adjustments in this structure, much of it remains the same as it was conceived in 1947.

Although most Americans seemed oblivious to the changed international environment, the United States was striving to establish a coherent strategy. The inability of the British to continue their worldwide commitments led to their withdrawal from Greece, which, in turn, led to the Truman Doctrine for the United States. Concerned about the possibility of a Communist-led revolution against the Greek government, President Harry S Truman declared that "we must assist free peoples to work out their own destinies in their own way. I believe that our help should be primarily through economic and financial aid which is essential to economic stability and orderly process."[78] With the collapse of the Czechoslovakian democracy and the onset of the Cold War, Americans became more sensitive to the Russian threat. What emerged was the primacy of Europe in American security policy and a policy of strength based on America's nuclear monopoly and economic and financial strength. Moreover, the United States entered a period in which it attempted to expand its influence and to counteract the Soviet Union by becoming a partner with a number of other nations through a series of multilateral and bilateral treaties. The United States made a series of commitments to the defense of a variety of areas around the world. The most serious and clearest commitment was to Europe through the North Atlantic Treaty Organization (NATO). With some minor shifts of direction, NATO remains today as it was originally conceived, a counterforce to the Soviet Union. Paralleling this early and continuing commitment to Europe, the American military focused most of its attention on the defense of Europe in the context of NATO.

The Soviet Union's acquisition of nuclear weapons dramatically shifted America's strategic calculations. Eisenhower, like Truman, viewed the Soviet Union as the major threat, and communism as a monolith encompassing much of Eastern Europe and China, with its heart in the Soviet Union. The defeat of the Nationalist Chinese and the Korean War simply confirmed what most Americans feared—an expansionist Soviet Union and an aggressive ideology that threatened the West and the United States.

It soon became apparent that a new grand strategy had to be adopted which would respond more effectively to the new international situation.

Earlier, George Kennan had suggested a containment policy in his now famous "Mr. X" article.[79] Although ignored by the Truman Administration, this policy became feasible, particularly in light of the nuclear environment and American superiority in nuclear weapons. It basically sought to contain the Soviet Union within the limits of Eastern Europe and to limit its expansion in other parts of the world. This was backed by a "New Look" military strategy.

America's search for an effective and economical military posture to challenge the Soviet Union evolved into a strategy based on the presumption that ground forces had become virtually irrelevant in major wars. Nuclear weaponry and the ability to deliver nuclear warheads on enemy targets were the keys to success. The threat of nuclear devastation against any aggressor became the basis for American global strategy. It quickly became apparent, however, that such a strategy was both naive and dangerous in light of Soviet nuclear capability. To threaten to drop nuclear bombs in an invasion of a power friendly to the United States would open the door for nuclear retaliation on the United States itself. Clearly, such a strategy considerably limited American options.

By the late 1960s it became apparent that the Soviet and American nuclear weapons inventories and technology were balancing each other, creating a nuclear "stand-off." The "balance of terror" became a useful concept, with deterrence emerging as the most realistic nuclear strategy for the United States. The presumption was that if the United States had a sufficient supply of nuclear weapons capable of destroying major parts of the Soviet Union, nuclear war could be avoided. According to this view, both sides would recognize that such a war would be too costly for either side to accept. Moreover, it became clear that the "bigger bang for a buck" concept of military strategy could not work in limited war contingencies. In unconventional and revolutionary wars, such a strategy was irrelevant: "In the spring of 1954, when the Department of Defense was concentrating its greatest efforts on developing our capability to strike massive atomic blows, we very nearly found ourselves involved in a bloody jungle war in which our nuclear capability would have been almost useless."[80]

America's military posture had changed little from World War II to the Korean War. The focus remained on European-type wars, although the military remained on a peacetime basis, performing occupation duty in Europe, Japan, and Korea. The demobilization of the military forces immediately after World War II necessitated a long, arduous rebuilding process. At the same time, strategy and organization were remolded around nuclear warfare. As a result of the cutback in defense appropriations and the reduction of forces, the armed services were placed in a position to seek out their proper roles and to struggle against each other for their share of the defense budget. For the Army, doctrinal principles stressed the use of firepower and maneuver, with tank warfare playing a major role. Although helicopters were coming into use, it was the Marine Corps that seriously undertook to study the use of helicopters in war. The Air Force and Navy jockeyed to gain control of strategic forces. Internally, the Air Force was trying to define the role of tactical and strategic air forces. The Navy began its never-ending debate regarding the role of battleships, aircraft carriers, and submarines.

The involvement of the United States in the Korean War came only a few years after World War II. In light of its peacetime role and occupation duty in the Far East, the initial period of the Korean War found the U.S. Army woefully unprepared. As General Matthew B. Ridgway commented, the "Army was in a state of shameful readiness when the Korea War began."[81] After the Chinese entered the war, it became clear that certain doctrinal changes were necessary. The infiltration of American positions by the Chinese at night, followed by attacks from the rear and the use of mass frontal assaults combined with guerrilla war in the rear, were new phenomena to the American military. Nonetheless, the massive use of American firepower, supported by unchallenged control of the air and the seas around Korea, provided the American military with an advantage rarely seen in war.

Although the Korean War showed weaknesses in America's military capability, particularly in terms of limited war, little was done to correct them. Moreover, the nuclear capability of both superpowers mutually canceled any nuclear advantage. As General Ridgway pointed out, "Under these conditions, national objectives could not be realized solely by the possession of nuclear capabilities alone as sufficient, either to prevent, or to win a war."[82] Yet it was during the same period of time that the Army tactical doctrine was refashioned around nuclear war, almost to the neglect of other contingencies.[83]

In a statement that was both candid and prophetic, General Ridgway wrote to Secretary of Defense Charles E. Wilson in 1955, identifying major flaws in American military capability.

In general, the foregoing commitments express the intent of the United States:

a. To meet force with force.
b. To be prepared to meet and defeat limited aggression in small perimeter wars, whether or not nuclear weapons are used.
c. To be capable of defeating Soviet Bloc military forces if general war should occur, whether or not nuclear weapons are used, and in widely varying terrain and climates.

In my view, the present United States military forces are inadequate in strength and improperly proportioned to meet the above commitments, specific or implied.[84]

The American experience in Korea was translated into a doctrine of preparation against the Soviet Union. Mass frontal attacks were presumed to be the Soviet style of land warfare. At the same time, America's land forces were reorganized and restructured around the concept of nuclear war. Such a strategy produced a doctrine relegating land forces to a distinctly secondary role in war such as defense of key installations and home guard duties. The Air Force and Navy became the primary instruments for "offensive" warfare. Nevertheless, the reorganization of the Army around Pentomic Battle Groups was an attempt to synthesize a ground forces role with strategic weaponry. Battle Groups, units that were larger than battalions but smaller than regiments, were organized as self-contained, nuclear war-oriented units. The purpose of the ground forces was to engage the remnants of enemy forces and occupy the enemy areas following a nuclear exchange.

The deterrence strategy and balance of terror, although making nuclear wars less likely, as some presumed, made nonnuclear wars more likely. Indeed, after the end of World War II, nonnuclear conflicts had occurred frequently. Nonetheless, well into the 1960s, America continued to view the Soviet Union as the major challenge. This view was reinforced by the Cuban Missile Crisis in 1962 and the subsequent Soviet policy to match and surpass the United States in strategic capability. Only a few recognized the emerging threats to the United States in non-European areas. The focus of the military remained fixed on the grand battles in Europe against the Soviet Union: "Even though all of America's military conflicts since World War II have been outside Europe, the Army and the nation have invariably refocused their concerns after these conflicts upon the defense of Western Europe. And doctrine for the postwar Army has centered on a European-type battlefield."[85]

As David Halberstam points out, the American view of the world shaped its foreign policy, which in turn provided the strategic guidelines for America's military posture.[86] Unfortunately, the American view of communism remained basically unchanged over a decade of major changes in the international field. Thus, according to Halberstam, our view of the Southeast Asian turmoil was guided more by 1950s perspectives than by 1960s realities.

The essence of good foreign policy is constant re-examination. The world changes and both domestic perceptions of the world and domestic perceptions of national political possibilities change. It was one thing to base a policy in Southeast Asia on total anti-Communism in the early 1950s when the Korean War was being fought and when the French Indo-China war was still at its height, when there was, on the surface at least, some evidence of Communist monolith, and when the United States at home was becoming locked into the harshest of the McCarthy tensions. But it was another thing to accept these policies quite so casually in 1961 . . . when both the world and the United States were very different. By 1961 the schism in the Communist world was clearly apparent: Khrushchev had removed his technicians and engineers from China.[87]

The involvement in Vietnam was, therefore, primarily a reaction to American perception of the grand design of a Communist monolith. In this respect, a number of "bright" young men, according to Halberstam, intellectually rationalized the policy of containing communism, while classic intellectuals took a passive role, not questioning U.S. policy.

Classic intellectuals stayed where they were while the new breed of thinkers-doers, half of academe, half of the nation's think tanks and of policy planning, would make the trip (to Washington), not doubting for a moment the validity of their right to serve, the quality of experience. They were men who reflected the post-Munich, post-McCarthy pragmatism of the age. One had to stop totalitarianism, and since the only thing the totalitarians understood was force, one had to be willing to use force. They justified each decision to use power by their own conviction that the Communists were worse, which justified our dirty tricks, our toughness.[88]

The Kennedy Administration adapted a new strategy based on the military's ability to respond across a wide spectrum of contingencies. The military had to be prepared to respond not only with devastating nuclear power but also in a conventional as well as unconventional way. Kennedy revitalized the Special Forces and took a deep interest in counterinsurgency. During this period of time, the Army regained some of its stature vis-à-vis the Air Force and Navy. This became particularly important in terms of conventional land warfare in Europe. "Flexible response" presumed that the American military had the ability to react quickly with adequate forces in a variety of contingencies. It also presumed that American forces could be adequately trained and equipped for such contingencies. The weakness of the flexible response strategy was revealed in Vietnam. Its critics were quick to point out that such a strategy was based on incrementalism rather than on the proven military axiom of overwhelming firepower and force at the point of decision. In Vietnam, it was argued, American military forces were increased and committed only gradually, allowing the enemy to readjust and respond at each phase of increased American involvement. This was the case, according to these critics, not only in terms of ground forces but also with respect to the use of the Navy and Air Force.

Other critics argued that the posture of American forces in all the services was such as to preclude successful counterinsurgency. Organized around conventional guidelines with military professionals whose view of war evolved from traditional roots, critics argued that the American response in Vietnam was based on unconventional rhetoric with conventional operations.

The American military entered the Vietnamese conflict on the presumption that overwhelming firepower and mobility, combined with control of the air and sea, would ultimately defeat the enemy and that such a battlefield victory would not be prolonged. Moreover, many American professionals felt that they were prepared for the kind of unconventional war taking place in South Vietnam. Many had read about such wars and had familiarized themselves with Mao's works on the subject. Some had also completed short courses on counterinsurgency.

American political leaders had presumed that the fate of South Vietnam was inextricably linked to American security interests. That is, saving the South was essential to the containment of communism in Southeast Asia and important to the defense of the Pacific area. The need to become involved in Vietnam was reinforced by the feeling that the American military had the necessary strength to defeat, relatively quickly, the Vietcong as well as any North Vietnamese units that could be deployed in South Vietnam.

The commitment to Vietnam extended over a period of time beginning in the 1950s. While there were shifts in approaches, American presidents felt that the American presence was necessary to prevent a Communist victory:

The basic American commitment to Vietnam was set, internally and publicly. Over the years the precise rationale was to take some interesting twists and turns, and the military was to jump off the bandwagon for a while, but the top political leadership of the executive branch never wavered from the objective of preventing a Communist takeover.[89]

These civilian and military presumptions, however, ignored at least three essential elements of the Vietnamese conflict. First, America entered the conflict on a limited war basis. That is, American military action was aimed at limiting the hostilities to South Vietnam, with the air war extended into the North but on a severely limited basis. Targets were limited, the boundaries for ground action were limited, and the use of massive weapons of destruction was limited, the B–52s notwithstanding. Most importantly, American purposes were limited—the survival of the South, not defeat of the North.

According to many military men and civilians, this limitation precluded the American military from bringing to bear its most effective capability, offensive operations against the enemy heartland. North Vietnam, and secondarily Cambodia and Laos, became for all practical purposes sanctuaries of strength for enemy ground forces. The Cambodia incursion was basically a "sideshow," and the use of B–52s and massive bombing, while disruptive, was never conclusive, particularly against a nonindustrial country. In fact, the experience of air war in World War II should have provided sufficient evidence of this fact. Thus, American mobility in the air, ground, and in sea operations was aimed primarily at the immediate battle area in South Vietnam. There is some truth in the observation that had it been aimed at North Vietnam itself, the outcome of the war may have been different.

Yet, the limited war was a function not only of deliberate American policy, but also of the fear of expanding the war beyond acceptable boundaries, since it was felt that the Chinese would never allow North Vietnam to be defeated by American forces. The experience of the Korean War was not lost on most American commanders and civilian policy makers. At the same time, however, the Vietcong and North Vietnam viewed the conflict as a total war. To them it was a matter of survival. Thus, the war was asymmetrical, with the psychological advantage in the hands of the Vietcong and North Vietnamese. In this respect, the political-military context of the conflict was established long before the Americans arrived and in most respects was immune from American influence.

The center of gravity of the political-military operations of the Vietcong and North Vietnamese was on the political-psychological consequences. American forces were guided by conventional military criteria, assessing the progress of the conflict according to body count, prisoners, and weapons captured, and whether or not the enemy military operation succeeded.

Second, American democracy placed political-psychological constraints and limitations upon the American military. Americans expected their soldiers to behave in acceptable patterns on the battlefield. This almost took on the air of "gentlemanly behavior" against the foe. Thus, "rules of the game" were imposed that had little relevance in revolution and counterrevolution. Reinforcing these democratic expectations was the fact that American military men evolved from a culture that stressed the importance of the individual; humanity, dignity, and justice. The culture in Vietnam into which American military men were immersed was considerably alien to Americans. Thus, American military men had a difficult time understanding their ally and their enemy.

Third, in contrast to the Second Seminole War and the Philippines, Americans in Vietnam had little control over the politics and political system of the target area. On a larger scale, Vietnam represented more the difficulties associated with the Punitive Expedition. In any case, political efforts, programs, and policies in the Vietnamese conflict were not coordinated with the military efforts. On the one hand, the South Vietnamese tried to control and affect the politics of the area; on the other, Americans tried the same thing in the military arena. Thus, while the South Vietnamese political efforts were frustrated time after time, the Americans would win battles with no apparent impact on the total situation.

The American military found this war frustrating. It was one thing to find and fight a conventionally postured enemy; it was another to engage in operations that were supposed to pacify the countryside, create a sense of loyalty to the South Vietnamese government, and establish a legitimate order in the South. While battle after battle might be won, the political payoffs seemed to be going to the Vietcong and North Vietnamese Army. Most American military men operated with a conventional mind set; yet they were trying to find answers to an unconventional conflict. Exacerbating the problem was the fact that pacification efforts could succeed only if the South Vietnamese themselves could implement them within their own country. Even after battles were won and the enemy scattered, it did not take long for the Vietcong to reestablish themselves in the same area.

The costs of involvement in Vietnam were high for America, and much greater for the South Vietnamese and the revolutionaries. For Americans, there were over 57,000 deaths and over 250,000 wounded. No true estimate of casualties can be made of the civilian populace and of the other forces involved, both South Vietnamese and revolutionaries, but these run into the hundreds of thousands. Aside from World War II, the Vietnam War was America's most expensive war in dollar costs: it came to more than $120 billion (in 1973 dollars).

Finally, the protractedness of the war, the seemingly endless series of battle victories that did not bring the end of the war any closer, and the realization that the South Vietnamese ally was far from secure in the control of their own country, gradually eroded American military and civilian morale, and convinced many Americans that withdrawal was the only alternative remaining.

SUMMARY

The changing international environment after World War II caused the Army to reexamine its warfighting posture. Reorganizations, introduction of new weaponry, changing balances between armor, mechanized, and infantry, and rethinking concepts of defense and offense occurred in every decade since the war. Indeed, the wars in the Middle East became mini-European-type wars and provided additional justification for the American Army to concentrate on conventional armored battles in Europe. Battle in the central plains of Europe became the cornerstone of Army doctrine. Faced with an overwhelming number of Soviet tanks and artillery, the Army doctrine stressed active defense and later, in a European context, fighting outnumbered and surrounded. More recently, battles in depth have become part of the doctrine.

The Army's attention to counterrevolutionary warfare hardly matched its concern with conventional operations. The grand battles of Europe, with their wide-ranging sweeps and envelopments of one mobile force by another; battleships and aircraft carriers with their massive firepower, engaging in sea battles reminiscent of the Leyte Gulf victory in World War II; and the air battles and dogfights over Europe during World War II—all of these remain cornerstones of the conventional professional orientation. Although in the post-Vietnam period, military professionals are involved in strategy and tactics of the electronic battlefield, laser weapons, and space warfare, the fundamental cornerstone of the professional perspective remains linked to the glorious battles of the immediate past.

Special or elite units such as the Army's Special Forces remain outside the mainstream, not only in strategic and tactical concepts, but also in terms of careers and professionalism. Attention to unconventional warfare, counterrevolution, or what the military calls "low-intensity conflict," remains on the periphery of professional education and military training. But as America's long history shows, the most difficult and frequent combat has been of a non-European and unconventional type.

It was not until 1983 that the Department of the Army took the first hesitant steps to centralize its special operations structure. It organized the 1st Special Operations Command at Fort Bragg, North Carolina, consisting of Special Forces, Rangers battalions, Civic Action and Psychological Warfare units. Special units of the Air Force and Navy were designated to operate with this Command. At the same time, the Army established special operations as an official career field. Nonetheless, the fact remains, in the decade of the 1980s, the most promising career patterns for military professionals remain in standard command and staff channels.

Yet, the Army had organized the Special Forces as an arm of unconventional warfare in response to guerrilla warfare in the early period of the Korean War. Initially made up of an odd mixture of members of the World War II Special Services and Ranger battalions and a sprinkling of new officers, the 10th Special Forces eventually developed into a highly professional and effective unconventional warfare group. This unit was organized in the early 1950s. Since that time a number of other Special Forces Groups have been organized, trained, and deployed.

The original purpose of the Special Forces, however, was to engage in insurgency behind enemy lines. Moreover, the traditional elements within the military looked with dismay upon the "foreign" atmosphere associated with the Special Forces. For example, it took many years before the Special Forces were authorized their own insignia and "Green Berets." Even in Vietnam, the conventional posturing of American forces and the professional orientation of most military men supported the traditional view that the unorthodoxy of Special Forces was a threat to the effectiveness and capability of American military forces.

The Army did include unconventional warfare training as part of the standard unit training. In addition, in the 1960s, officer education and training included attention to counterinsurgency. Unfortunately, these efforts did little to develop an effective counterinsurgency capability. American military professionals, educated and trained in conventional military terms, and oriented towards nuclear war and major land battles in Europe, had to redirect their thinking and professional orientation to a type of warfare that was incompatible with the long tradition of military professionalism. Thus, the attempt at reeducation was at best superficial and incomplete.

Ignoring the long history of American involvement in unconventional conflict, most American military officers were prone to read the works of Mao Tse-tung as the best preparation for combat in Vietnam, neglecting the difficulties of translating these into operational realities. Counterinsurgency became a reemphasis on small-unit tactics, devoid of the kind of political-social strategy and tactics and police-intelligence necessities that are fundamental in dealing with revolutionaries at the operational level. The serious study and practice of unconventional war remained limited to small detachments of Special Forces. Such skills and knowledge rarely penetrated conventional army units.

In all fairness, however, it may well be that American military men could not effectively train and prepare for counterrevolutionary war outside the conventional framework without violating some basic tenets of democratic society. Reinforced by cultural traits and intellectual perspectives, these constraints were to prove important in determining the outcome of the American involvement in Vietnam.

Thus, the United States became involved in the Vietnam War with a military posture that was based on a conventional threat and that perceived the enemy as similarly postured and armed. The initial impact of American military assistance was to structure the South Vietnamese Army according to American Army doctrine. The ground was prepared to engage in counterrevolutionary war with conventionally postured military forces and with a professional perspective that all but ignored the essense of revolution. What made the problem even more difficult was that American civilian policymakers were generally ignorant of the political-military history of Vietnam and of the dimensions of revolution and counterrevolution.

CONCLUSIONS

Regardless of the period of history, the American military establishment usually prepared for the "last war," but rarely in the case of unconventional conflicts. Preparations for war, professional training and education, and military formations and doctrine reflected a close linkage with European-type systems. Almost immediately upon emerging from the Revolutionary period, the American military system linked its effectiveness and capability with how well it could stand up to British regular military formations. Subsequently, the grand battles in history provided the guideposts for the military establishment. The historical view and professional training and education relegated unconventional wars to historical sideshows, unrelated to the development of American military professionalism.

The earlier European focus and the later conventional orientation were perpetuated by the relationships between the military and society. In an American democratic system, involvement in unconventional war was difficult to rationalize in terms of maintaining the American military system, except in a law and order capacity. Thus, peace on the frontier and coastal defense became prime movers of the American military establishment prior to the turn of the century. But peace on the frontier was primarily an adjunct to westward expansion and the vastly expanding commercialization and industrialization of the country. The military was used as a frontier police force; yet the underlying thrust was to develop traditional doctrine reflected in European armies.

The American military system has usually been in an uncomfortable position with respect to the political system. From the very beginning the Founding Fathers struggled over the proper role and position of the military in American society. The prevailing theme in the American political system and the democratic value system was and is that the military is clearly subordinate to civilian leaders and, among other things, plays a secondary role in political-military strategy. Until the end of World War II, the American military usually faced a critical Congress which consistently limited resources for military expenditures. In most instances political-military policy evolved with little correlation to the capability of American military forces, except in times of war. In the cases examined here, America considered itself at peace or, at most, in a limited conflict situation. In each case, including the first years of the Vietnam conflict, American concern was focused on different foreign areas, different issues, or both.

The struggle between Regulars and militia which emerged during the early years of our country has continued in one form or another ever since that time. The proper role and adequacy of the reserves, both National Guard and reserve units, remain an issue today. In earlier years, questions of the battlefield competency of Regulars and militia was a major issue. Serious debates took place as to where the main reliance should be placed, on Regulars or militia.

Even with its experience in unconventional warfare and its reliance during earlier years on the militia and a citizenry in arms concept, the primary core of military posture rested on conventional postures: conventional doctrines and weaponry. Emerging from the Revolutionary period, the American military system adopted the European style of warfare and later based military professionalism on its own experience in the Civil War and the two world wars. Instruction in military history and strategy and tactics at the service academies owes its formulation to the grand battles in history. From their very inception service schools aimed their instruction primarily at teaching officers to be commanders and staff officers in the traditional mode of European staff systems.

Until World War II, the American military remained consistently behind European armies in development of weapons, tactics, and organization. The exception was the U.S. Navy, at least through World War I. The rush for disarmament and arms control during the period between the two world wars limited the developments in maritime warfare. Yet, the U.S. Navy had a relatively well-established strategic doctrine long before the American Army was able to break out of its coastal defense and Indian-fighting orientation. Thus, the major thrust of military professional education and the character of the military system was aimed at European-type armies and battles. The limitations placed upon the military by Congress and the American people as a whole constrained the ability of the military to develop military capabilities or the organizational scope of most European armies.

If we relate these developments to the cases examined here, we see that the American military's response, at least initially, followed conventional patterns. Enveloping columns in Florida, trench warfare during the Spanish-American War, enveloping columns during the Punitive Expedition, and battalions in the attack in Vietnam—all reflected a conventional view of warfare reinforced by traditional training and operations. Even in the Philippine-American War, where the enemy did initially engage in trench warfare, and in Vietnam, where conventional conflict at first seemed appropriate, American forces remained conventionally postured long after the conflict became unconventional and the adversary developed wide-ranging guerrilla tactics. Most importantly, in the conflicts examined here a revolutionary system was challenging an existing system, with all of the political-social and psychological struggles this entailed. From the beginning, such conflicts confronted the United States with problems outside of the traditional political-military arena.

The American military has historically underestimated the capacity of its adversaries in unconventional conflicts, not only because of the traditional mind set and conventional posturing of forces, but also because the complexities and difficulties of unconventional war were never fully understood by either the military or civilians. The military criteria for successful doctrine and operations rested with those that emerged from the set piece battles of Europe or the Civil War. Unconventional conflicts were not perceived as being the kinds of wars that could seriously threaten

American security. These became conflicts on the periphery of American professional training and education, and American policymakers usually dismissed them as insignificant and inconsequential to American policy. The American military inherited this perspective, which reinforced its own view of such conflicts.

The American military establishment did eventually respond to the challenge of revolutionary war. In terms of battlefield performance, there is little to fault, although battle victories in the conventional sense were infrequent, even in Vietnam. But the successful conduct of counterrevolutionary war remained elusive to most military professionals because the tactics of revolution and counterrevolutionary warfare were not necessarily related to battlefield victories. The democratic culture, providing the guidelines for the military establishment, limited the ability of the military to respond to the kind of challenges counterrevolutionary warfare posed. The "victories" that did occur were largely a reflection of the overwhelming use of manpower and firepower, and, in some instances, the degree to which the military went beyond the boundaries of ethical and moral behavior inherent in democratic systems. The posture of the military reflected the state of the nation and established the posture and mind set with which the military entered the counterrevolutionary conflict. These reinforced the already existing conventional mind set and traditional doctrine.

In sum, from the very beginning of America's military establishment, the basis for strategy, tactics, and doctrine rested on a European model. After America established its own position as a world power, the American military establishment based its professional mind set on the grand battles of major wars. More recently, the American posture has been based on nuclear and nonnuclear war against major adversaries presumed to be postured similarly to American forces. Such a posture and mind set has been perpetuated by civilian leaders whose socialization and commitment to democratic values have made it difficult for them to understand the nature of revolution and counterrevolution.

In any case, the national leadership and the views of the American people directly affect military posture. The traditions of civil-military relations have made the military sensitive to society's attitudes and, in some respects, have fostered a desire to isolate the military instrument so that it can better prepare for conflict without the continuous oversight of civilians.

NOTES

1. As quoted in Clinton Rossiter, *The Political Thought of the American Revolution* (New York: Harcourt, Brace and World, 1963), p. 126.

2. J. P. Mayer (ed.), *Alexis de Tocqueville, Democracy in America* (Garden City,

N.Y.: Doubleday Anchor Book, 1969), p. 651. See also T. Harry Williams, *Americans at War: The Development of the American Military System* (Baton Rouge: Louisiana State University Press, 1960), pp. 17–21.

3. Roy P. Fairfield (ed.), *The Federalist Papers* (Garden City, N.Y.: Doubleday Anchor Book, 1966), 2d ed., p. 69.

4. Ibid., pp. 119–120.

5. Ibid., p. 62.

6. Maurice Matloff, *American Military History* (Washington, D.C.: Office of the Chief of Military History, U.S. Army, 1968), pp. 105–106.

7. As quoted in Rossiter, *Political Thought*, pp. 126–127.

8. As quoted in Russell Weigley, *History of the United States Army* (New York: Macmillan, 1967), p. 85.

9. Fairfield, *Federalist Papers*, p. 69.

10. Weigley, *History of the United States Army*, p. 154.

11. Ibid., p. 131. See also pp. 129–131 for a discussion of these battles. Also see Harry L. Coles, *The War of 1812* (Chicago: University of Chicago Press, 1965), pp. 152–163.

12. Coles, *War of 1812*, pp. 159–160.

13. Henry Adams, *History of the United States During the Administration of Jefferson and Madison*, 9 vols. (New York: Scribner's, 1889–1901), VIII, 45. As quoted in Weigley, *History of the United States Army*, p. 117.

14. Matloff, *American Military History*, pp. 117–118.

15. William S. Coker, "The Spanish Floridas and the United States," in James R. McGovern (ed.), *Andrew Jackson and Pensacola* (Pensacola, Fla.: Jackson Day Sesquicentennial Committee, 1971), p. 41.

16. Weigley, *History of the United States Army*, p. 160.

17. Ibid., p. 131.

18. Ibid., p. 160.

19. John K. Mahon, *History of the Second Seminole War, 1835–1842* (Gainesville: University of Florida Press, 1967), p. 119.

20. C. Robert Kemble, *The Image of the Army Officer in America* (Westport, Conn.: Greenwood Press, 1973), p. 36.

21. Mahon, *History of the Second Seminole War*, p. 118.

22. Ibid.

23. Ibid.

24. Ibid., p. 119.

25. Ibid., p. 118.

26. Ibid., p. 116.

27. Ibid., p. 117.

28. Arthur W. Thompson, *Jacksonian Democracy on the Florida Frontier* (Gainesville: University of Florida Press, 1961), p. 35.

29. R. Ernest Dupuy and Trevor N. Dupuy, *Military Heritage of America* (New York: McGraw-Hill, 1956), pp. 207–210.

30. Julius W. Pratt, *A History of United States Foreign Policy* (Englewood Cliffs, N.J.: Prentice-Hall, 1960), p. 237.

31. Ibid.

32. Ibid., p. 279.

33. Ibid.

34. Matloff, *American Military History*, p. 280.

35. Ibid., p. 301.

36. Weigley, *History of the United States Army*, p. 262.

37. Robert M. Utley, *Frontier Regulars: The United States Army and the Indian, 1866–1891* (New York: Macmillan, 1973), p. 411.

38. Weigley, *History of the United States Army*, p. 268.

39. William Addleman Ganoe, *The History of the United States Army* (New York: D. Appleton-Century, 1942), pp. 298–355.

40. Ibid., p. 355.

41. Ibid., p. 356.

42. Graham A. Cosmas, *An Army for Empire: The United States Army in the Spanish-American War* (Columbia: University of Missouri Press, 1971), p. 6.

43. Ibid., p. 14.

44. Ibid., p. 19.

45. Weigley, *History of the United States Army*, p. 305.

46. Utley, *Frontier Regulars*, p. 410.

47. Ibid., p. 397.

48. Kemble, *Image of the Army Officer*, p. 120.

49. Ibid., p. 130–131.

50. Ibid., p. 131.

51. Utley, *Frontier Regulars*, pp. 21–22.

52. Weigley, *History of the United States Army*, pp. 252–253.

53. Ibid., p. 265 and Matloff, *American Military History*, p. 281.

54. Ganoe, *History of the United States Army*, p. 357.

55. Cosmas, *Army for Empire*, p. 19.

56. Ibid., p. 44.

57. Matloff, *American Military History*, p. 349.

58. Weigley, *History of the United States Army*, p. 320.

59. Emory Upton, *The Military Policy of the United States from 1775* (Washington, D.C.: U.S. Government Printing Office, 1904).

60. Weigley, *History of the United States Army*, p. 334.

61. Ibid., p. 336.

62. Ibid., p. 281.

63. Ibid.

64. Ibid., p. 222.

65. Ibid., p. 340.

66. Ibid., p. 400.

67. Ibid., p. 321.

68. Williams, *Americans at War*, p. 115.

69. Pratt, *History of United States Foreign Policy*, p. 370.

70. Weigley, *History of the United States Army*, p. 399.

71. Matloff, *American Military History*, p. 409.

72. William Addelman Ganoe, *History of the United States Army*, p. 482.

73. Ibid., p. 483.

74. Ibid., p. 490. See also Williams, *Americans at War*, p. 85, in which the author states, "Americans always turn quickly and eagerly from a war at its close and put its experience behind them."

75. Weigley, *History of the United States Army*, p. 420.

76. Samuel P. Huntington, *The Soldier and the State* (New York: Vintage Books, 1964), p. 234.

77. Ibid., p. 233.

78. Paul Hammond, *Cold War and Detente: The American Foreign Policy Process Since 1945* (New York: Harcourt, Brace, Jovanovich, 1975), p. 38.

79. George Kennan, "Sources of Soviet Conduct," *Foreign Affairs* 25, No. 4 (July 1947): 566–582.

80. Matthew B. Ridgway, *Soldier: The Memoirs of Matthew B. Ridgway* (New York: Harper & Brothers, 1956), p. 275.

81. Ibid., p. 191.

82. Ibid., p. 325.

83. Major Robert A. Doughty, *Leavenworth Papers: The Evolution of U.S. Army Tactical Doctrine, 1946–76* (Fort Leavenworth, Kans.: Combat Studies Institute, U.S. Army Command and General Staff College, August 1979), pp. 12–19.

84. Ridgway, *Soldier*, p. 327.

85. Doughty, *Leavenworth Papers*, p. 46.

86. David Halberstam, *The Best and the Brightest* (New York: Random House, 1972).

87. Ibid., p. 121.

88. Ibid., p. 43.

89. Leslie H. Gelb and Richard K. Betts, *The Irony of Vietnam: The System Worked* (Washington, D.C.: Brookings Institution, 1979), p. 183.

4

Nature of the Conflict

CONQUEST AND CONSOLIDATION

The Second Seminole War had its immediate roots in the War of 1812 and more remote origins in the turmoil associated with the Spanish and British occupations of Florida. The primary cause of the Second Seminole War, however, was the Indian removal policy followed by the Jackson Administration. The nature of the conflict confronted America with its first major unconventional war. Many elected officials and military leaders, as was the case with the rest of the country, felt that the Seminoles in Florida posed no threat and that the disturbances they caused would be quickly resolved. The conflict became deadly and difficult, however, as the Seminoles fought in defense of their land and way of life.

For the American military, even in the aftermath of a number of disgraceful episodes in the War of 1812, the militia system was still the mainstay in times of national emergency. Some improvements took place in the military with the establishment of a staff system. However, the military retained its conventional posture paralleling the European organizational structure, and this was reflected in the conduct of the war.

The military forces used in the Second Seminole War were led by a succession of American generals, each with his own views on the conflict. There was continual discord between Regulars and volunteers, not only regarding the way the war should be fought, but also with respect to the roles played by the various forces and the ability of the various commanders. Disagreements between state and local authorities, and the federal government and commanding generals were constant obstacles to effective military operations.

The primary cause for the internal dissension was the strategy and

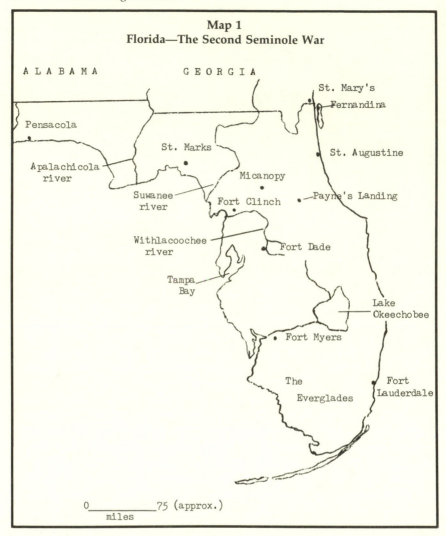

Map 1
Florida—The Second Seminole War

ALABAMA   GEORGIA

St. Mary's
Fernandina

Pensacola

St. Marks   St. Augustine

Apalachicola
river

Micanopy

Suwanee   Payne's Landing
river   Fort Clinch

Withlacoochee   Fort Dade
river

Tampa
Bay

Lake
Okeechobee

Fort Myers

The   Fort
Everglades   Lauderdale

0_____75 (approx.)
    miles

tactics initially followed by the military in the conduct of the Second
Seminole War. Following their European orientation and regular battle
drill, American officers deployed their troops in conventional columns
and enveloping movements. Such deployment was guided by the presumption that the enemy was vulnerable to conventional tactics. But
such tactics were ill-suited for the task. Not only was there lack of
mobility and of coordination and communications between columns,
but also logistical support was not up to the task. The terrain was difficult
and unknown, and the men unaccustomed to the rigors of warfare in
the swamps and dense underbrush. Fighting an enemy who knew every
nook and cranny of the terrain and who generally refused to stand up

and fight, the American columns did little but exhaust themselves and expose themselves to continual harassment by the Indians. Unfortunately for the Americans, they had forgotten the lessons of the Revolutionary War in which Americans had used unconventional warfare with great success against the British. It was the Americans who now faced an unconventional enemy.

It was only later in the war (and after difficult and costly experience) that the use of large columns was abandoned by the military and "search-and-destroy" detachments were used. Detaching themselves from the main body, these highly mobile units sought out the Indian on his own ground. Their tactics eventually led to the destruction of much of the Seminole's war-fighting capacity.

The combat during the Seminole War was characterized by ambushes and raids by the Indians against small detachments of forces and against various white settlements. When faced with large forces, the Seminoles usually faded into the brush. A volunteer officer who had served in the Seminole Campaign notes, for example, "Having scoured the hammocks in every direction, and stationed troops at every point where the Indians were likely to escape, we find that they have nevertheless given us the slip."[1] The same officer also described the results of General Scott's use of three columns in an attempt to strike at a large band of Seminoles.

...the Campaign has turned out a failure. For, though it went forth whizzing and shining like a rocket, it has come back like the rocketstick, falling low, a dull, heavy, inert, burnt out thing. We are not inaptly compared to a prize-ox, stung by hornets, unable to avoid, or catch, his annoyers; or we are justly likened to men harpooning minnows, and shooting sand pipers with artillery....And why did the Campaign fail? Ah! This is a fruitful mystery, and may receive as many solutions as the French Revolution had origins, and all as different. To my view, the most prominent cause of failure was to be found in the *face of the country*, so well adapted to the guerrilla warfare which the Indians carry on, affording ambushes and fastnesses to them, and retardation to us....A second source of failure arose from the *climate*....A third cause...was *the deficiency of the means of transportation*. A fourth...was the *conduct of the General Government, and of the Generals in the field* (italics in original).[2]

To make matters more difficult, hardly anyone knew anything about the interior of Florida. The interior had not been penetrated by white men. There were over 58,000 square miles with many parts covered by swamps and dense forests with hardly anything more than some trails traversing the ground. The climate had little more to offer. The semi-tropical climate created hot and humid summers, with heavy rains. But in some areas during the winter, the temperature dropped to zero. Insects and reptiles abounded. It was hardly a place soldiers trained in European fashion would find hospitable to their training, organization, and physical well-being. For the Seminoles on the other hand, it was home: an area they knew intimately and a climate to which they were well accustomed.

Even as late as the 1880s, little was known about Florida and the Seminole Indians, and there was little improvement in communications in the interior of Florida. After searching for the Seminoles, an American official in 1884 stated, "Owing to the ignorance prevailing even in Florida of the location of the homes of the Seminole, and also to the absence of routes of travel in Southern Florida, much of my time at first was consumed in reaching the Indian country."[3] Not only the climate and the geography of Florida contributed to the character of the war, but the Seminoles' political system, culture, and history were particularly important factors.

Prior to the arrival of the Spanish, there were approximately 25,000 Indians of various tribes in western and northern Florida. The Spanish occupation of Florida was the first contact between Indians and white men. By the beginning of the eighteenth century, however, most of the tribes had disappeared, leaving Florida in a virtual vacuum, except along some areas of the East Coast.

The Spanish, fearing domination by the English, sent expeditions north of the Florida territory to induce Indians affiliated with the Creek Confederation to move into Florida. By the end of the eighteenth century, a number of Indians had moved into the lower peninsula and had amalgamated into the Seminole group. Taken over by the English in 1763, Florida was evacuated by the Spanish, who took a number of Indians with them.

Another migration into lower Florida occurred in the aftermath of the Creek War of 1813–14. Beginning as a civil war between the Lower and Upper Creeks, it ended in a war between the Indians and white men, linked to the War of 1812. As a result of General Andrew Jackson's successful campaign against the Red Sticks (the war faction of Upper Creeks), much of the fighting power of the Creeks was destroyed.[4]

The Creeks had to cede much of their land to the U.S. government. The remainder of the Red Sticks moved into the lower Florida peninsula and affiliated with Lower Creeks, and for all practical purposes the Red Stick faction had separated itself from the Creek Confederation. As early as 1777, the groups that had moved into the lower peninsula of Florida had been named Seminoles by a British Indian agent, the name meaning the "wild people" because of their desire to be separate from the other Indian groups. By the early nineteenth century, embittered groups from the Upper Creek area had joined with those in the lower peninsula. Thus, over a period of years, a number of Indian groups or strains had evolved into the Seminole tribe.

But whether Muskogee- or Hitchiti-speaking, whether Upper or Lower Creek, whether Apalachicola, Apalachee, Chiaha, Eufaula, Tallahassee, Talathili, Oconee, or something else in origin, all but the Yuchi were of the Muskogean family, all shared the Creek culture, and all had earned the designation of Seminole because they had broken away from the settled northern towns and migrated southward.[5]

The Seminoles had no centralized political system. They were loosely organized into about 25 villages, each with a headman. Usually, each village represented a clan, which was the primary social organization. Clans were the basis for daily rituals and for maintaining social order, to include meting out punishments to offenders. The Seminoles' organization followed matriarchial lines; that is, when a warrior married he went to live with his wife's clan. It was the mother's clan that was the basis for any hereditary status; chiefs were chosen through the female clan. Nonetheless, the father's clan, according to Seminole practice, had to be treated with respect.

The basis for individual status and privilege in Seminole society was prowess in war. A man could not pass into manhood until he accomplished some feat in war. Such achievement was considered a *rite de passage* into manhood and status as a warrior. Until the man could achieve such status, he would even be required to do manual labor with the women—a humiliating task.

War provided an opportunity to become a warrior and allowed the man to achieve power and fame:

...he might become the leader of a band and be entitled to the designation "emathla." Or he might by the same avenue be chosen a war leader and be called "tustenuggee." ...Reckless courage might bring a warrior the name "hadjo;" notably fearless conduct, the title "fixico."[6]

Since there was no central authority, individual leaders within the clan usually made the decision to go to war. If such leaders were unable to get support from the Clan council, they could recruit their own following to make up a war band. Warriors were not obliged to join one or the other war party. The most popular leader usually attracted most of the warriors. This decentralized structure carried over into combat operations. Rarely did the Seminoles operate according to a central and coordinated plan. War bands usually decided upon their own battle tactics and tactical operations. Even in such instances, persuasion was needed to convince leaders within the war band to undertake a particular operation. During the Dade massacre, for example, several leaders within the group that conducted the ambush debated the proper tactical course before undertaking the action.

War bands performed a variety of war rituals before conducting war. This required the purification of the flesh. The medicine man had a major role in conducting this ceremony since it required not only the taking of a medicinal potion to cleanse the warrior, but also adherence to religious rituals. "Purity, being synonymous with abstemiousness, was essential to victory."[7] Thus, for the Seminoles, the clan organization provided social cohesion, with war providing the necessary rites of passage to manhood and warrior status. A decentralized political system allowed a considerable amount of freedom for each clan, and within the clan warriors and leaders had a considerable degree of freedom to act individually in the conduct of war. Even within the economic system, there was some individual initiative. The Seminole economic system was a mixture of the communal and private. Although land could not be privately owned, the individual warrior could own slaves and cattle. Within various clans, warriors and leaders could amass a considerable degree of wealth.

Of particular importance was the view held by the Seminoles regarding their land in Florida; they felt that the Florida land was theirs in perpetuity through their ancestors. Removal of the Seminoles from Florida therefore represented a break with their ancestors and their gods. As one Seminole representative had told white negotiators in 1820, "An hundred summers have seen the Seminole warriors reposing undisturbed under the shade of his live oak, and the sons of one hundred winters have risen on his ardent pursuit of the buck and the bear, with none to question his bounds or dispute his range."[8] And in 1826, describing the importance of land to the Seminoles, "Tuckhose Eathala, called John Hicks by the White men, vividly stated the pull of their connection, 'here our navel strings were first cut and the blood from them sunk into the earth, and made this country dear to us.' "[9] In sum, the Second Seminole War was a matter of survival to most Seminole Indians. For Americans, it was seen as a minor skirmish and a minor irritant (at least initially) standing in the way of progress and consolidation of lands east of the Mississippi.

The Dade massacre in December 1835, which a number of historians identify as the beginning of the Second Seminole War (although the Battle of Black Point was the opening salvo of the war), reflected the character of the war.[10] Major Dade and his command of 112 men, on a march from Tampa Bay to Camp King, were ambushed by a Seminole band led by Micanopy. According to M. M. Cohen, "The enemy lay concealed in the high grass and saw palmetto, and commenced with a most destructive fire by which nearly the whole advance guard was cut down...of the whole command, consisting of 112 men, only three escaped."[11] The column, not expecting an attack, marched in almost leisurely fashion. Although it was divided into an advance guard, main body, and rear guard, no flankers were out. Thus, security to the flanks of the column was almost nonexistent.

The column marched in two files into open terrain. The Indian band was positioned on the west side of the road with a pond directly opposite on the east side of the road. Thus, it would be difficult for any members of the advancing column to escape. The soldiers were in their sky-blue uniforms wearing overcoats which would make it difficult to get at ammunition pouches. Once the trap was sprung, Dade's men managed to remain in good order and slowly retreated into a small thicket of woods keeping up a steady fire, and with the help of a six pounder cannon were able to keep the Indians at bay. By late afternoon, however, the 180 Indians had overwhelmed the column. Although the Seminoles took food, clothes, and ammunition from the column, they did not scalp or loot. It was their Negro allies who killed the wounded and looted the dead.[12]

The systematic use of torture was absent in this war, although there were many atrocities, notably, the killing and scalping of prisoners or the wounded. Although the Creeks had been noted for torturing prisoners, by the first part of the nineteenth century this had changed. According to one account, there was no evidence of the use of torture and rape during the later period.[13]

While the Dade massacre was characteristic of the kind of war in which American forces were to be involved, there were several engagements that can be considered battles in the conventional sense. The battles of Withlacoochee in 1835 and Lake Okeechobee in 1837 are cases in point.

The Battle of Withlacoochee in December 1835 marked the Seminole War as something more than light Indian skirmishes. It also tended to institutionalize certain perceptions by both whites and Indians regarding the war and their opponents. In December 1835 approximately 250 Seminole warriors including about 30 Negroes fought an American force of 750, of which there were 250 Regulars. Five hundred volunteers were from Florida. After reaching the Withlacoochee River, General Duncan L. Clinch had his Regulars cross, since the objective of the force was a Seminole settlement on the other side of the river. Using the only available river transport, "a leaky Indian canoe," the Regulars crossed the river and prepared to attack. They were ambushed by the combined Seminole-Negro force which inflicted casualties of 4 killed and 59 wounded, or about 25 percent of the regular force. Meanwhile, the volunteers remained on the far bank. After the battle, recriminations followed with accusations being hurled at the volunteers for refusing to come to the aid of the Regulars. The volunteers, on the other hand, charged the Regulars with improper tactics. The volunteers also pointed to the fact that it was their fire which kept the Indians at bay until the Regulars could be extricated. As John K. Mahon concludes, this battle showed the "gap between regulars and citizen-soldiers which was to hamper operations many times during the coming war."[14]

Escaped Negro slaves made an important contribution in the Seminoles' struggles against the white man during the war. Many of the escaped slaves had formed a political system of their own, living in an alliance with the Seminoles.

Even though the Seminoles regarded the Negro race as inferior, everyone knew that the Negro influence with the natives was great. At the start of the war certain Negroes were among the top war leaders.... they were armed and willing, for they had everything to lose if the Seminoles agreed to leave the peninsula.[15]

The Battle of Lake Okeechobee in 1837 is considered to be the largest battle of the war. Colonel Zachary Taylor, the commander of one of General Thomas S. Jessup's columns, led his forces against the Seminoles in one of the few pitched battles of the war. The outcome brought fame to Taylor and no doubt was instrumental in developing his reputation as a strong leader and combat soldier.

The Indians had prepared their position with great care. Not only had they occupied a position with good defense characteristics, but they had also cut down sawgrass in the swamp to make firing lanes. The position was protected in the front by a swamp with Lake Okeechobee in the rear. The swamp had mud and water three feet in depth with sawgrass standing five feet tall. Approximately 400 Indians occupied the position and waited, certain of their ability to repel the Americans.[16]

Taylor, after a conference with his officers, decided on a frontal attack. This decision was to be the cause of much criticism by the volunteer units in his command. The Missouri Volunteers were in the first attack wave. Following them was an attack force made up of the 4th and 6th Infantry, with the 1st in reserve. The attack was on foot since the terrain made it impossible to mount a cavalry charge.

The general public's first reaction to the news of the battle was shock and dismay, in light of the heavy American casualties and the inability to capture the main body of Indians. But General Jessup quickly countered such criticism by pointing out that the battle was "one of the best fought battles known in our history."[17] Undoubtedly, such praise and comment was based on the fact that it was one of the few engagements, and certainly the largest, that forced the Seminoles to engage in conventional battle. The president praised and thanked Taylor for his conduct, the commanding general commended him, and Taylor won a brevet commission as brigadier general.

While such battles were the exception, they are important in understanding America's military posture and conduct on the battlefield. The

European orientation and the conventional approach to the battlefield were the main characteristics of military posture and reflected professional orientation towards combat.

The most effective tactic, however, was implemented later in the war. The use of columns was abandoned and replaced by more mobile and smaller detachments which veered off from the main force to engage bands of Indians. This early version of search-and-destroy operations was accompanied by a pacification campaign aimed at controlling specific operational areas and depriving the Indians of their food and lodgings. Devised by Colonel Taylor, the operational area was divided into districts that were 12 miles square—hence the label of "squares." Each square or district had a stockade and a garrison commanded by a district commandant who was to comb his district on alternate days. Colonel Taylor was not able to follow through on these tactics. Following orders from the War Department, Taylor ceased further operations. The Indians, taking advantage of the respite, went on the offensive. Out of frustration, Taylor asked to be relieved of his command.[18]

Succeeding Taylor, Colonel William Jenkins Worth was to make this tactic of "squares" more effective by vigorously pursuing pacification and search-and-destroy operation aimed at the Seminoles' food production and dwellings. Worth devised a plan aimed specifically at the enemy's economic livelihood and support structure, expanding on Taylor's plan. He campaigned throughout 1841, regardless of the weather, and destroyed much of the Seminoles' crops and dwellings. The constant harassment prevented the Indians from staying in one place long enough to grow more crops. Although Colonel Worth's men paid a high price in sickness and disease, the operations succeeded to a great extent. The Seminoles had to disperse into small bands and spent much of their time trying to subsist rather than engaging in serious organized resistance.[19]

One of the final battles of the war occurred in 1842, the year that the Second Seminole War was officially ended. A detachment of 102 men from the 2d Infantry under the command of Major Joseph Plympton made contact with a band of Seminoles near Dunn's Lake east of St. John's. The detachment had been pursuing this band of fifteen warriors since they had raided a settlement, killed four people, burned two buildings, and taken a quantity of loot. Forming into a skirmish line, the Americans attacked, but as usual the Seminoles had abandoned the position earlier and waited in the rear.

For over an hour the battle was intense. Eventually, however, the Indians were driven from their position. But the Americans were unable to catch them, and no prisoners were found. The real battle was the Americans' efforts in seeking out the Seminoles prior to the battle. According to Major Plympton's official report, many weeks were spent in constant marching over rough terrain with little comfort for his men. He praised them for their discipline and effort.[20]

The geographical characteristics of Florida posed great difficulties in communications, supply, and tactical movements for the American military. The configuration of Florida and the fact that it was bordered on three sides by water provided the opportunity for the fledgling U.S. Navy to become involved in the kind of warfare that it was to face in a similar environment almost 150 years later and thousands of miles away.

The U.S. Navy's role was to support ground operations. Its role also involved operation of landing parties, and at times both sailors and marines served as infantrymen. Patrolling the coastal waters, the Navy controlled communications along the coast and helped prevent arms from being smuggled from Cuba or being delivered from one part of Florida to the other. This was the first time that the Army and Navy had cooperated effectively against an enemy. This cooperation provided valuable training and added an important dimension to operations against the Indians.[21]

SUMMARY

Regardless of the problems in preparing for the Second Seminole War, the American military establishment was able to bring the combat zone a substantial number (in light of the times) of soldiers and sailors. The organizational structure and command system of the military establishment developed into a reasonably effective one, not only in conducting joint operations with the Navy, but also in integrating state militia and volunteers with the regular system (even if at times this created antagonisms between the citizen-soldiers and the Regulars). John K. Mahon points out that the Seminoles could not match this organizational and resource capability. Most, including President Jackson, underestimated the Indians. The Seminoles, numbering 1,000 to 1,500 warriors, fought for survival. This disadvantage gave them their tenacity and will to engage in combat.[22] The war officially lasted six years and was costly in both manpower and dollars.

The Second Seminole War had been guerrilla warfare, of a kind the Army was not equipped to fight. The effort depleted the Regular Army so seriously that in July 1938 its authorized strength had to be increased from around 7,000 to about 12,500 men. A total of about 10,000 Regulars and perhaps 30,000 short term volunteers had been engaged. Almost 1,600 men had lost their lives in battle from disease and about $30 million had been spent in order that 3,800 half-starved Indians might be shipped West.[23]

John Tebbel and Keith Jennison have pointed out that the Seminoles have attempted to maintain their integrity through the generations: "In the Second World War most of them refused to register for the draft. They were not, they explained, citizens of the United States. They were members of the Seminole nation, an independent state. It appears that the Second Seminole War will never end."[24]

A number of lessons may be drawn from the Second Seminole War—lessons that Americans had to relearn each time they were involved in this type of war. Perhaps the most important lesson, and one that characterizes all four of the cases studied here, particularly Vietnam, is the need to understand and appreciate unconventional war. This understanding and appreciation must be institutionalized within the professional educational system. But as Russell Weigley points out, American cultural patterns and the military professional value system prevented the kind of understanding of unconventional and revolutionary war necessary to conduct the most effective counterrevolutionary operations. From the American historical perspective, it was one thing to be a revolutionary and another to be a counterrevolutionary.[25]

As noted earlier, many political, social, and economic changes took place in America from the period following the Second Seminole War to the end of the century. The U.S. military engaged in a war with Mexico and also went through a devastating civil war. Following the Civil War, the Army, again reduced considerably in strength, was initially involved in Reconstruction and was later scattered in a variety of posts throughout the West fighting Indians and assisting in expanding American civilization westward. Only in the last decade of the century was the West settled and the Army began to regroup from its Indian-fighting days. It was during the same period that the Army became involved in quelling domestic disturbances and establishing the basis for military professionalism. By the turn of the century, America looked outward, using the U.S. Navy as its main instrument in the conduct of foreign policy and protection of trade. The Army remained wedded to a coastal defense and internal stability role. Nonetheless, the Spanish-American War thrust the Army into a foreign war extending from Cuba to the Philippines. Thus, it had to quickly emerge from its internal orientation to a war footing against a foreign foe in a land 7,000 miles away. The adjustment was not easy, particularly since the military was to be faced with a difficult climate and terrain, unknown people, and guerrilla war.

MANIFEST DESTINY AND THE CIVILIZING MISSION

Arriving in the Philippines in the early part of the sixteenth century, the Spanish set out to get their share of the spice trade, open up trade with Japan and China, and convert the Filipinos to Christianity. Ironically, it was only in the last goal that the Spanish were reasonably successful. They followed a policy of bloodless conquest, more or less, trying to avoid the problems that developed out of their occupation of parts of the American mainland. Thus, church and state became partners in establishing Spanish control. Although they succeeded in expanding Christianity, the Spanish met with stiff resistance from the Muslims in the south and the Igorots in the north, preventing the expansion of Christianity in the Moro areas.

At the turn of the century, most of the population in the Philippines was in rural areas. The Filipinos had little contact with the Spaniards except through the local friar or priest, who generally spoke the local language. Most Spanish officials lived in Manila, with others located in various towns. Adopting a policy of indirect rule, the colonial administration allowed the traditional system of administration to continue, with some colonial revisions. The countryside was organized at the local level around the barangay (barrio) ruled by a datu or headman. The next higher unit of rule was the pueblo, made up of several barangays. The highest Filipino official was the petty governor of the Pueblo. The next higher level was the governor, a Spanish official, who controlled the province, reporting directly to Manila. The governor was responsible for all administrative, military, and judicial affairs in his province. The role of the church was crucial in the conduct of government.

Although most Filipino peasants were not directly affected by Spanish economic policies, the impact of colonialism opened up new opportunities for the hereditary Filipino elite and the Chinese *mestizo* groups. These developed into a landholding elite which eventually challenged the hold of the church in the rural areas. By the late nineteenth century, the church and landholding aristocracy had established a secure position in the colonial system and with this was created a widening gap between the peasants, the landholding elite, the local Spanish priests and friars, and the colonial government. It is from these political and economic conditions that the Filipino nationalist movement developed. The Philippine revolution against Spain began in 1872 following a mutiny of Filipino garrison troops and the subsequent suppression by the Spaniards, which included the execution of three Filipino priests. The revolution grew and was a part of the political landscape when the United States intervened in the Philippines, complicating the nature of the conflict faced by the Americans.

The scope of American military operations in the Philippines included three types of combat conditions correlated with three different types of enemies. The first phase was combat with regular Spanish forces which was short and relatively bloodless. This established the basis for the next two phases. The second phase was warfare against the Filipino

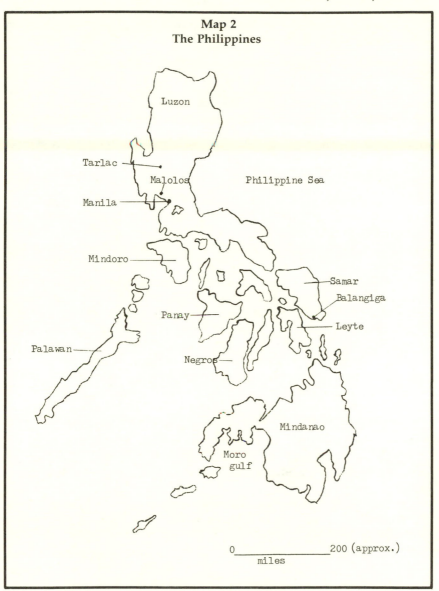

Map 2
The Philippines

Luzon

Tarlac

Malolos

Manila

Philippine Sea

Mindoro

Samar

Balangiga

Panay

Leyte

Palawan

Negros

Mindanao

Moro
gulf

0   200 (approx.)
miles

nationalists, which included both conventional and unconventional war. The third phase was a protracted war against the Moros in the southern Philippines, which was primarily unconventional. Our main concern is with the last two phases.

The Army entered the Spanish-American War using the Regular Army, state militia, and volunteers. Immediately following the armistice with Spain, however, President McKinley ordered the mustering out of about

100,000 volunteers, with the regiments in the Philippines remaining until 1899, ending the first phase.

McKinley applied pressure on the army to end the war in such a way that the anti-imperials could not make capital out of it. Volunteer regiments were sent home to be replaced by regulars, who were more tenacious and resolute. The fight became a struggle to win the minds and hearts of the villagers who supplied the guerrilla bands and offered them bases and sanctuaries.[26]

The second phase of the war, the Philippine-American War, was fought primarily by American Regulars. This war (second phase) passed through three periods before it finally ended in 1902, with each period reflecting a particular type of conflict: the conventional war in 1899; the unconventional (guerrilla) war under Emilio Aguinaldo until 1901; and the fragmented unconventional (guerrilla) war in the post-Aguinaldo period until 1902.

A conventional war was fought from the outbreak in early 1899, through the capture of the first Filipino capital at Malalos and later the one at Tarlac, and the establishment of a secret headquarters by Aguinaldo in the mountain areas of northeastern Luzon. The second period began after the destruction of General Gregorio del Pilar's insurgent band defending Tilas pass, sacrificing itself to allow Aguinaldo to escape.

Realizing the futility in trying to combat American forces, whose firepower and organization proved to be superior to anything the Filipino Army could bring to bear, Aguinaldo shifted his tactics. Proclaiming a guerrilla war in December 1899, he instructed his army to disband, go home, and conduct guerrilla operations against American forces. His strategy was to protract the war and attempt to erode the will and morale of the American Army while playing on the public opinion of the United States.[27]

The third period of the war began with the capture of Aguinaldo and the final capitulation of the last remnants of the Filipino guerrilla force in Samar and Batangas in 1902.

As noted earlier, the second phase began on a conventional note. Filipino revolutionary forces used trench warfare and massed troops against American forces. The battle around Manila was typical. Hostilities between American and Filipino forces began in February 1899. It is not clear what provoked the conflict, but it appears that an insurgent patrol challenged an American guard post near Manila on the eve of the signing of a peace treaty with Spain. The Philippine revolutionary government under Aguinaldo was, of course, incensed at the American's insistence that Filipino forces not enter Manila. American military forces blocked Filipino forces from entering and also conducted peace negotiations with Spain based solely on American interests.

In any case, the American VIII Corps under General Elwell S. Otis reacted promptly to the challenge, and eventually all American units were in action against the 40,000 Filipino Army around Manila. Extensive operations were conducted in conventional military formation against a foe who was also conventionally organized and positioned. William T. Sexton describes the hostilities that would last three years:

A bloody battle was to take place in Manila in which the Insurgents were to be driven from their entrenchments and scattered into the surrounding territory. . . . February was to mark the beginning of the three-year struggle in which the United States was forced to employ two-thirds of its armed forces to quell an insurrection and establish peaceful civil government in the Islands.[28]

The forces of the VIII Corps consisted of volunteers and Regulars. The Battle of Manila proved that the volunteers in the American forces could operate effectively when led properly. The battle also showed that regardless of numbers and the protection of trenches and redoubts, the insurgent forces could not or would not stand up before the American forces, particularly when American attacks were supported by artillery and naval gunfire. Considering the large scale of the battle, American casualties were relatively light: 59 killed and 278 wounded versus an estimated 3,000 casualties for the Filipinos.[29]

Immediately following the Battle of Manila, American forces commenced offensive operations against various formations of the Filipino forces. Time after time, American forces in conventional combat dislodged and defeated the insurgent forces, who persisted in conventional formations. Aside from the Battle of Manila, the insurgent operations around their capital of Malolos were a prime example of their conventional posture. The insurgents constructed what Leon Wolff calls a "Hindenberg line of entrenchments between Caloocan and Malolos, and positioned about 16,000 Filipino insurgents to block any American advance."[30]

An American force of over 11,000 officers and men composed of a mix of volunteer and regular units, advanced with supporting artillery on the insurgent capital. After a series of sharp skirmishes along conventional lines, the force entered Malolos. The description of the capture of the city reads like a standard operation of conventional forces in a built-up area. A series of earlier defeats, however, had left the insurgents in a precarious position by the time they had retreated to their capital.

After a week of steady fighting which cost the Americans 534 casualties, the city was occupied, although attempts to surround the rebel forces failed. As usual, Otis directed MacArthur to stop where he was and to abandon a plan to drive the natives eight miles north to the line of the Rio Grande Pampanga.

With the capture of Aguinaldo's capital city the war was as good as over; so
calculated General Otis.[31]

By the end of 1899, the American Army numbered almost 60,000.
With this number of troops and with the acknowledgment by Aguinaldo
that the Filipino Army could not successfully fight the Americans in
open warfare, General Otis proclaimed that the war in the Philippines
was over. Before the end came, however, another two years were to
pass with more than 6,000 additional American casualties.[32]

Following the capture of Malolos, American forces eventually captured
Tarlac and forced Aguinaldo to flee to the mountain areas in northeastern
Luzon. Once established in a secret headquarters in November 1899,
Aguinaldo after a meeting with his advisors disbanded the Filipino na-
tional Army and shifted to guerrilla warfare.

The guerrilla warfare was initiated by insurgent leaders, possibly at the sug-
gestion of General Aguinaldo who also planned to organize his own guerrilla
force in the mountains of Benguet. The remnants of the insurgent forces that
dispersed and took to the hills provided the nuclei for these guerilla units that
sprang up in various parts of the country.[33]

The difficulty of the unconventional second phase is reflected in the
number of American casualties, which doubled. The number of wounded
remained about the same. The fatalities had increased because of the
changed nature of the war, that is, by ambush and close-in fighting,
and sudden attacks on small groups of U.S. soldiers: "The Americans
were not fighting a uniformed army. They were fighting determined
groups of men who tilled the fields by day and stalked outposts by
night. The new type of warfare was infinitely more dangerous."[34]

General Otis continued his operations using conventional tactics, although the insurgent forces had now scattered to begin unconventional
warfare. Moreover, Otis used the equivalent of modern search-and-
destroy tactics. Rather than securing the territory, American forces would
strike into an area thought to contain revolutionaries. After the operation, American forces would return to Manila. Revolutionary forces would
simply move back into the area vacated by the Americans and reorgan-
ize. Americans were to face similar situations in Vietnam during the first
years of the war and responded in the Otis pattern with similar results.[35]

Otis's handling of military operations began to provoke some questions. He evidently misunderstood the nature of the revolution and
misunderstood the culture and society of the Philippine Islands even
more. Sending optimistic reports to the War Department upon completion of virtually every operation, General Otis misinterpreted the impact
of such operations: "Over and over he reported to the War Department

that the natives had been 'scattered.' But as soon as the Americans left, the rebels moved back in. Soon another expedition had to be laboriously fitted out to quell them."[36] Six decades later American military men were to find amazingly similar conditions and submit equally optimistic reports about the Vietcong in South Vietnam.

General Otis asked to be relieved after he became weary of trying to defeat the revolutionaries in the Philippines. He came to realize the difficulties of counterrevolutionary war. Trained and experienced in conventional wars, he could not adapt to the needs of counterrevolution and all of its unconventional tactics and political-social elements. General Arthur MacArthur took command and was later succeeded by General Adna R. Chaffee. It was under General Halleck that a civilian administration was established in the islands under William Howard Taft.

Part of General Otis's difficulties, no doubt, stemmed from reports provided by newspaper correspondents who had been highly critical of his handling of military operations. Newspaper correspondents then, as later in Vietnam, were some of the first to question the efficiency of American military operations in the Philippines. For example, a correspondent of the *New York Evening Post* cabled his editor, as follows:

The loss is usually given in the ratio of twenty to one. The twenty is guesswork.... But what of these "glorious victories"? Wherein lies the glory of killing "niggers"? It seems to take very little nowadays to make a glorious victory.... There are towns here which have been "captured" again and again, each time with a "glorious victory." Today it is unsafe for an American to go even ten miles from the city of Manila.[37]

The second period of the Philippine-American War also saw a shift in American tactics. In countering the guerilla forces, the organization of American forces changed "from that of a divisional tactical organization to that of a territorial occupational system of organization."[38] Four departments were established: the Department of Northern Luzon, the Department of Southern Luzon, the Department of the Visayas, and the Department of Mindanao. Manila was placed under a separate command. As military governor of the Philippines, Otis was given overall command of these departments.[39] Later, General MacArthur, taking over from General Otis, implemented a new pacification policy aimed at isolating the guerrillas from their logistical and support bases in the villages (barrios). It was also intended to break the political-psychological bond between the villages and the guerrillas.[40] With the election of McKinley in 1900, General MacArthur could be assured of the continuation of a policy of pacification in the Philippines.

Using General Order 100, issued in the American Civil War, as a legal basis, General MacArthur gave instructions that guerrillas who disguised themselves as civilians would be treated as rebels, losing their status as soldiers. During the Civil War the Adjutant General's Office issued General Order 100 stating that "war rebels" who rose in arms against the "occupying or conquering army" were to be "treated summarily as highway robbers or pirates."[41]

The standard procedure to deal with the Filipino populace upon capturing a town was to establish a native government. This procedure was based on the presumption that the Filipinos would gladly opt to govern themselves under the protection of Americans. However, as Americans again were to relearn decades later, this was but a superficial and unrealistic approach to counterrevolution.

The guerrilla forces established their own system of administration, dividing the islands into various districts, zones, and local units, each under the control of a guerrilla commander. Tactics were determined by the local commanders. In the classic fashion, long before Mao's revolutionary doctrine, the guerrillas used the local populace as supply and intelligence channels. Moreover, local commanders were instructed to establish parallel governments. "In many instances the same officials employed by the Americans were also serving the guerrilla units. This set-up enabled the guerrillas to use the money collected as taxes by the Government."[42] Thus, the Filipinos would establish, almost simultaneously, a shadow government or revolutionary system each time the Americans established a native government.[43] The revolutionary government was the real government in most instances. Most Filipinos whom the Americans had installed to govern usually refused to accept the appointment or passively resisted American attempts to impose their authority on the islands. The guerrillas enforced their authority by killing or threatening death to those who cooperated directly with the Americans, although passive cooperation was acceptable.[44]

General MacArthur commented on the difficulties of the guerrilla war:

Wherever throughout the Archipelago there is a group of the insurgent Army it is a fact that beyond dispute that all contiguous towns contribute to the maintenance thereof. . . . Intimidation has undoubtedly accomplished much to this end; but fear as the only motive is hardly sufficient to account for the united and apparently spontaneous action of several millions of people.[45]

The unconventional nature of the war created difficult problems in treating prisoners on both sides. There was a great deal of evidence suggesting that Americans and Filipinos alike brutally handled a number of their prisoners. American dead were found mutilated and American prisoners were badly mistreated.[46] For their part Americans were charged with varying degrees of torture and mistreatment of their prisoners. For example, in order to elicit information on the Filipino military activities, it was alleged that some Americans "became specialists in the 'water cure.' "[47] According to Welch, this method of torture "consisted of forcing four or five gallons of water down the throat of the captive, whose 'body becomes an object frightful to contemplate,' and then squeezing it out by kneeling on his stomach."[48] This was done over and over again until the captive talked or was killed in the process. Many accused General Otis of conducting a brutal campaign reminiscent of the Spanish campaign in Cuba—the very reason America went to war against Spain.

American troops usually reacted swiftly and brutally upon learning of abuse of American prisoners or their wounded. In one account, a reporter with American forces described what occurred after a mutilated body of an American was found. An American scouting party after finding the body turned against the nearest Filipino village, burning it and killing every native who looked as if they might have something to do with the killing of the American.[49] Such actions did little to win over potentially friendly Filipinos to American rule. Moreover, the American public, who hardly understood guerrilla war, was likely to be critical of American battlefield behavior.

Revelations about American abuse of Filipinos came as a shock to most Americans. Even if many allegations were untrue, it did suggest that something had gone amiss with America's civilizing mission in the Philippines. To correct any abuses, President McKinley decided to turn over the administration of the islands to a civilian, appointing William Howard Taft as the governor-general. The presumption was that taking the control of the islands from the military would ease the problems of countering the revolutionaries and provide a quickened pace of assimilation of the Filipinos into an American-controlled system. The military was now limited to military operations. Subsequently, a number of improvements were made in schools, sanitation, and taxation, and a system of representative government was established. By the end of 1901 the U.S. Army had established itself throughout most of the islands, a civil administration was conducting civil affairs, and the U.S. Navy controlled all major ports. Yet, it was the same year that the revolutionary war reached its highest pitch: "There were 1,026 engagements, 345 Americans killed, 490 wounded, 118 captured; while 3,854 rebels had been killed, 1,193 wounded, and 6,572 captured."[50] But the war was not all one-sided. In September 1900 "an entire company of the 29th Volunteers was ambushed on the island of Marinduque, east of Luzon, and forced to surrender."[51]

Americans in general did not fully appreciate or understand guerrilla war. Most had been led to believe that there were only a few bands of Filipino outlaws and that these would be defeated handily. The optimistic reports by General Otis reaching Washington were made public. As was to be the case in the early years of America's Vietnam involvement, it was felt that America's role was moralistic and necessary, and that the war would end quickly and easily. Moreover, the differences that were found in the environment in Manila were in direct contrast to the real war in the countryside. The impressions received in Manila supported the view that the war was a minor one bound to be won by the Americans in short order. American activities in Manila appeared to take on the air of a gigantic social affair. Wives of American officers had come to Manila to stay; a luxurious Army and Navy Club was established as was a civilian counterpart, the University Club.

The cultural and linguistic differences between American and Filipino kept them separate and in their own worlds, with little social contact between the two.[52] Moreover, Manila appeared to be in a separate world from the fighting taking place in the countryside: "From the suburbs of the capital one might still occasionally hear the muffled, somewhat chilling, crackle and boom of distant gunfire. Within an amorphous zone between ten and thirty miles from the Walled City, the war went on."[53] If one were to substitute Saigon for Manila and Vietnamese for Filipino, the same descriptions would apply to the American involvement in Vietnam in the early 1960s.

It became clear that the military occupation of the Philippine Islands would not end the revolution. Americans became convinced that in order to defeat the Filipinos, their leader Aguinaldo had to be captured or killed. And indeed, Aguinaldo was captured by Colonel Frederick Funston in a ruse that was to be heralded as a great American victory. Aguinaldo's call for Filipinos to carry on with unconventional war against the Americans brought a continuous flow of Filipino reinforcements into his headquarters area. Colonel Funston devised a plan based on deception and infiltration, using Maccabebe Scouts. The Maccabebes who were from Pampanga Province, had been used by the Spanish as mercenaries against other Filipinos, and now the Americans used them the same way. The basis for the animosity of the Maccabebes towards other Filipinos was not clear, but the fact was that they were willing and eager to assist the Americans. Colonel Funston with four other American officers formed an expedition, in which the Maccabebes posed as Filipino reinforcements and the Americans acted as their captives.

Since the Maccabebes were indistinguishable from other Filipinos, they had no trouble in penetrating the ranks of the revolutionaries. Going through a hundred miles of unknown country under control of the revolutionaries, the expedition entered Aguinaldo's headquarters village of Palanan. Welcomed as heroes along the way and also by Aguinaldo's own guards, the expedition, which outnumbered the entire garrison of Palanan, captured Aguinaldo and killed several of his guards. The expedition returned to American-controlled territory without incident, and for many Filipinos, the revolution seemed lost. What made matters worse for the Filipinos was the proclamation by Aguinaldo, issued while in captivity, for all Filipinos to lay down their arms.

Although the capture of Aguinaldo seriously damaged the Filipino revolution, guerrilla warfare continued throughout the various provinces under other leaders.[54] According to one account, the revolution took on the character of a mass movement, although operations became haphazard and disjointed.

Some military commanders, more attuned to mass aspirations, did not heed Aguinaldo's proclamation of capitulation....Of course, the people's resistance during the early years of the American occupation did not leave for posterity the elaborate constitutions, programs, and tables of organization that the *illustrados* were so adept at preparing. Moreover, the contemptuous attitude of the Americans towards these movements—an attitude inherited by Filipino colonial officials—precluded any serious historical interest in them....The chronology of the numerous skirmishes and battles, ambushes and raids that the resistance fighters mounted is not of primary importance...it is still possible to glean from accounts of the tactics of the guerrillas and also of the American-directed Constabulary just what the people's attitudes to the resistance forces were.[55]

The third period of the Philippine-American War began with odds against further Filipino resistance. By early 1901 American forces had secured control of all of Luzon. At the same time, the Filipino middle class and many other Filipinos had become weary of the conflict. Divisiveness within the Filipino political system made it increasingly difficult to maintain an effective nationalistic movement. Nonetheless, the third period was important in manifesting Filipino resistance to American occupation:

Throughout the first decade of American occupation, the facade of stability barely concealed the resistance that continued to rage in various parts of the country. It is true that most of the resistance groups, particularly the quasi-religious ones, did not have clear political programs. Nevertheless, the people manifested their protest through these organizations which in a primitive sense sought freedom from foreign rule.[56]

Although conflicts continued throughout the first decade and the Moro resistance became more threatening to the Americans, the Filipino aspect of the war was officially ended in 1902.

American commanders eventually realized the difficulties of counterrevolutionary war. It was one thing to fight conventionally postured armies, but it was another to fight a revolutionary who blended into the countryside. As Americans were to learn over and over again, conventional tactics were inadequate in such types of wars. The tactics that were eventually employed deviated considerably from standard operations.

But guerrilla resistance had become the nightmare of American troops. Being incessantly booed and fired upon from cover, was, if anything, more nerve-racking than out-and-out fighting. As a rule the Filipinos allowed their foes to capture any town they wished. Later they would attack by surprise or lead them into the outskirts, fully armed and sometimes even in uniform. It was infuriating, but there was little militarily that could be done about it. Everyone was an *amigo*! "Everyone was against us," grumbled General R. P. Hughes; and since it was impractical to kill off the entire native male population the problem might go on indefinitely, or at least until Aguinaldo was captured.[57]

The viciousness and unconventional nature of the latter parts of the second phase of the war is well illustrated by the incident at Balangiga in 1901. Company C of the 9th U.S. Infantry occupied the small coastal village of Balangiga. There were 74 men assigned to the company, housed in public buildings. The company was composed of many veterans of the campaign in Cuba, the insurrection in Luzon, and the Boxer campaign. Soldiers lined up for mess, the only time they did not carry their weapons. The entire male population of Balangiga, supported by 80 natives from surrounding hills who were part of the insurgent General Vicente Lukban's forces, massacred the Americans. The town officials and populace had earlier appeared friendly, putting the Americans "off guard." Fighting almost bare-handed against bolo-swinging Filipinos, the Americans did manage to kill 250 attackers. The American troops in turn suffered 36 killed, 8 wounded who died later, 22 wounded, 4 missing, and 4 unhurt. Company G of the 9th Infantry formed a relief expedition to Balangiga, drove the insurgents out, and burned the town.[58]

Subsequently, Brigadier General Jacob Smith was given the job of pacification. Upon giving the mission, General Smith proclaimed to his men: "The policy to be pursued in this brigade will be to wage war in the sharpest and most decisive manner possible....No civilized war, however civilized, can be carried out on a humanitarian basis."[59] He ordered a battalion of Marines to clean up the island. "I want no prisoners, I wish you to burn and kill; the more you burn and kill, the better it will please me."[60]

The operations produced a new wilderness, according to one account, and eventually led to congressional hearings on the conduct of the war and to a court-martial of the officers involved in the Samar pacification campaign.[61] But the policy was apparently successful. The forces of Lukban were harassed and chased all over the island of Luzon. Lukban was captured in February 1901, and by April the remaining insurgents in the field surrendered.

Eventually, the tactic of "Benevolent Pacification" and zones of protection brought the end of the second phase.

In every instance when the army stormed and destroyed a village, it promptly rebuilt it, reopened its market, hacked out new roads, and set up a school. It was an effective military policy. "Benevolent pacification" and "beneficent administration" were key words in McKinley's vocabulary, and the emphasis of the army was always on reform rather than control."[62]

Zones of protection were established in which American forces gathered the populace into controlled areas and food outside of these areas was confiscated. Filipinos who did not enter into protected areas were considered enemy. With American forces searching outside protected areas and operating on search-and-destroy type missions, insurgent bands had to scatter.

So the insurrection faded away in the manner of all such struggles, a minor sequel to a comic-opera war, lost in the clamor and shuffle of greater events; and the United States found herself in possession of an Asian archipelago which under other circumstances, might well have been spurned.[63]

According to official sources, in a period of slightly more than three years, there were over 2,800 separate battles and actions.[64] In most of these engagements American troops had been ambushed.

After the end of the second phase, American troop strength in the Philippines was reduced from about 70,000 to 35,000. Before the conflict ended, virtually all elements of the Regular Army ground forces had served in the Philippines. In addition, 25 regiments of volunteers and 19 organizations of state troops had augmented the Regulars.[65]

The second phase, the Philippine-American War, had not been a "splendid little war." The cost of the war was $400 million. But the cost in lives and suffering was much greater. It was estimated that over 126,000 American servicemen served in the Philippines during the period and battle losses amounted to 4,200 killed and over 2,800 wounded. For the Filipinos, it was estimated that 16,000 to 20,000 soldiers were killed, with approximately 200,000 Filipinos dying of illness, disease, and other war-related ills.[66]

But the third phase of the Philippine campaign began almost before the second ended. This phase was different from either the conventional conflicts with Spanish forces or the struggle with Filipino nationalists. As Richard O'Connor has concluded, "No deadlier, longer, or stranger war was ever fought by the American Army in proportion to the numbers involved than the intermittent jungle campaigns between 1900 and 1914 against the Moros in the southern Philippines." Few Americans paid attention to this conflict, except when the Moros made last ditch stands in their forts. Then a hue and cry would be raised by American "humanitarians" about the massacre of Moro women and children by American forces "with the 'civilize 'em with a Krag' philosophy."[67]

With respect to the Moro phase of the Philippines revolution, Leon Wolff concludes: "oddly enough, they were to be the last and most ferocious holdouts against American authority."[68]

In past centuries the Spaniards had been forced to leave those feral heathen more or less alone, but the United States was intent upon assimilating them no less than the Tagalogs and Visayans and the rest. When the Mohammedans found their provinces suddenly teeming with white Christians, they took to the warpath in earnest.[69]

Moro society was fragmented. No single chief or sultan could negotiate or speak for all of the Moros. As was the case with the American forces in their dealings with the Seminoles, any negotiations required discussion with a variety of sultans and datus (religious leaders). In this respect, it was also difficult to "win" in the traditional sense. One defeat by the Moros, no matter how costly, did not spell defeat of the Moros as a whole. Rather, it required continual campaigning against a variety of relatively self-sufficient Moro communities. "So many groups existed— each independent and under its own arbitrary, often despotic, chief— that to win the allegiance of one meant little towards winning the others. Even friendly Moros rarely used their influence to make others friendly; their whole tradition of independent living precluded it."[70]

The Americans learned, as the Spanish had earlier, that the Moro country was more difficult to pacify than the northern islands. While the Spanish succeeded in converting most of the Filipinos to Christianity and pacified most of the islands, the Muslims conducted a long and successful struggle against them.[71] The Muslim Moros resisted the Americans as they had the Spanish and delayed complete pacification of the islands for more than a decade after the collapse of the Filipino resistance.

Moro Province consisted of Mindanao, Basilan, Jolo, and a number of islands that extended across the Sulu Sea to Borneo. These islands were sparsely settled, consisting of approximately 500,000 people: 325,000 Moros, 85,000 Filipinos, and 105,000 headhunters. As Haldeen Braddy observes, "The province was so far from pacification and civilization (outside the Lake Lanao district) that the United States had considered separating the Moro Archipelago from the rest of the Philippines."[72]

To assist in its campaign against so-called outlaw Moros, the Philippine Constabulary was organized. Composed of loyal Filipinos from the main islands, the Constabulary acted as a police force. However, there were many occasions when the police forces were unable to cope with Moro activity. Such a situation occurred in 1906 when the services of the 6th U.S. Infantry were needed:

In the Philippines, the army had to be called into activity to quell disorders with which the constabulary and scouts were unable to cope. Notably, Colonel J. W.

Duncan took a detachment of the Sixth Infantry against the stronghold of Bud-Dajo. The attack of the place was fraught with some of the most desperate fighting known in the army's many engagements in the islands. It looked for some time as if the place could not be carried.[73]

The American campaign against the Moros was a mixture of "carrot and stick." While it was clear that the Moros had to be pacified, it was also clear that this could not be done peacefully or with a short campaign or programs that proved to be successful in the northern islands. Thus, a policy had to be designed which would induce Moro acceptance of American authority without challenging their traditional life-style.

The story of the American campaigns against the Moros revolves in no small part around the operations and activities conducted by John H. Pershing. At first a captain and later a brigadier general, Pershing served tours of duty in the Philippines extending from 1899 to 1903 and from 1909 to 1913. During his first tour he served primarily as a military officer conducting military operations. In his second tour he was governor of Moro Province. Indeed, he was the last military governor in the Philippines.

Pershing laid the groundwork for his general success with the Moros during his first tour as a captain. He did not try to conquer the Moros solely with military force. Pershing felt that an understanding of Moro customs and habits was essential in successfully dealing with them— and he went to extraordinary lengths to understand Moro society and culture. Pershing socialized with Moro sultans and tried to treat them as equals, which was not a popular position for those times.

General Pershing observed at close hand the character of the Moros and their view of themselves and their environment:

The almost infinite combination of superstitions, prejudices and suspicions blended with his character make him a difficult person to handle until fully understood. In order to control him other than by brute force, one must first win his implicit confidence, nor is this as difficult as it would seem....He is jealous of his religion, but he knows very little about its teachings....As long as he is undisturbed in the possession of his women and children, and his slaves, there is little to fear from him.[74]

The Moros learned of Pershing's respect for their customs and religion and of his fair and firm dealings with them. Pershing with a few scouts and interpreters entered the "Forbidden Kingdom" of the Moros, Lake Lanao, to speak and confer with the Moro sultans and datus, something never before done by a white man. To the surprise of the American community and the Filipinos themselves, Pershing succeeded in his mission. Just prior to his departure for the United States in 1903, Pershing was given an honor not shown to any other white man: he was made a Moro datu. In accepting this honor, Pershing had to take part in a solemn ceremony in the midst of Moro country around Lake Lanao.

Pershing was to be in many ceremonies in his life—before kings, presidents, emperors, educators, and churchmen. But this ceremony in the wilds of Mindanao above shimmering Lake Lanao, squatting on his heels and chewing betel nut, swearing fealty on the koran, was "the most unique ceremony in which I. . .ever participated."[75]

This picture of Pershing is in stark contrast to that of the firm disciplinarian in World War I.

In his second tour of duty in the Philippines, Brigadier General Pershing as governor of Moro Province commanded 5,500 officers and men, of which 2,500 were Filipinos of the Philippine Constabulary. Charged with pacification of the province, he put into practice what he had learned during his first tour as a captain. He understood well the necessity of having American forces involved at the grass roots levels of Moro society. In this respect, he was sensitive to the political-social goals, even if it meant subordinating the military goal.

He stationed small detachments of soldiers throughout the interior, to guarantee peaceful existence of those tribes that wanted to raise hemp, produce timber, or farm. It was a scattershot method of bringing peace, and dissipated the large garrison into minuscule detachments. Pershing admitted that his method did not promote military efficiency, but he argued, "No influence can ever reach these people except the influence that comes by contact."[76]

Aided by a few friendly Moros, the detachments were able to drive off the bandits and restore peace in many areas. Pershing's tactics were not so successful, however, as to prevent continued depredations by outlaw Moros.

American detachments found themselves chasing raiding parties or seeking to rescue women kidnapped by Moros. Moreover, American lives were continually threatened by "Juramentado," in which a Moro whipped up to a religious frenzy would attack a white Christian with a bolo, regardless of the odds. A number of American officers and men were victims of "Juramentado." The depredations by Moro bands became impossible to counter without drastic action. General Pershing concluded that complete pacification would come only after all of the Moros had been disarmed. Issuing necessary orders, American units began implementing the new policy. Predictably, the Moros resisted, and this led to the final campaigns in the Philippines.

The Moros' "last stand" so to speak took place at Bud Dajo and Bad Bagsak, major Moro strongholds. Pershing sent a 1,000-man force against the main Moro cotta (fort) at Bud Dajo, a sanctuary atop a mountain.

This was the same cotta that was attacked by General Leonard Wood five years earlier with great loss of life, including women and children. Casualties at that time were estimated to be 600 Moros and 100 Americans. This time the force laid siege to the cotta, and eventually a number of Moros surrendered and others faded into the countryside. In another part of Mindanao, action was taken against another major Moro stronghold at Bad Bagsak. The battle was different. While it was not known how many Moros were in the large cotta, it was estimated that about 5,000 had been chased into the forts. It was a well-defended position atop an extinct volcano protected by trenches. The battle lasted five days. The American forces consisted of 1,200 officers and men. Several units of Philippine Scouts were composed of Moros commanded by American officers. In the end, after vicious hand-to-hand fighting, the effective use of artillery, and instances where Americans had to climb hand-over-hand up mountain sides, the Moros were defeated. The casualties for American forces were 15 dead and 25 wounded. For the Moros, 500 lay dead with an unknown number wounded. The dead and wounded included a number of women and children.[77]

There again was an outcry in the United States against the killing of women and children. Under the circumstances, it is difficult to see how some of these casualties could have been avoided. The Moros, as was their custom, took their women and children with them to their cottas. Since about 75 percent of the Moros on Bad Bagsak were noncombatants, it speaks well for the American forces that noncombatant casualties were held to 5 to 10 percent. Nevertheless, the American people decried such actions:

Even those who favored American custody of the Philippines regarded the killing of women and children an unpardonable crime against humanity. The protestants were, of course, ignorant of the special conditions of combat in the southern islands. A soldier being fired upon in the heat of battle has neither the time nor the inclination... to differentiate by age or sex whoever is trying to kill him. The only alternatives were to call off the battle (since Moro warriors refused all pleas to release the women and children from a surrounded fort) and give the Moros their way, or to attempt a separation of the men from their families.[78]

While the Moros conducted guerrilla-type warfare, their tactics eventually hinged on their ability to defend their cottas or forts, which were usually located in mountainous areas or on tips of volcanos. When they took up such a defense, it was usually with their families, women, and children. In any case, the campaigns against Bud Dajo in 1911 and Bad Bagsak in 1913 marked the final days of the Moro campaigns, although as late as 1917 there was another Moro uprising on Mindanao.

By the middle of the second decade of the twentieth century, American control of the Philippine Islands was well established. While there were some minor disturbances, the American policy of benevolent pacification and the focus on improving the quality of life appealed to many Filipinos. This eventually led to Philippine independence immediately after World War II, almost 50 years late according to some Filipinos.

SUMMARY

American military forces in the Philippines were again led by a succession of generals. As in the case of the Seminole War, the force was conventionally organized and reflected a certain degree of discord between volunteers and Regulars. The Filipino revolutionaries, after declaring an independent Philippine nation, were first organized and launched military operations in a conventional style. The Filipino Nationalist Army, in fact, controlled the islands, and, although they had not managed to occupy Manila, they had besieged it. At first the American strategy was influenced by the conventional style of their opponents: they used advancing columns and fought battles from fixed positions (for example, they used trenches to launch actions against defended towns). Defeated in this type of warfare, the Filipinos changed their strategy to unconventional warfare—to which the Americans responded by using the columns to encircle and then engage the nationalists. As in the case of the Seminoles, the columns proved to be ill-suited to the task. Communications and the coordination of movements between the columns were erratic, supply problems marred their speedy movement, and the terrain—damp swampland—caused health and equipment problems. The use of columns for envelopment was eventually abandoned and was replaced by a strategy that favored "quick, decisive blows" and "search-and-destroy" missions. These missions were accompanied by a pacification system in the form of a geographical occupation network: the population was relocated in protected areas or protected villages. A major factor in the success of the second phase was the capture of Aguinaldo. The war ended with the capture of the few remaining insurgent leaders.

The last phase of the conflict in the Philippines shifted to the southern islands against the Moros. Although the Moros were not fighting a revolutionary war in the same sense as the Filipinos, the nature of the conflict followed a similar pattern. The Moros, fighting to preserve their way of life and their control over parts of the southern islands, fought primarily in unconventional fashion, although their tendency to engage in conventional war, defending their "forts" in a last-stand fashion, proved their downfall.

Finally, sporadic skirmishes continued as the Philippine Constabulary, led by American officers, took on the major share of law and order duties in the Philippines. In the end, what the Filipinos could not gain by revolutionary struggle, they achieved by the development of a reasonably effective democratic system, eventually leading to an independent Philippine Republic. The fact remains that the Philippine-American War was a major effort in the Filipinos' drive towards independence.

BANDIT CHASING

The U.S.-Mexican border is about 1,000 miles in length covered by a variety of terrain. Even today, Americans find it difficult to patrol. In the first decade of the twentieth century, not only was this border troublesome, but events in Mexico provided opportunities for conflict and created incidents exacerbating relationships with the United States. Mexico embarked on a bloody revolution in 1910 after the dictator Porfirio Diaz was overthrown. He was replaced by Francisco Madero who was murdered and replaced by General Victoriano Huerta who was subsequently ousted by foreign diplomatic pressure and a revolt led by Emiliano Zapata, Alvaro Obregon, and Pancho Villa. Each of these successful revolutionaries had his own private army and controlled his own area of Mexico as warlord. Pancho Villa controlled the largest Mexican state of Chihuahua. By 1916 Venustiano Carranza had managed to maneuver himself to a position where he proclaimed himself the "First Chief" of the Mexican government.

Up until the revolution, most Mexicans lived in a state of serfdom. Except in the major cities and towns, much of Mexico was sparsely settled, particularly the state of Chihuahua. Living in small settlements centered around a square and a Catholic church, the peons of the countryside usually scratched out a living from the soil or worked for foreign mining interests. Communications were nonexistent except between major towns. After the experience with the occupying French forces, few Mexicans had any use for foreigners. Part of the revolution was aimed at clearing Mexico from foreign control. It was also true that no central government really controlled the countryside. Warlords such as Zapata and Villa held sway and, being from the "people," commanded loyalty, if not out of respect, certainly out of fear. The private armies of Zapata and Villa also played on the traditional Mexican activity of banditry, supposedly robbing the rich to help the poor. In any case, the armies of Zapata and Villa were from the people and were from the land in which they operated. Villistas knew every nook and cranny of the state of Chihuahua. They were also acclimated to the weather and terrain, and were accustomed to living off the countryside.

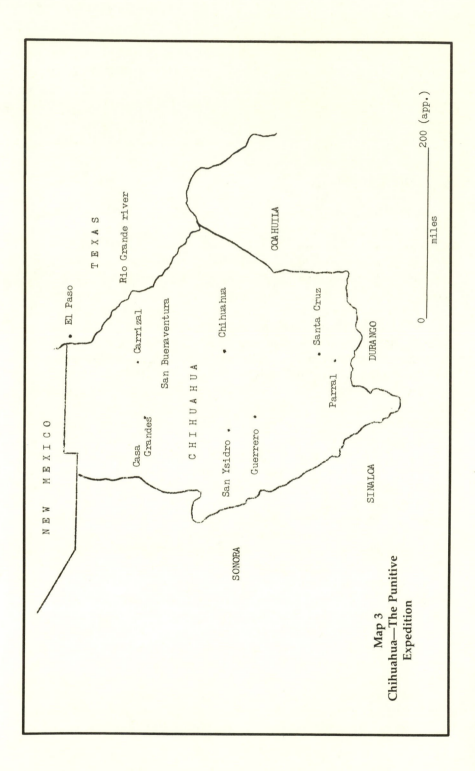

Map 3
Chihuahua—The Punitive
Expedition

During the period 1910 through 1916, revolutionaries roamed through the countryside, each of the major factions attempting to gain control of Mexico:

A variety of men made the Mexican revolution—rich and poor, Indian and peon, bandit chief and intellectual, guerrilla and European-trained general—each commanding a loyal faction. More political parties and splinter groups circulated around this revolution and civil war than around any other of North America's political disaffections. But no matter what the passion or the tactic, each of these men and factions had the same goal: to take Mexico back from the foreigners.[79]

Both the Madero and Carranza revolutions tended to be anticlerical, primarily because in the view of the revolutionaries the Catholic Church represented a foreign presence. The revolutionaries at times reacted violently against the Church. The Catholic Church in the United States did not take kindly to the Wilson Administration's support of the Mexican revolutionaries.[80] In the process, American lives were lost, property taken and damaged, and border incidents became commonplace. American business interests and groups living close to the border began to put pressure on the American government for some action.

In 1913 General Huerta's government had been recognized by a number of foreign governments. President Wilson, after receiving reports from his own investigators, concluded that Huerta "besides owing his position to brute force, would not serve the interests of 'the submerged eighty-five percent.' He let it be known that he would recognize Huerta only if the latter would agree to hold a fair election in which he himself should not be a candidate."[81] General Huerta refused and to show his displeasure arrested over 100 members of the opposition party of the Mexican Congress.

President Wilson embarked on a campaign to rid Mexico of Huerta. By 1914 through political pressure and arms sales to Huerta's opponents, Wilson had created an environment that eventually led to Huerta's resignation. This left the way open to Carranza who was former governor of the state of Coahuila and "who had taken up arms against Huerta after Madero's death."[82] The Constitutionalists (Carranza's forces) occupied Mexico City, and Carranza declared himself the "First Chief." Zapata in the South and Villa in the North disputed his rule, and the revolution continued.

The United States thought that Pancho Villa, who appeared to be a native of the soil and was supported by the Mexican peasants, could be a viable successor to Carranza. This was particularly appealing since Villa controlled Chihuahua, the state adjacent to Texas. Moreover, after the incident at Tampico and the occupation, albeit temporarily, of Vera Cruz by a force of 8,000 Americans, Wilson searched for an alternative to Carranza.

In 1914 Villa appeared to be at the height of his power, with an estimated 40,000 relatively well-armed men including artillery and adequate supplies, much of which came from American mining interests. At that time, American interests prompted a meeting between Pancho Villa, General John Pershing, and General Alvaro Obregon. Relationships between the United States and Villa appeared to be good, particularly since Villa had refused to move against the United States when American forces occupied Vera Cruz.

Following this meeting, Pershing maintained his brigade on the border in a constant state of preparedness. This concern had originally been prompted by the Vera Cruz incident. In the meantime, Zapata and Villa continued their struggle against Carranza. Their forces occupied Mexico City, but eventually the Carranza General Obregon defeated Villa's forces and pushed him back into Chihuahua. Carranza appeared to be on the way to success in consolidating Mexico. Zapata was pushed to the south and Villa was limited to Chihuahua. The Wilson Administration maintained a position of "watchful waiting." By 1916, however, Wilson felt that Carranza was the wave of the future for Mexico. Reinstating an arms embargo against Villa and allowing Carranza forces to pass through American territory, Wilson made it clear whom he and the American government supported. Neither the Congress nor the American people were consulted on these presidential actions. American defensive lines along the Texas-Mexican border were coordinated with Carranza forces. As a result, Villa's forces were badly defeated when they tried to take Agua Prieta, a Mexican suburb of Douglas, Arizona. Villa was pushed further south, and his ability to gain access to supplies from the North was severely curtailed. It was a humiliating defeat for Villa, who now blamed the Americans.

Villa retaliated by raiding Columbus. This raid was preceded by a variety of attacks on Americans and American property: "In January 1916, in the state of Chihuahua where Villa held sway as a war lord, seventeen American miners were murdered in cold blood by his men at Santa Isabel. Two months later Villa himself led the raid at Columbus against American territory."[83]

The reasons for Villa's raid are much disputed. They range from Villa's need for supplies, resentment against the Americans for recognizing Carranza, to Villa's desire to make himself a folk hero in his own country.[84] It has even been suggested that Villa may have been an agent of German intrigue.[85] In any case, the continual depredations against Americans and American property had thoroughly angered most Americans. The Columbus raid appeared to be the last straw.

Theoretically, American forces entered Mexico with the permission of the Carranza government. Although Carranza was sympathetic and cooperative in his tone following the raid on Columbus, he may not have given direct permission for American forces to pursue Villa. It appears that such permission was only for Villa's future invasion of American territory.[86] Nonetheless, whether Carranza's note was badly translated or was seized upon by American officials as an excuse for military intervention into Mexico, American reaction was swift. Pershing was ordered into Mexico for the purpose of capturing Pancho Villa.

While there are various estimates of the forces available to Villa in his struggles with the United States during the Punitive Expedition, it appears that the numbers rarely went above 1,000. Most of the time his forces when gathered numbered around 500.

The conflict in which the American forces found themselves after their move into Mexico had at least three major dimensions: the pursuit of Villa and combat with the Villista forces; the problem encountered in trying to comply with the dictates of the Carranza government and avoid war with Mexico; and the external issue of tensions in Europe and the possibility of American involvement in the European war.

In the countryside of Mexico, the main confrontation was with the Villista forces. In the villages and towns, difficulties also arose with the Carranza government. Most Mexicans, regardless of political orientation or loyalties, were antagonistic toward the American forces. The Americans faced many obstacles in capturing Villa:

Chances of catching Villa were slim. The expedition operated in an unfamiliar country, which was sparsely settled by ignorant people who feared reprisals. For information it depended on frightened, unwilling natives or on untried American employees. With Villa, exactly the opposite was true. He knew every foot of Chihuahua and could depend on natives for reliable information on every step Pershing took. Villa traveled light, lived off the country, rode his mounts hard, and replaced (or stole) them whenever he needed fresh stock.[87]

In the state of Chihuahua, where most of the peons were sympathetic toward Villa, and those who were not were afraid of providing any information to the Americans, Pershing was operating in a virtual intelligence vacuum. Indeed, "probably most anti-Villa Mexicans hated the Americans more than they hated Villa."[88]

There was at first some cooperation between Americans and Carranza forces. On orders from the Carranza government, however, the expedition under Pershing was limited to the state of Chihuahua. It could not use the Mexican railroad system, nor was it allowed to enter any towns or villages without permission. Thus, American forces had to rely on poor country roads and trails, on mule and wheel transport isolated from the population, and on what little amenities they might receive by permission, from villages and towns.

General Pershing's task through the whole campaign was, to speak mildly, awkward. He had to advance with litte transportation through the most trying part of a tensely hostile country. He was allowed to attack one party but not the other, while both were equally antagonistic. He was in the position of the man who had to walk into a hungry leopard's cage with orders to beat Mr. Leopard, but under no conditions resist Mrs. Leopard with her cubs.[89]

The third dimension was the European war which had begun in 1914; the longer it lasted the more likely it appeared that America would be involved. Thus, to be involved in a serious occupation or war in Mexico would have jeopardized America's ability to protect its own interests in what appeared to be a much more crucial area. Therefore, while the conflict in Mexico involved American forces, the main American concern was Europe.

In Mexico, the initial American response was, as in the past, to use two advancing columns to encircle and then engage the Villa forces. Although these columns never did succeed in capturing Villa, they were not entirely unsuccessful. They managed to engage the Villa forces in a series of running battles and killed or captured significant numbers of Villa's men. It is likely that these columns, despite the problems of supply, communication, coordination, and reinforcement, could have captured Villa if they had been allowed to pursue him in an unrestricted fashion. Since they were forbidden to do so, the strategy changed to a pacification or geographical occupation system. Chihuahua was divided into areas that were patrolled and in which "search-and-destroy" missions were launched. Although successful in those areas, these actions were unsuccessful in a larger sense because Villa avoided those areas and launched actions in areas forbidden to the American forces.

By the time of Villa's raid on Columbus, much thought had already gone into debating the issues of American preparedness and preparing the American officer corps for modern war. Moreover, the concentration of an American maneuver division on the Mexican-American border in 1911 provided a nucleus for a force ready to take the field. But the United States was not militarily prepared.

Organizing the expedition proved a daunting task. Despite her vast financial resources, America did not possesss a single military unit ready or equipped for operations in Mexico. In fact the *Detroit Free Press* felt that the country was indebted to Villa for revealing that its army "was not prepared even for a fourth-class skirmish."[90]

General John J. Pershing was placed in command of the expedition which consisted of about 10,000 officers and men organized into two columns: the East Column, which included one cavalry squadron, two infantry regiments, an artillery battalion plus one battery, and the 1st

Aero Squadron consisting of eight aircraft; and the West Column, which included two cavalry squadrons (less two troops) and one battery of field artillery.[91]

It is almost an article of faith that the Punitive Expedition was a ponderous, slowly moving column, hampered and handicapped by its wagons and wheeled artillery, and about which the swiftly moving Villista guerrillas rode at will. . . . (This is) simply not true. . . . It was a game of hare and hounds, with Villa and his bands in the uncomfortable position of the hare.[92]

Upon the receipt of information about Villa's whereabouts, the West Column formed into three smaller detachments and proceeded south to seek out Villa. As the American forces were to learn over and over again in their campaign in Mexico, accurate information on the whereabouts of Villa and his forces was difficult, if not impossible, to gather. Much of the information had to come from local inhabitants who were reluctant to give any information to the Americans. Maps were inaccurate, the terrain was difficult, and the population hostile. The restrictions placed upon Pershing by the American government at the insistence of the Carranza government in Mexico made his task enormously more difficult. Complicating the situation still further was the fact that the Mexicans were in revolutionary turmoil, trying to establish a republican form of government. Yet individual warlords were in power: Zapata in the South and Villa in the North.

American units had. . .been unsuccessful in eliciting accurate information on Villa. . . . Even Carranzistas frankly admitted that they would consider it a national disgrace if the Americans rather than their own *federales* should capture the Conventionist rival. Mexicans of whatever political convictions challenged the right of American troops to move through Mexico itself. To counter this, American commanders carried copies of an official permit signed by the Carranzista General Obregon to enter the country.[93]

In any case, the pursuit of Villa began by moving into the state of Chihuahua. In the meantime, Villa had moved from one location to another, easily evading or defeating Carranzista forces. In March, Villa's forces attacked three locations: Guerrero, Minaca, and San Ysidro. At the first two locations, the Villista forces surprised the Carranza garrisons and captured stores of guns and munitions. At San Ysidro, however, the Carranza garrison commander had fortuitously strengthened the garrison the night before and easily repulsed the Villista attack. In their pursuit of the Villista forces, however, the Carranza forces in turn were set upon by another Villista force. Although the Carranza forces were defeated, Villa was wounded and taken by his men to Guerrero. This set in motion an American-Villa battle that was to shape the nature of the campaign during the remainder of the American intervention.

One of the American detachments from the West Column learned of Villa's wounds and headed for Guerrero. But as was the usual case, their native guide took a roundabout way, thereby delaying the American arrival until late in the day. The detachment commander had to wait until daylight for his attack on Guerrero.

Upon catching sight of the Americans, the guerrillas hurriedly saddled and fled the town. In the ten-mile running fight that ensued, the fugitives purposefully separated and scattered in various directions towards the mountains and safety. The cavalrymen nonetheless killed thirty Villistas near Guerrero, at the expense of only four American enlisted wounded.[94]

As described by Richard Goldhurst, the attack by Colonel George Dodd's detachment against Villistas at Guerrero "cheered the United States Congress. . . . But Guerrero was as near as any of Pershing's columns ever came to capturing Villa, and the campaign was to last almost another year."[95] Villa had left Guerrero several hours earlier to Parral to have his wound attended.

It was estimated that in the actions leading to this first encounter with the American forces, Villa had his forces organized into two bodies totalling 450 men. The advance body consisted of 80 men, and the remainder were with the main body.

The fight at Guerrero was the first contact between the Punitive Expedition and Villa's forces. Their feeble resistance, together with the element of surprise, even though the surprise was not as complete as Dodd had hoped for, gave the measure of their combat quality against American Regulars. In fact, the Villistas offered almost no resistance: their one ambition was to escape. Their fire was wild and uncoordinated, their cohesion almost nonexistent.[96]

As a result of the fight at Guerrero, Villa's forces were scattered over the countryside. They were unable to regroup until several months later and only because Pershing's forces were tied down by a variety of political considerations.[97]

In the following months, Pershing's forces penetrated deeper into Chihuahua and rushed off into various directions chasing down remnants of Villa's forces. The initial actions received the cooperation of Carranza forces, contrary to the later months of the Punitive Expedition. The force of Pershing and Carranza actively cooperated in looking for Villa: "During the search the two forces inflicted many casualties on Villista forces. Including some 113 raider casualties at Columbus, the tally eventually numbered 273 guerrillas presumed dead and 108 known wounded. From the standpoint of damage inflicted on guerrilla rebels, Pershing's Punitive expedition began encouragingly."[98]

Upon reaching the area around Parral, about 200 miles into Mexico, Pershing became concerned lest the presence of American forces so deep in Mexican territory create political as well as military difficulties. His fears were well founded. Viewing the Americans as another foreign invader, most Mexicans united behind the Carranza government which now made it clear that it wanted the Americans to leave. Thus, in the process of the Punitive Expedition's penetration into Mexico, the Americans eventually had to face four enemies: the countryside, the people, the Villista forces, and the Carranza government.

An encounter took place at Parral, which more than convinced Pershing that his force had reached the limits of its usefulness and that the Mexicans were now united in actively opposing the Americans. In the process of searching for Villa deep in the state of Chihuahua, Pershing gave orders to Major Frank Tompkins, commander of a cavalry squadron from the 13th Cavalry, to "Go find Villa wherever you think he is."[99] This led Major Tompkins and his men to Parral. Major Tompkins's force, close on the heels of Villa halted at the outskirts of Parral. Villa had by then reached the safety of the mountains, but Tompkins needed supplies and fodder for his horses. Tompkins's presence at Parral was the deepest penetration into Mexico by American forces. Although there were Carranza forces in town with whom Tompkins tried to negotiate, it soon became evident that the Americans were not wanted. Moreover, the American forces were warned that the Carranza forces in conjunction with the townspeople would attack if their forces were not immediately withdrawn. The worst occurred. The Americans were fired upon, and several Americans wounded. Tompkins managed an orderly and slow withdrawal, although he was wounded and the horses exhausted. Rear guard actions by small detachments of Americans kept the Mexicans at bay. Tompkins's force made it to Santa Cruz where he took up a defense perimeter and held off the Mexicans until a relief column from the 10th Cavalry arrived. American casualties were six dead and six wounded. Yet, about 600 Carranzistas were held off at a loss of 40 attackers killed. Certain aspects of Tompkins's encounter at Parral remain unclear to this day.[100]

Even though there was confusion regarding the events at Parral, the incident convinced Pershing of the futility of trying to chase Villa all over the countryside, particularly since it was clear that Pershing could no longer depend upon the cooperation of the Carranzistas. He was also convinced that it would be impossible to make contact with any large group of Villistas. This marked a change in the political-military situation. It was now clear that the Carranza government had shifted from cooperation with American forces to outright hostility.[101] There now appeared to be an implicit Carranza-Villa alliance to rid Mexico of American forces. As a result, Pershing was faced with a delicate political and military situation. He hesitated to vigorously pursue Villa forces for fear of further political consequences with respect to the Carranza government. Thus, he settled on deploying his military forces against the remnants of the Villa band without extending beyond the current military deployment.[102] Pershing established five military districts, each commanded by a regimental cavalry commander with the mission of clearing his district of Villista forces. In the meantime, President Wilson had learned of the encounter at Parral and of the threat by Carranzista forces. He now feared a war with Mexico and was preparing to call up the National Guard.

Another encounter took place, however, which again changed the course of events and eventually led to the withdrawal of American forces from Mexico. Troops K and C, with 76 officers and men on reconnaissance, under the command of Captain Charles T. Boyd, attempted to pass through the town of Carrizal in June 1916. The Mexican commander of the town refused permission. Enraged, Captain Boyd attempted to force his way through Carrizal. By that time, the Carranzistas had 200 men with rifles in entrenched positions. The Americans attacked in two separate groups over open ground. Over a two-hour period they encountered brisk and deadly fire which killed 14 Americans, including Captain Boyd. More than 30 Americans were wounded and 25 captured. It was the worst defeat suffered by American troops in Mexico—and this was not at the hands of Villistas, but by townspeople and Carranzista forces. A relief force from the 11th Cavalry rounded up survivors who were now all on foot.

Although under pressure from Wilson who demanded an explanation and who urged action against Mexican forces, Pershing waited for a full report and found that Captain Boyd's men performed as well as could be expected, and perhaps could have succeeded in extricating themselves had they not panicked. In the final part of his report, he concluded, "Too much praise cannot be given Boyd and Adair for personal courage in their gallant fight against overwhelming odds in which both died like the brave American soldiers they were."[103]

Another authority writes, concerning Carrizal, "it is enough to say that two understrength troops of the 10th Cavalry with their officers killed or wounded, inflicted casualties almost equal to their own total strength, and that the Carranza government changed its tone immediately after the fight."[104] But, according to Ronald Atkin, the battle at Carrizal was a disaster for American forces: "Boyd led his Negro cavalrymen forward on foot across open ground into what can only be called a miniature Balaclava; fewer than a hundred utterly exposed troops against 400 entrenched Mexicans armed with machine guns." Accordingly, this battle turned out to be the last action of the Punitive Expedition.[105]

A short time following the encounter at Carrizal, the American secretary of state sent Carranza a note demanding release of all American prisoners. At the same time concern for involvement in the war in Europe made Wilson wary of pushing the issue too far with Mexico. Carranza also recognized that a conflict with the United States could lead to his own destruction since he was already hard pressed in action against Zapata in the South. This eventually led to guarantees by Carranza that the border would be secured for America and the withdrawal of the expeditionary force.

In assessing the Punitive Expedition, Atkin concludes that the Villista bands met defeat in every encounter with the American forces. He argues that the Villistas were surprised in every encounter, which says a great deal about the ability of the Villistas to conduct guerrilla warfare.[106] Nevertheless, the fact remains that the nature of the environment and the conditions under which American forces conducted the campaign were unconventional, particularly in terms of the enemies faced, which ranged from the people and countryside to the government in power, as well as Villistas.[107] The Villistas' unsuccessful guerrilla warfare is primarily a reflection of Pershing's tactics and American troop quality, the undisciplined manner of Villista operations, and the inability of Villa to exploit the unconventional nature of the conflict.

After the American withdrawal, Villa's forces were able to reassemble and again threaten northern Mexico. Thus, many wondered about the consequences of the Punitive Expedition. While some criticized not only the military intervention, but also Wilson's policy towards Mexico, others felt that some punishment had been meted out to Villa. But more important, some felt that the Punitive Expedition provided an invaluable experience for the American people and the Army prior to America's entry into World War I.[108]

For both the Carranza forces and Villa, the ultimate aim was to get rid of the American forces. For Carranza, the use of Americans might be useful in the short term, but he knew that Mexicans would not stand for an indefinite or highly visible presence of Americans. Even though Americans entered Mexico with Carranza's presumed permission (although this is disputed), they entered what ultimately became hostile terrain with a hostile populace and a highly suspicious, indigenous government. In the end, the American forces had to face the forces of both Villa and Carranza, and were hated by almost all the Mexicans.

The action of the Punitive Expedition revealed a number of things about the American military, perhaps none so revealing as the character of General John Pershing. He understood the main objective which subordinated all others—to stay out of war with Mexico. His experience in the Philippines and his understanding of the workings of the military system gave him the sophistication needed to deal with a dangerous political-military situation. Pershing's leadership and views regarding operations within Mexico, by and large, reflected an understanding of the meaning of limited war, unconventional war, and the priority of political objectives, even at the risk of unsuccessful military operations.[109] American leaders were to try to learn the same lessons—fifty years later.

From the political point of view, America's involvement in Mexico in 1916 and 1917 revealed a perspective and policy preferences that carried into the post-World War II period and were to haunt the American military. The Mexican intervention revealed the underlying basis of American policy which held a messianic view, resting on liberal and moralistic principles. Such perceptions governed American expectations of their military forces. And in Mexico, it was the basis for supporting the revolution. Unfortunately, most revolutions do not conform to the American model, nor do battlefield conditions lend themselves easily to liberal and moralistic principles. "Most revolutionaries are neither liberal nor reasonable . . . they impose on their countries their own vision, which may range from the need to realize prophecies of dialectical materialism to the need to free peons from serfdom to *gringos.*"[110]

Nonetheless, the operations in Mexico provided experience for those who would command American forces in World War I. Logistics, administrative support, organization, and operations under combat conditions were put to good use in preparing and training the American Expeditionary Forces and in leading them into combat. Given the difficulties of the times, however, part of the experience in Mexico was soon forgotten. The peculiarities of the conflict, the difficulties of operating in an alien culture against not only an unconventional enemy, but also the people of the entire area, and the political-social dimensions of American military intervention were lost in the haste and pressures of America's entry into the European war. Given America's past, however, it is reasonable to conclude that even if there were no foreign pressures, it is unlikely that the lessons of the Punitive Expedition would have penetrated beyond the conventional posturing of American forces.

THE LOST CRUSADE

The American involvement in Vietnam has been examined by a variety of scholars, journalists, military men, and policymakers. The why's and wherefore's of the Vietnamese conflict have been explored endlessly, and answers run the whole gamut on the ideological spectrum. Even the movie industry has taken a hand in trying to explain the Vietnam War in such films as *The Deerhunter*, *Apocalypse Now*, and *The Green Berets*.

America's involvement in Vietnam had its roots in the misunderstanding of revolution and the attempt to respond to revolutionary war through conventional lenses. Even those who understood the complexities of revolution and counterrevolution found it difficult and, at most times, impossible, to translate policy into effective strategy and tactics. It is also true that in Vietnam Americans forgot the lessons of history and perhaps relearned too late what they had experienced earlier in the Seminole War, the Philippines, and the Punitive Expedition. Compounding the problem is the fact that democratic society and cultural patterns are not oriented to fighting counterrevolutionary wars.

The Vietnam War was perplexing to the American people: it could not be understood in conventional terms, and it could not be won using conventional methods of warfare. Consequently, it was difficult for administration spokesmen to communicate the purposes of U.S. involvement in Vietnam. This led to an apparent confusion as to purposes, disagreement as to means, and search as to causes. And in every case, one could find experts and a rationale for almost any point of view.

Even as late as 1969, there was little understanding of the war and what to do about it: "Thus the Vietnam conflict continued, with no fundamental changes in the positions of the major parties. The same erroneous premises that provided the rationale for the faulty judgments of those whose decisions led the United States to project its power into Vietnam still governed American policies."[111]

Under President Diem, the war remained primarily a Vietnamese conflict. After his assassination and coincidentally that of President Kennedy in 1963 and the coming into office of President Lyndon Johnson, the war became Americanized. Still later, during the Nixon Administration, the war reverted to the Vietnamese. Thus, the war came full cycle from Vietnamization to Americanization to Vietnamization.

The nature of the conflict in Vietnam, as has been suggested, was complex and multidimensional. It was not only a revolutionary war with unconventional tactics, but at times the war became quite conventional and a number of outside powers became involved, some directly, others indirectly. In addition, there is some truth in the observation that the war in Vietnam included several wars, classified according to geography (that is, the North or in the Delta), to the type of enemy involved (that is, the Vietcong, North Vietnamese Regulars, or mixes of both), and to the tactics (unconventional, conventional, mixes of both).

Americans, civilian and military alike, were most confused by the political context of the conflict which included a mix of communism, nationalism, democracy, religion, personalism, colonialism, imperialism, and external forces. Moreover, the political context was controlled and influenced by the Vietnamese themselves, with Americans viewed as intruders who simply replaced the French colonial troops. Thus, on

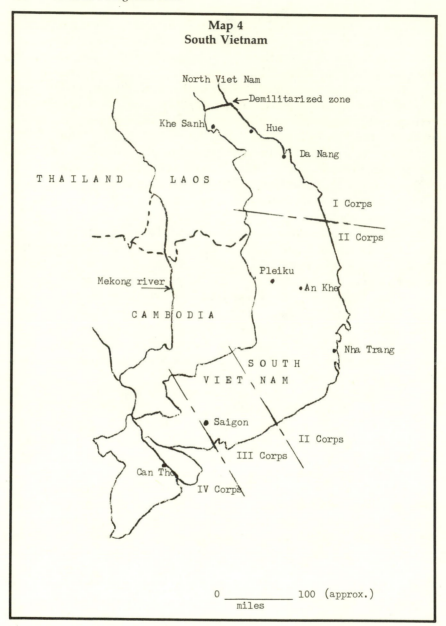

Map 4
South Vietnam

North Viet Nam

←—Demilitarized zone

Khe Sanh

Hue

Da Nang

THAILAND   LAOS

I Corps

II Corps

Pleiku

Mekong river

•An Khe

CAMBODIA

Nha Trang

SOUTH

VIET NAM

Saigon

II Corps

III Corps

Can Tho

IV Corps

0 _____ 100 (approx.)
        miles

the one hand Americans had a major military impact, and on the other, they could never control the political context, which in the long run proved to be the key to the conflict. But the political and military issues in Vietnam could not be realistically separated. To understand the problems associated with the American involvement, we need to understand the characteristics of the Vietnamese political-military context into which American forces were committed in strength beginning in 1964.

THE BEGINNING

U.S. interest in the Indochina peninsula (Cambodia, Laos, North and South Vietnam) had been minimal until the Communist domination of Mainland China in 1950. Up until that period, the United States had no military commitments, little political or economic interest in Southeast Asia in general, except perhaps for the Philippines. The loss of Mainland China to the Communists coincident with the outbreak of the Korean War in 1950 and the increasing French involvement in military actions in Tonkin (Northern Vietnam) caused concern and directed the attention of the United States toward the Southeast Asian area in general and Vietnam in particular. In this respect, one could argue that the French attempt to reestablish their colonial empire precipitated the initial involvement of the United States in Vietnam. There is also a reasonable amount of evidence to suggest that the French policies towards Vietnam did much to destroy the basis for a truly nationalistic and non-Communist Vietnamese government.

On September 2, 1945, Ho Chi Minh declared the Democratic Republic of Vietnam an independent state including all of Vietnam. Following this declaration, the French, with the assistance of British occupation troops, returned to Vietnam and took over the reins of government in most of Annam (Central Vietnam) and Cochin China (Southern Vietnam).[112] Simultaneously, the French military prevented Ho Chi Minh's followers from establishing control over these areas. Tonkin remained under control of Ho Chi Minh, for all practical purposes. This set the stage for the French-Vietminh War (the first Vietnam War).

President Roosevelt expressed disapproval of the French policy in Indochina. Following his death, the United States turned its attention almost exclusively to Europe and the European defense alliance. These concerns were sufficiently pressing to subordinate the Indochina issue. Consequently, during the Truman Administration the United States gave passive approval to the French policy in Indochina. This approval shifted to indirect assistance and economic aid in 1950 as the French military became increasingly involved in fighting in North Vietnam against Ho Chi Minh and his followers (the Vietminh).

In 1948 France and Vietnam signed an agreement establishing the state of Vietnam within the French union. This was followed by decrees of the emperor of Vietnam, Bao Dai, formally establishing the state of Vietnam in 1949. The following year Great Britain and the United States extended *de jure* recognition to Vietnam. With the outbreak of the Korean

War, the United States and France declared their mutual concern and association in Southeast Asia.[113]

As a result of the increasing intensity of the French-Vietminh war, the United States increased aid to France. In a communique issued in September 1953, it was agreed that "the United States will make available to the French Government prior to December 31, 1954 additional financial resources not to exceed $385 million. This aid is addition to funds already earmarked by the United States for aid to France and the Associated States."[114]

The military actions covering the early years of the 1950s to Dien Bien Phu in 1954 have been addressed at length elsewhere.[115] Briefly, the French were convinced of the superiority of their forces in conventional battles and made attempts to maneuver the Vietminh into such a situation. However, the Vietminh, following the classic outlines of revolutionary wars through various phases, created a condition in which the French controlled only the main cities in the delta region, while the Vietminh, for all practical purposes, controlled the population and the countryside. The high point of French military actions was at Dien Bien Phu. The French, sensing a situation in which their conventional forces and superior firepower could finally be brought to bear, placed themselves in a militarily disadvantaged position. General Nguyen Giap, staking his reputation and that of the Vietminh forces on the outcome of the battle, committed the bulk of his forces at Dien Bien Phu, overwhelming the French. The French lost about 9,000 men, killed and wounded. In addition, about 7,000 men were taken prisoner by the Vietminh.[116] Against the French garrison of 13,000 to 15,000 troops, the Vietminh had committed close to 50,000 men in addition to a like number of support troops.

But even after the battle, France retained control of much of South Vietnam and still had large military formations available for battle. Nonetheless, the political repercussions in France were overwhelming and precluded the further prosecution of the war. The defeat at Dien Bien Phu combined with the ongoing Geneva talks created a sense of resignation which sealed the outcome of French involvement in Indochina.

In reviewing the period immediately following World War II and ending with the Geneva Agreements in 1954, we can identify several important factors in respect to the long-range influence on U.S. involvement. Prior to 1954 the United States had already established a precedent for assistance in Vietnam. This assistance was channeled primarily through the French government; by July 1954 the United States had provided nearly $1 billion in aid for use within the Indochina peninsula. During the Dien Bien Phu crisis in 1954, serious consideration was given for U.S. military actions in Vietnam in support of French forces. The objections of Great Britain, the unwillingness of France to grant complete independence to Vietnam, and the serious questions raised by certain congressional leaders and American military officers were sufficient to preclude U.S. military involvement at that time.[117]

The United States also appeared to view the Indochina peninsula, with special reference to Vietnam, as one of the mainstays for the perceived struggle against Communist China. The American involvement in the Korean War and the French in Indochina were viewed as part of the same struggle and appeared to be part of the design of Chinese Communist policy to rule all of Asia. The fact that French troops had fought side by side with U.S. troops in Korea reinforced the relationship between these areas of conflict. Nonetheless, a number of military men opposed a land war in Asia. General Matthew Ridgway, Army Chief of Staff in the 1950s, was particularly outspoken in his opposition. In 1954 he correctly predicted what would be required in terms of troop strength, if the United States were to become involved in a land war in Southeast Asia.[118]

The 1954 Geneva Agreements provided for the temporary partition of Vietnam along the 17th parallel creating a North and South Vietnam; imposed regulations on foreign military personnel and bases; provided for countrywide elections in 1956; established an International Control Commission to supervise the implementation of the agreements; and provided for the free movement of peoples either north or south for a period of 300 days.[119] The Agreements also created the environment and forces which attracted direct U.S. involvement in Vietnam.

The French defeat and withdrawal from Indochina led to the formation of the Southeast Asian Treaty Organization (SEATO) at the insistence of the United States through the personal diplomacy of Secretary of State John Foster Dulles. The SEATO Treaty, although falling short of commitments prescribed in the North Atlantic Treaty Organization (NATO), did provide a legal instrument for active American participation in Southeast Asia. Briefly, the treaty pledged joint action against armed attack on any territory or state in the area. The Indochina peninsula (Cambodia, Laos, and South Vietnam) was included as part of the treaty area, although the constituent states were not signatories.

Perhaps more important from the point of view of the direct and immediate involvement of the United States was the letter from President Dwight D. Eisenhower to President Diem of South Vietnam in October 1954. Until the Geneva Conference, U.S. assistance was through the agencies of the French government. In his letter, President Eisenhower expressed "grave concern regarding the future of the country temporarily divided by an artificial military grouping, weakened by long and exhausting war, and faced with enemies without and by their subservient collaborators within."[120] The president concluded the letter by offering U.S. aid directly to the South Vietnamese government, in essence supplanting the French as the main support of the government.

By the time of the Geneva Agreements, the stage had been set for a deep American involvement in Vietnam. The period following Geneva brought Ngo Dinh Diem to power in South Vietnam and the beginning of a period of rule that was to lead to repression and military coups. The French military presence was also removed following the Geneva Agreements. By 1956 the United States became the only important foreign presence in South Vietnam.

THE POLITICAL CONTEXT

The conclusion of the Geneva Agreements in 1954 closed one chapter and opened another in the history of modern Vietnam. The new chapter began with the emergence of two seemingly independent states, North and South Vietnam. The political conditions in South Vietnam following the Geneva Agreements were chaotic. After years of warfare the economic situation, administrative structure, and governmental control were in a state of collapse. The religious sects, Binh Xuyen, Cao Dai, and Hao Hao, effectively contested the control of the Saigon government in areas throughout the South. The Binh Xuyen for all practical purposes controlled Saigon proper. All of these sects had relatively effective armies, which had been supported by the French, and formed the basis for autonomous regions within the South. The influx of approximately 900,000 refugees from the North created immediate problems with respect to housing and food. (Later, these same refugees were to be the mainstay of the Diem government.) In addition, the armies of North Vietnam appeared to be poised to strike at the South. Ngo Dinh Diem inherited a chaotic administrative structure, an incompetent Army, and an economically and politically prostrate nation.[121]

To the surprise of many, including the United States, Diem destroyed or brought under control the religious sects, administered a relatively effective refugee program, and brought under his control the Army of South Vietnam which proved surprisingly effective against the Binh Xuyen, Cao Dai, and Hao Hao. By 1956 Diem had established what seemed to be the basis for a stable and effective government and the foundations for economic growth.

Although a number of journalistic accounts reflected unfavorably on Diem's capacity to govern and the future of South Vietnam, several American spokesmen were convinced of the importance of South Vietnam and of its stability and potential for development. Senator John F. Kennedy, for example, stated in 1956:

Vietnam represents the cornerstone of the Free World in Southeast Asia, the keystone to the arch, the finger in the dike. Burma, Thailand, India, Japan, the Philippines and obviously Laos and Cambodia are among those whose security would be threatened if the red tide of Communism overflowed into Vietnam.

Vietnam represents a proving ground of democracy in Asia. Vietnam represents the alternative to Communist dictatorship.

The key position of Vietnam in Southeast Asia, makes inevitable the involvement of this nation's security in any new outbreak of trouble.[122]

Senator Mike Mansfield stated that "Diem's star is likely to remain in the ascendancy and that of Ho Chi Minh to fade—because Diem is following a course which more closely meets the needs and aspirations of the Vietnamese people."[123] This statement followed along the lines of the official position of the United States.

Vietnam today, in mid-1956, progressing rapidly to the establishment of democratic institutions by elective processes, its people resuming peaceful pursuits, its army growing in effectiveness, sense of mission, and morale, the puppet Vietnamese politicians discredited, the refugees well on the way to permanent resettlement, the countryside generally orderly and calm, the predatory sects eliminated and their venal leaders exiled or destroyed.[124]

This initial surface stability and relative calm began to fade as the confident Diem government embarked on policies which, coupled with existing but latent insurgent structures in South Vietnam, soon created all of the ingredients for another Vietnam War.

Perhaps the first outward movement toward insurgency was a result of Diem's Anti-Communist Denunciation Campaign initiated in 1956 and 1957. The purpose of this campaign was to destroy the Communist cadres in the South and the Vietminh sympathizers. Instead of concentrating on attempting to win public support and hence neutralize the effectiveness of the Communist cadres, the Diem government engaged in a massive manhunt, which Jean Lacoutre characterizes as a "witch hunt."[125] By 1956 Diem had not made any attempt to hold general elections. This combined with the Anti-Communist Denunciation Campaign dispelled Northern hopes of reunification of Vietnam through a nonviolent process.[126]

Some historians have suggested that Ho Chi Minh was convinced that the South would never be able to develop into a stable state, particularly in light of Diem's policies which were alienating the population. Even with the passing of the election deadline, Hanoi continually counseled moderation, preferring to wait for Diem's fall through his own devices. In any case, the events in 1956 and 1957 appear to have convinced the North Vietnamese leaders that the South would have to be reunified through other than peaceful means.[127]

Previously, the North had established certain organizational apparatuses to publicize the cause of reunification. The Vietnamese Fatherland Front, designed to rally all Vietnamese to the cause of reunification, was founded in the North in 1955. In addition, a National Preparatory Committee, speaking for the new Front, indicted the United States for its obstructionist role in "peaceful" unification.[128] The existence of these organizations combined with the events taking place in South Vietnam set the stage for a more forceful unification policy.

The first evidence of the Second Indochina War appeared sometime in 1957–58. Bernard Fall provides statistics which indicate that a pattern of systematic assassinations of government officials on the village level developed in 1957: "During the year 1957, a total of 472 small officials were killed by the Communists, according to a statement by President Diem himself."[129] This figure doubled in 1958–59.

Accounts also began appearing in Saigon newspapers concerning the deterioration of security in the countryside.

Today the menace is heavier than ever, with the terrorists no longer limiting themselves to the notables in charge of security. Everything suits them, village chief, chairmen of liaison committees, simple guards, even former notables . . . In certain areas, the village chiefs spend their nights in the security posts, while the inhabitants organize watches.[130]

In another account, a Saigon newspaper stated, "The security question in the provinces must be given top priority; the regime will be able to consolidate itself only if it succeeds in finding a solution to this problem."[131]

During the period 1957–60, it was estimated that over 5,000 total incidents occurred and 1,700 officials were killed, while another 2,000 officials were kidnapped.[132] It was also estimated that about 10,000 civilians were kidnapped. Ominous signs appeared in the countryside providing some evidence that villages were being deserted for the relative security of the urban areas. All of these pointed to the growing ability of the revolutionaries to isolate the government from the masses of the people and limit the government's control of the countryside. By the end of 1958 widespread terrorism had developed, particularly aimed at hamlet and village chiefs, teachers, local security officials, and other government officials. The Vietcong had become more visible: "By this time, too, the Vietcong had begun to set up their own administrations in the villages, run by cadres who were in charge of indoctrinating the population and collecting taxes—both money and rice—and creating new espionage nets."[133]

The developments in 1957–58 represented a major step in revolutionary war and a significant failure on the part of the Diem government. A more enlightened policy towards the peasants as well as a more realistic policy in the campaign against the Communist cadres, and a broadening of the base of support for the Diem government may well have eliminated many conditions conducive to insurgency: "It was thus by its home policy that the government of the South finally destroyed the confidence of the population, which it had won during the early years, and practically drove them into revolt and desperation."[134]

It was only in 1959 that the Diem government began to appreciate the immensity of the revolutionary struggle that had developed in Vietnam. Law 19/59 was passed, which provided for "repression of acts of sabotage, and infringements of national security."[135] Special tribunals were established to pass judgments of hard labor or death with no provision for appeal. This law in effect legalized the actions of Diem's police and Army. It was perhaps a manifestation of Diem's pronouncement earlier in the year that "at the present time, Vietnam is a nation at war."[136]

The peasants' expectations of peace and a better life under an independent Vietnam were shattered. Diem's policies and the increasing violence and repression resulting from the counterrevolutionary conflict made the peasants a pawn between the protagonists. "Caught between state and Communist reprisal operations, and generally dissatisfied with unfulfilled promises of land reform and social justice, the masses could discern little difference between current plight and what they had experienced during the colonial years."[137]

By 1963 the situation in South Vietnam had reached crisis proportions. The inability of the South Vietnamese Army to cope with main force Vietcong units and the increasing alienation of the Diem government from the countryside appeared to be the beginning of the phase three period of revolutionary war. It also reinforced the observation of many that the South Vietnamese government under Diem had outlived its usefulness and was incapable of conducting a counterrevolutionary program under its existing leadership.

The first sign of the unraveling of the Diem regime was the Buddhist revolt in 1963. The Buddhist revolt began in Hue and quickly spread to Saigon, where Diem's Special Forces troops attacked pagodas and arrested Buddhist monks. This act served as a catalyst and resulted in thousands of students joining ranks with the Buddhists in demonstrating against the Diem government. The universities of Hue and Saigon were closed along with all secondary schools in Saigon. The effect was to punish the children of the elite as well as the children of many military officers. This added to the dissatisfaction of many officers who felt that Diem's personal control of the military and his brother Nhu's role in the government were undermining the efficiency and effectiveness of the

South Vietnamese Army. Furthermore, the Buddhist revolt was given widespread media coverage in the United States and for the first time, raised some serious questions regarding the situation in South Vietnam.[138]

The United States became increasingly disenchanted with Diem. The new American ambassador to Vietnam, Henry Cabot Lodge, on arriving in Vietnam during the height of the Buddhist crisis, protested against the outrages. President Kennedy expressed his great concern during a press conference and television interview over the situation in Vietnam. This culminated in demands by Congress to withhold aid from Diem's government until the repression ceased. A number of South Vietnamese military officers felt that the United States was ready for a change.[139]

The Vietcong and the Buddhists had brought the Diem regime to the brink of military and political disaster, but it was Diem's own army which put an end to his rule. The colonels and generals who organized the coup were anti-Communists motivated not so much by democratic convictions or revolutionary zeal as by their concern over the regime's inability to combat and defeat the Vietcong. Furthermore, the men who overthrew Diem were fully convinced that their project, although never publicly endorsed by any authorized U.S. spokesman, had the blessings of the U.S. Government.[140]

A number of factors created the environment in which Diem found himself in 1963. Basically, the policies regarding land reform and the means to implement them were ineffective and eroded by graft and corruption, alienating the peasants. Treatment of the Buddhist majority, combined with the overreliance on the Catholic minority, personal friends, and relatives, with little attempt at mass appeal, not only discredited Diem, but also stultified the administration and dissipated any innovations or serious mobilization that may have been created for the counterrevolutionary war. These factors, exacerbated by Diem's lacklustre personality, enmeshed in mandarin symbolism, precipitated widespread revolts in the countryside as well as urban areas which culminated in the coup d'etat of 1963 and the death of Diem. With the demise of Diem and the collapse of his government, the Second Indochina War entered into a new and perhaps more perplexing phase as far as the United States was concerned.

The downfall of the Diem regime ushered in a period of coup followed by countercoup, creating political instability and allowing the increased control of the countryside by the Vietcong. General Duong Van Minh became head of state and government by virtue of his chairmanship of the Military Revolutionary Council. Through this instrument, the key ministries were controlled by the generals. General Minh was displaced by General Nguyen Kahn, followed by attempts to establish a civilian government which were unsuccessful as a result of Catholic and Buddhist demonstrations. This political instability continued until June 1965, when the Armed Forces Council, the select group of generals controlling the state and government, established an all-military National Leadership Committee. Air Marshal Nguyen Cao Ky, a Buddhist, became the prime minister. General Nguyen Van Thieu became chief of state. Under Ky's leadership, there was an attempt to increase the military effectiveness of the South Vietnamese armed forces, combined with attempts to place the country on a war footing. In the meantime, however, the Buddhists had organized the Struggle Movement which soon attracted a variety of critics of the military government, particularly students. Political instability inherited from the Diem period combined with infighting among military officers continued. Ky reacted with strong military and police countermeasures against the Struggle Movement, reducing its political importance. As late as 1970 the Buddhists had not reappeared as a strong political force.

U.S. demands for constitutional government and the increasing need to broaden the power base of the existing government led to the calling of a Constituent Assembly to draft a new South Vietnamese constitution. The Constituent Assembly elections, in which 81 percent of the registered voters turned out in areas under government control, seemed to indicate that there was an undercurrent of movement towards greater and more meaningful participation in the political process within South Vietnam. A constitution was promulgated which led to national elections in 1967.[141]

As a result of a secret meeting of generals, it was decided that General Thieu would head the military ticket and Ky would run as vice-president. Although the Thieu-Ky ticket won, the Peace Candidate, Trong Dinh Dzu, made a surprisingly good showing. Following the elections, politics in South Vietnam remained characterized by political manipulations and intrigue manifested in such factors as a continuing Thieu-Ky feud, manipulations within the National Assembly and the Senate, replacement of a number of officers appointed by Ky, and attempts by Thieu to consolidate his political power. By 1970 Thieu appeared to have gained a measure of confidence in his own ability and to have established a semblance of stability in the political system of Vietnam. Nevertheless, fears of military coups still remained part of the political picture in Vietnam.

From the Ky period, the nature of the war had undergone change. The Vietcong had demonstrated their ability to attack and, in most cases, succeed in defeating the South Vietnamese. The political infighting compounded the problems and training within the South Vietnamese Army. By the end of 1965 most observers felt that the South Vietnamese government was on the verge of military defeat.

It is within this context that the U.S. involvement must be viewed.

As suggested earlier, from the end of 1964 the South Vietnamese government was faced with its most serious crisis. It was during 1964, however, that the United States became involved in a series of decisions that led to the commitment of U.S. ground troops to South Vietnam and for all practical purposes provided a temporary solution to the crisis in military inability of the South Vietnamese.

Although there were over 23,000 U.S. personnel in South Vietnam by 1964, the United States had maintained that its role was purely advisory and that it was only an indirect participant. A major shift in this attitude was a result of the events in the summer of 1964 associated with the Gulf of Tonkin. Following the attack of a U.S. destroyer by North Vietnamese torpedo boats, retaliatory air action was taken against port and fuel facilities in North Vietnam. Subsequently, Congress passed the Gulf of Tonkin resolution by a vote of 414 to 0 in the House and 88 to 2 in the Senate.[142] The first step toward Americanization of the war had been taken.

Later in 1964 the Vietcong focused attention on U.S. military installations and personnel. Bien Hoa was attacked followed by attacks on a U.S. officer's billet in Saigon itself. Early in 1965 the U.S. military compound in Pleiku was attacked. The increasing tempo of military activity and the determination of the U.S. government to respond to attacks on U.S. personnel and installations shifted the advisory role of the United States to that of active participant. This shift was signaled by the start of bombing attacks on the North and the dramatic increase in the number of U.S. troops in 1965, whose role now included active ground combat. Certainly, the declining ability of the South Vietnamese Army and the resulting instability of the Ky government were basic to the reassessment of the U.S. role. By the end of 1965 U.S. troop strength increased to 184,000, and casualties for that year rose to 1,369 killed and 6,114 wounded. During the same period the South Vietnamese suffered 11,243 killed and 23,118 wounded. The war in 1965 had become an American as well as Vietnamese war.

The increasing involvement of the United States, particularly as reflected in casualty statistics, aroused increasing opposition to the war in the United States. As early as 1965 citizen groups were demonstrating against the war. In November 1965, 20,000 demonstrators joined in a nonviolent "March on Washington for Peace in Vietnam." These initial demonstrations were only harbingers of things to come. The uneasy political mood and the development of opposition towards the war were also reflected in the growing questions in Congress regarding Americanization of the war. A major debate on Vietnam took place in the Senate during hearings of the Senate Foreign Relations Committee in 1966. During this period, a growing schism developed between President Johnson and congressional critics. The administration maintained its position that the United States must honor its commitments, Communist aggression must be halted, Communist China contained, and South Vietnam must remain independent, while critics pointed to a corrupt South Vietnamese government and mismanagement of the U.S. involvement.[143]

In 1967 and continuing into 1968, the United States increased its troop strength in South Vietnam, which in turn led to increasing opposition both in Congress and in demonstrations throughout the nation. By this time certain initiatives had been taken regarding peace negotiations. Although there were a number of temporary truces in 1967, no permanent settlement evolved. Demonstrations against the Vietnam War continued, including a march on the Pentagon in October 1967.

The Communist Tet Offensive in January and February of 1968 was a key event in the Vietnam War.[144] Although many military men would argue, with justification, that it was a Communist military defeat, it could also be argued that it marked a major political and propaganda victory for the Vietcong. Prior to the offensive, there was a degree of optimism regarding the increasing stability of politics in South Vietnam and the increasing impact of U.S. and South Vietnamese military operations against the Vietcong. The Tet Offensive dispelled all doubts concerning the ability of the Vietcong to mount military operations and destroy security, even in the U.S. Embassy in Saigon. It demonstrated that, regardless of the efforts of pacification and U.S./South Vietnamese military operations, the Vietcong had the ability to attack and seize, albeit temporarily, major cities in South Vietnam. The credibility of U.S./South Vietnamese pacification and security efforts had become highly suspect. Military solutions to the war had become unattainable.

Within the United States, Tet coalesced the opposition that had been growing throughout 1967 as the war had continued, seemingly without end. President Johnson's initial support eroded on both right and left—the former demanding an end to the war through escalation and the latter through deescalation, if not outright withdrawal (sometimes, in fact, the same people held both views).[145]

Subsequent to the Tet Offensive, General William C. Westmoreland, commander of U.S. forces in Vietnam, admitted that a military victory in the classic sense was not possible because of our national policy in not expanding the war. President Johnson's surprise announcement in March 1968 that he would not seek another term as president was followed by his announcement that a bombing halt would be put into effect covering 90 percent of North Vietnam. During 1968, demonstrations on the campus, in cities, and opposition in Congress had produced an environment in which the decision-making capacity of government and the credibility of the Executive Office were seriously challenged. The problems of urbanization, poverty, race, youth, the economy—all seemed to stem from the resources being used by the Department of Defense in conducting the war in Vietnam. Draft card burning and attacks on the ROTC, induction, and selective service offices reflected the growing disenchantment not only with the administration, but also with the military. Within the military, a growing number of personnel were associated with antiwar groups. The American Servicemen's Union and the coffeehouse culture associated with Army bases emerged during this time.

From 1965 through the Tet Offensive, political control of South Vietnam moved from one set of military men to another, even with the elections in 1967. The fragile political structure had a negative impact on the ability of the South Vietnamese military. The dangerous situation in 1965 prompted U.S. involvement with ground combat troops, temporarily stabilizing the military situation. Nonetheless, the political situation in the South frustrated attempts to consolidate efforts in the countryside. Moreover, the post-Tet political-military situation generated little optimism in American circles regarding the successful conduct of the war. American withdrawal was beginning to appear as the only viable alternative.

THE MILITARY CONTEXT

In 1965, with the first commitment of large-scale American combat troops into Vietnam, the conditions in South Vietnam and the posture of the Vietcong and North Vietnamese forces in the South were in the stage two phase of Mao's revolutionary strategy. That is, the revolutionaries had elevated the war to large unit operations, prepared to combat South Vietnamese forces on an equal footing and in conventional battles. American forces responded in kind, adopting the "fire brigade" approach first used in Korea—the use of highly mobile units to quickly respond to military threats. By 1966, with the addition of many more American units, the American forces were able to take the offensive and stabilize the combat area. Thus, for the initial phase in Vietnam, American forces operated in conventional patterns employing brigade or larger sized units against Vietcong and North Vietnamese forces. These tactics had little impact on pacification, since they were aimed primarily at finding enemy units, destroying them, and then returning to base— shades of General Otis in the Philippines!

When the second phase of the war began in about 1967, the effort turned toward the use of smaller units in search-and-destroy efforts. Operational areas were established, usually at brigade levels, and commanders were given the mission of clearing their area of the enemy. By 1968, however, the term *search and destroy* fell into disuse, and clearing and secure operations were implemented. The idea was to clear the area of the enemy and to secure the area for pacification efforts by the Vietnamese forces and government.

Regardless of the tactical posture adopted by American forces, the main purpose remained to find the enemy and destroy him. The idea of pacification and civil-military operations, while receiving a great deal of verbal commitment, was not carried out with the same effort and enthusiasm as conventional operations. Perhaps this was to be expected. American forces, even with all the verbal articulation about counterinsurgency, were conventionally postured and based on a military professionalism resting on a conventional mind set. Moreover, the enemy evolved into a highly mobile, well-armed, battle-wise opponent. The Vietcong forces had deeply penetrated South Vietnamese society and the political system. Their access to local resources and the indigenous people gave them significant advantages over Americans, who could hardly hide within the populace or become one of the "fish in the sea." To be sure, the North Vietnamese found the environment in the South alien. But under the guidance of the Vietcong who knew the country well, North Vietnamese forces were able to operate effectively.

At the same time, American forces were faced with different kinds of wars in various areas of Vietnam. In the North (I Corps area) the war became a more or less conventional confrontation between American forces and the North Vietnamese. In Central Vietnam (II Corps), the confrontations were between highly mobile Vietcong forces, the North Vietnamese, and American forces—a mixture of conventional and unconventional war. In the areas around Saigon and some southern parts of Vietnam (III Corps), the war remained primarily between the Vietcong and the American forces, while in the Delta (IV Corps) it was a rice paddy war, primarily unconventional in nature. Thus, in the southern part of Vietnam, unconventional patterns prevailed. In the North, conventional battles were more frequent.

The Tet Offensive in 1968 was a turning point in the war. The enemy showed that he was willing to take heavy casualties in standup battles with American and South Vietnamese forces. It also showed that the enemy had adapted well to the principles of revolutionary warfare—the political objective was more important than military success. Thus, while American forces had inflicted a major military defeat on the enemy, the enemy had achieved a great political victory. Previous to the Tet Offensive, pacification efforts seemed to be progressing reasonably well. Americans had again proclaimed the light at the end of the tunnel, and there began to develop a generally optimistic attitude regarding the outcome of the war. The Tet Offensive destroyed all of that. The fact that the enemy could penetrate even into the American embassy in Saigon was not lost on the populace. American forces had to turn their attention to enemy attacks in major areas, cities, and towns; the countryside had to be virtually abandoned. The political-psychological impact on the Vietnamese was far-reaching. The Vietcong and North Vietnamese forces could control the countryside, almost at will, even after all the efforts of the American forces. Americans at home became disillusioned as they learned of an enemy who, regardless of American efforts, could penetrate the very center of the Vietnamese capital. It was clear to many that the Tet Offensive proved that the enemy's "great mobility and unpredictability frequently forced the free world forces to conduct search-and-destroy operations or fight major battles in areas that had supposedly been freed from enemy influence."[146]

The battles, skirmishes, and ambushes that took place in Vietnam during 1965–70 provide abundant material for military historians. Defying any particular patterns, the war during these years has best been described by S.L.A. Marshall: "The sure thing proves to be an empty bag. The seeming flash-in-the-pan turns into a major explosion. Elephant guns are used to bang away at rabbits. Tigers are hunted with popguns."[147]

A sampling of engagements illustrates the complexity and character of the Vietnam War. The fight at Ia Drang in October-November 1965 was one in which relatively large American units were in action against large concentrations of the enemy. Brigade-size units of the 1st Cavalry Division engaged regimental-size units of the enemy.

It was during the week before Thanksgiving, amidst the scrub brush and stunted trees of the Ia Drang River valley in the western sector of Pleiku Province along the Cambodian border, that the war changed drastically. For the first time regular North Vietnamese regiments, controlled by a division-size headquarters, engaged in a conventional contest with U.S. Forces. The 1st battalion, 7th Cavalry 1st Cavalry Division (Airmobile) took the lead in this battle.[148]

The battle became one of maneuver and countermaneuver, with the North Vietnamese trying to outflank elements of the 3d Brigade, which had relieved the 1st Brigade. The battle turned into murderous firefights between platoons and companies. Artillery was used in close support to ward off enemy units. At times, enemy fire was so heavy that helicopters could not land at various landing zones.

U.S. Army official history reflects the nature of the battle:

When the North Vietnamese of the flanking force, estimated as company size, entered the dry creek bed that ran headlong into the rest of Company A, Nadal, eager to join the fray, had moved the remaining two platoons forward. First to meet the enemy in the creek bed was the 3rd Platoon. The firing was at very close range, the fighting savage. Recoiling from the first shock, the men of the left half of the 3rd Platoon climbed onto the creek bank where, along with the men of the 1st Platoon they poured a murderous fire into the enemy.[149]

At intervals during the night, enemy forces harassed and probed the battalion perimeter in all but the Company D sector, and in each instance well-placed American artillery from Falcon blunted the enemy's aggressiveness. Firing some 4,000 rounds, the two howitzer batteries in the landing zone had also laced the fingers and draws of Chu Pong where the lights had been seen. Tactical air missions were flown throughout the night.[150]

The enemy eventually withdrew from the area after unsuccessfully trying to overrun an isolated American unit and without penetrating defense perimeters. With the help of artillery, tactical air, and B-52 strikes, the area became a death trap for enemy units. Aside from the great amount of munitions and weapons captured by American forces, it was estimated that the enemy suffered 634 known dead, 581 estimated dead, and 6 prisoners. However, it was costly to American forces, with 79 killed and 121 wounded.[151]

Ambushes along major highways and roads and ambushes of ground units were more common characteristics of the fighting in Vietnam. Periodically, American forces had to keep major roads open by moving through in armed convoys. Such movements were frequently ambushed as was the case along Highway 1 in October 1966. The 11th Armored Cavalry moved into its base camp a few miles south of the provincial capital of Xuan Loc, located north of Saigon in III Corps area. Convoys moved through Highway 1 and then onto Highway 2 into the base camp area.[152]

The Dong Nai Regiment of the Vietcong's 274th Regiment, a veteran unit, established ambush positions along Highway 1, west of Xuan Loc. This was midway between the province capitals of Bien Hoa and Xuan Loc. At this point, "Highway 1 dropped sharply to a stream bend and then rose to a gently rolling plateau. A dirt road running north and south intersected National Highway 1 at this point. Low hills rising only 10 to 20 meters above the road level began about 180 meters from the highway on both sides."[153] One side of the road was covered by tall grass with a banana grove lining the other side of the road. The concealment offered good positions for the Vietcong's main force of over 1,000 men.

A classic Vietcong ambush was prepared with heavy weapons at both ends of the killing zone—in this case 75–mm recoiless rifles. Along the killing zone, heavy machine guns were scattered for use against helicopters and jets.

The opening fire of the ambush was not well coordinated, however, since not all of the convoy was in the killing zone. Nevertheless, several trucks were damaged and destroyed. Men of the convoy took to the ditches, and heavy fire erupted all along the killing zone. Tactical air and helicopter gunships engaged the enemy almost immediately. Tanks and Armored Cavalry Assault Vehicles (ACAVs) (armed with a .50 caliber machine gun, two M-60 machine guns, and a 40 mm grenade launcher), which were almost like light tanks, had surrounded the ambush site. A relief force came upon the scene as the 274th Vietcong Regiment withdrew in a southerly direction. A total of thirty enemy dead were found. The American force had seven killed and eight wounded. Four trucks and two ACAVs had been destroyed.

From the beginning, the battle had not gone well for the Viet Cong. The ambush, designed to open with the crash of recoiless rifle fire and grenades, had begun with the sputter of small arms while half the convoy sped through unscathed. Alerted, most of the men entered the killing zone firing into the jungle on both sides of the road. Not until the middle of the convoy reached the killing zone had the enemy fired heavy weapons. Almost from the first, Blackhorse helicopters had struck from the sky. The ACAV, new to the men of the Dong Nai Regiment who had never seen a vehicle quite like it, poured more fire into the Viet Cong ranks than any other "personnel carrier" they had met. The clincher had come when the Ho Nai outpost flashed word that the relief force was on the way just minutes after the ambush struck. The regimental commander, whose troops were already beginning to flee south as jets came in to bomb, was obliged to order withdrawal when the fight had scarcely begun.[154]

When American forces met the enemy in battles such as those fought at Ia Drang and along Highway 1, they ultimately emerged as victors. In battle after battle, American forces usually proved to be effective and successful fighters, but not without taking casualties or difficult combat. In the end, however, battlefield victories appeared to be only incidental to the ultimate outcome of the Vietnam conflict.

More often than not, American forces became involved in sweeping operations such as *Operation Thayer* in September 1966 along Highway 1. The better part of the 1st Cavalry Division was involved. But what started out as a well-conceived plan to engage large units of the enemy ended up accomplishing little except causing American casualties: "Either the enemy was not there or, if present, was so adroit and clever that American genius and aggressiveness must be rated as something less than we believe. . . . Operation Thayer did not make sense to the soldiers who dealt with its stresses for almost a month."[155]

American military operations were characterized by a high degree of mobility and massive firepower. These were most effective when tracking and striking at enemy units that could be isolated. But in other instances, these may have hampered the key to successful counterrevolution.

In populated areas, it was difficult to distinguish between the enemy and the peasants. Finding enemy units was more difficult, and, if found, usually massive firepower was used against them. In the process many civilians were killed and hurt, and animals and ricelands that happened to be in the battle area were destroyed. Such tactics did little to develop and maintain sympathy for the South Vietnamese government or for American forces.[156]

Regardless of the battle victories and of the tactical doctrine characterizing American military operations, the psychological climate created frustration and alienation for many Americans. It was difficult for many to relate to the South Vietnamese as an ally or to the character and purposes of the enemy. In a psychological sense, Americans felt isolated from both, and battles took on a purpose and an end in themselves rather than being pursued for political and meaningful ends. This frustration and alienation was well expressed by an American soldier in Vietnam.

The G.I.'s are supposed to win the people's confidence, but they weren't taught any of that stuff. I went through that training and I learned how to shoot, but no one ever told me a thing about having to love people who look different from us and who've got an ideological orientation that's about a hundred and eighty degrees different from us. We don't understand what they're thinking. When we got here, we landed on a different planet. In Germany and Japan, I guess there was a thread of contact, but even when a Vietnamese guy speaks perfect English, I don't know what the hell he's talking about.[157]

The U.S. Navy, Air Force and Marines had substantial roles in the war. Any serious assessment of the military dimension of the Vietnamese conflict must include these services. The air war, tactical air support, naval gunfire (and naval support of riverine operations), and the Marines' ground war in the North are matters of importance in the history of the Vietnamese conflict. The complexity of these operations and the specific roles of the services are subjects in their own right and deserve their own studies. Nonetheless, it is useful here to glance at the Marine Corps operations in the North to develop a better understanding of the varieties of ground wars that occurred in Vietnam. The Marines operated primarily in I Corps or northern provinces against North Vietnamese Regulars. Most Marine Corps operations tended to take on conventional characteristics, with sweeps and operations along the northern coast. In some areas, the Marines found that fighting in towns was reminiscent of World War II's door-to-door and street-by-street combat. The North Vietnamese Regulars made no pretense at unconventional war. The fighting in Hue was typical of this type of combat.[158]

The battles in Hue involved not only the Marines but also army units such as the 101st Airborne Division and the 1st Cavalry, as well as units from the 1st ARVN Division (Army of the Republic of Vietnam). Indeed, as Michael Herr points out, in the final days of the battle for Hue, the

101st Airborne and the 1st Cavalry had heavy casualties: "in five days these outfits lost as many men as the Marines had in three weeks."[159]

Aside from these operations, the Marines tended to develop their own counterrevolutionary doctrine, almost separate from the doctrines being implemented in the rest of Vietnam by American forces. This included the integration of small detachments of Marines with Popular Forces within a village. The Marines lived and worked with the village forces and operated from within the village itself. This dispersal not only made the American presence more visible, but it also provided a sense of security for the villagers. However, dissipation of forces, pressures to engage in offensive operations, as well as the activity of revolutionary forces which eroded the Marine-village concept, prevented the carrying out of these tactics over the long range. The final impact of such an approach is still not clear. Some concern was expressed regarding the proper use of Marines. Oriented toward quick assault and penetration operations, some argued that the Marines were committed to missions in Vietnam which did not exploit their capabilities.

Another type of war was conducted by American Special Forces teams. While known mostly for their work among the Montagnards, Special Forces teams operated in a number of areas and conducted many types of operations, primarily aimed at the unconventional dimension of the war—mobile strike operations, border surveillance, long-range reconnaissance, and guerrilla operations against the enemy. One of the most important missions was establishment of the Civilian Irregular Defense Group. The purpose was to establish base camps among various minority ethnic groups in Vietnam, such as the Montagnards, for the purpose of conducting paramilitary operations against the North Vietnamese Army and Vietcong. These types of operations were well suited to the unique organization and training of the Special Forces. Some argue that the key to successful counterrevolutionary efforts rested primarily with units such as the Special Forces.[160]

The historical issue of regular versus elite units emerged in Vietnam. Historically, conventionally postured and trained military professionals normally have little use for special units. In no small part, this arises from the fundamental antagonisms between nontraditional professional perspectives, unconventional operations, and the traditional and conventional posture of most of the military system. According to Colonel Francis J. Kelly:

The Special Forces were continually conscious of mistrust and suspicion on the part of many relatively senior field grade U.S. military men. This state of affairs, which came about chiefly from a lack of knowledge of Special Forces operations, their limitations, and their capabilities, gave rise to many discrete efforts to bring the Special Forces either totally or in separate parts within the operational control of a U.S. Senior official. This desire to control Special Forces assets was not restricted to operational commanders, but was evident in many staff officers as well.[161]

Generally, little reference is made to the South Vietnamese military when analyzing American policy and military operations. This is probably because once American forces entered Vietnam in strength, they tended to take over the battle area as "frontline" forces. The South Vietnamese forces were left to play a secondary role, primarily concerned with pacification and mobilization efforts. In what is perhaps an irony of the Vietnam conflict, the major focus of the counterrevolutionary effort was left to the South Vietnamese military, although many Americans considered the South Vietnamese inferior to the enemy in ability and effectiveness. Perhaps the American military had no choice, since the Americans could hardly undertake mobilizing the South Vietnamese peasants. Yet, there is a nagging suspicion that, consciously or not, the enemy confronted Americans, and the Americans responded accordingly in those geographical areas and in the political-military dimensions that were fundamentally secondary to the center of gravity of revolution and counterrevolution.

For the most part, South Vietnamese military operations during the period examined here were separate from those of U.S. military forces. To be sure, there were many examples of joint operations that were successful. In addition, American advisors serving with South Vietnamese units brought some degree of coordination. American commanders remained reluctant to combine operations with South Vietnamese forces, however, not only because of the suspicions of Vietcong infiltration of such units, but because many felt that units of the South Vietnamese Army were poorly led, which could lead to military failures. Until the Vietnamization program began in earnest after the Tet Offensive, American commanders hardly considered South Vietnamese forces as frontline caliber—most felt that they were no match for NVA units or for veteran Vietcong units. This is not meant to overlook the fact that selected units of the South Vietnamese Army and special units fought as well as American units. It is also true that there were individual military officers in the South Vietnamese military whose skill and leadership were equal to any American military officer.

Following the Tet Offensive in 1968, American policy turned towards Vietnamization. Efforts were made to increase the effectiveness of the South Vietnamese forces and to develop a network of Regional-Popular forces capable of defending themselves and their areas. South Vietnamese troops were provided better equipment and were gradually injected into a "frontline" posture paralleled by an American attempt to gradually withdraw from active contact with enemy forces. As the 1960s ended, it seemed clear that the Americans were committed to a Vietnamization policy and withdrawal from active ground combat.

Although there were a variety of wars within South Vietnam, the major character of the conflict, particularly in the South, followed the classic lines of revolutionary guerrilla warfare: hit and run raids, assassinations, and, when the revolutionaries felt confident of success, conventional battles. Members of the Vietcong, particularly those at the district level, functioned as peasants during the day. At night or during special operations, they grouped into their Vietcong military units and conducted operations against the South Vietnamese Army, government officials, local security forces, and American units. The standard operation consisted of ambushes or hit and run raids against small units or detachments of "enemy" forces. Before help could arrive to relieve the counterrevolutionary forces, the Vietcong units usually faded into the rice paddies or the countryside; many returned to their homes in the villages and hamlets.

Trying to root out the Vietcong cadres became almost impossible without help from the villagers themselves. When a villager did take the initiative to point out enemy cadres to government forces, he and members of his family were sure to suffer the consequences from other Vietcong cadres. Officials of the South Vietnamese government as well as members of the South Vietnamese Army and local security forces found it impossible to spend a night in the countryside without adequate security. Americans also found it difficult to operate in the countryside except in organized units assured of reinforcement by helicopter-borne troops, artillery, and/or air strikes. The day belonged to the South Vietnamese and their allies, but the night usually belonged to the Vietcong. Two political systems were operating: the existing government by day and the revolutionary system by night. The Vietcong were, in Mao's classic phrase, "fish in the sea."

One of the most succinct observations regarding the conflict in Vietnam is recorded by an American officer. On April 25, 1975, the following conversation took place between Colonel Harry G. Summers, Jr., Chief Negotiations Division, U.S. Delegation Four Party Joint Military Team, and Colonel Tu, Chief North Vietnamese (DRV) Delegation, "You know you never defeated us on the battlefield," said the American colonel. The North Vietnamese colonel pondered this remark a moment. "That may be so," he replied, "but it is also irrelevant."[162]

It is unfortunate that many American policymakers, both military and civilian, have yet to grasp the essence of Colonel Tu's observation. It is even more unfortunate that American experience in revolutionary wars dating back to the Second Seminole War has been lost in the archives of military history. Even a cursory reading of the past may have provided insights into Vietnam and, just perhaps, may have prevented some policy miscalculations and misjudgments.

SUMMARY

It is difficult to sum up the military dimension of the Vietnam War, for it was so complex and multidimensional a conflict that no one summation can capture the essence of American involvement. Yet, in our comparative analysis, a number of points become clear.

One of the most telling problems was the lack of appreciation of the character and costs of revolutionary and counterrevolutionary war by many of America's political and military leaders. Lacking a sense of history and possessing a misconception of the Hanoi regime, most leaders felt that American technology and military strength were sufficient to defeat a Third World peasant society.

The surfacing of serious domestic problems and a rapidly changing social order within the United States coincided with its deepening commitment in Vietnam. While a number of civil rights groups tried to keep their separation from antiwar elements, the flood of protest and indignation over the war spilled over and seemed to capture protests against the injustices of society. Many protests became, in fact, antiwar protests. Draft evasion, equal rights, social justice, violent protest against the establishment—all seemed to become justified in the name of an antiwar posture.

All of these forces had an impact on the military profession and on the effectiveness of the military institution. The military professional became one of the most visible symbols of the establishment, and the military system was viewed as a coercive force outside of the mainstream of democracy. The anti-establishment attitude of many youth, and the highly critical commentary regarding American politics and society expressed by a number of intellectuals, religious leaders, and politicians, did little to engender a sense of patriotism or service to the country. The selective service system became a symbol of servitude. The involvement in Vietnam exacerbated the already antagonistic civil-military relationships, finally singling out the military as an instrument of oppression.

The American military posture and its combat effectiveness were seriously affected by these internal events. Even if American forces had been able to adopt a successful counterrevolutionary posture, while supporting the South Vietnamese military in the conduct of the war, the nature of American politics may well have prevented the effective prosecution of the war.

In addition, the international environment was rapidly changing, eroding much of the bipolar system and spheres of influence evolving from World War II. These changes made it increasingly more difficult to protect American national security interests, project American power externally, or identify and articulate clear foreign policy goals. This confusion and ambiguity was reflected in the military services, whose strategy and tactical doctrine shifted from one premise to another in Vietnam, while the organizational structure retained its traditional focus. Although there was a considerable amount of discussion regarding insurgency and counterinsurgency, the focus of military operations remained primarily conventional, with the few exceptions associated mainly with Special Forces units. The conduct of the war and its progress remained wedded to conventional norms, that is, the amount of real estate held, weapons and enemy captured, and body counts. The essence of the problem, however, was not in these conventional considerations, but in developing a political-social base around which an effective indigenous government could be developed.

The commitment of American ground troops to Vietnam changed the war into an "American" conflict. Instead of supporting the South Vietnamese military forces in developing combat effectiveness and a close interrelationship with South Vietnamese civilian teams to develop effectiveness in the countryside, the American military fought the kind of war for which they were best prepared—conventional and small-unit operations. Thus, much of the effort was taken from the South Vietnamese and placed in the hands of American military forces.

The 1950s saw the establishment of a conventionally oriented South Vietnamese military which was later perpetuated by American military forces. The South Vietnamese government, which initially appeared to provide the best hope for the South, eroded its political base by its lack of aggressiveness in carrying out much needed reforms and its inability to establish itself in the countryside. Thus, as American commitments grew, the South Vietnamese government appeared to become less and less effective in prosecuting the war. Part of the problem was the result of the Americanization of the war. But another part was the result of the internal fighting and personal aggrandizement of a number of South Vietnamese officials.

CONCLUSIONS

Study of the four counterrevolutionary conflicts reveals a number of common characteristics, perhaps the most important of which is their asymmetrical nature. American forces were first committed in what was considered to be a limited action. The attention of Americans was focused elsewhere, and the conflicts were viewed as sideshows. But for the adversary the conflict was a matter of survival and represented a total war. Even in the case of Pancho Villa, he and his forces were fighting for their very survival. They were soon to be joined by Carranza's forces and the people in the countryside who considered the Americans invaders and so regarded the Americans as a greater evil than Villa's ruthlessness against his own people.

Although all of the conflicts were unconventional, at times they included conventional combat. And in every case, the revolutionaries were fighting on their home ground, totally acclimated to both climate and terrain. In this respect, they were in an area in which the majority of the people supported their actions against those of the Americans. Even in areas such as Florida, which was mostly inhabited, American forces could not gather accurate intelligence, since few white men knew the interior of the area.

In each instance American forces tried, mostly in vain, to bring the revolutionary forces to combat in conventional settings. While this did occur from time to time, most of the battles took place either as running encounters, as in Mexico, or as the outcomes of ambushes and hit and run raids. Vietnam provided different examples in which the enemy did engage in conventional battles. Even there, however, such battles were primarily the result of the enemy's efforts to gain a propaganda victory and were political in their purpose rather than military. In other words, for the revolutionaries, the military outcome was incidental to the political-psychological consequences.

At the outset of each of the conflicts, American forces used conventional maneuvering and tactics to try to bring the enemy to battle. And in each conflict, American forces eventually had to adopt some kind of unconventional posture. This ranged from rudimentary search-and-destroy operations in Florida to a combination of search-and-hold and conventional combat in Vietnam. In this respect, the two conflicts in which American forces controlled not only the military but also the political instrument, the Second Seminole War and in the Philippines, were reasonably successful. In the case of the Punitive Expedition and Vietnam, the Mexican government and the South Vietnamese, respectively controlled the political instrument. In these latter cases, success was elusive, with some calling the Punitive Expedition a failure, and the other resulted in withdrawal of American forces and the defeat of South Vietnam.

Not only did the United States not control the political system or the political environment, but there was also outside aid to the revolutionaries. In Mexico, the aid given to Villa was directly from the peons in the countryside and indirectly from the Carranza government itself. In Vietnam, the apathy of many Vietnamese peasants to the struggle, and the suspicion of both the South Vietnamese government and the Americans made the counterrevolutionary effort extremely difficult. The aid given to the revolutionaries through the commitment of North Vietnamese Regulars, the supply of arms and munitions through China, and the sanctuaries afforded in North Vietnam, Cambodia, and Laos made it virtually impossible to isolate the revolutionary system. The contrast between these situations and those that faced the Americans in Florida and in the Philippines in no small part affected the outcome of the counterrevolutionary effort.

From the American military professional point of view, in none of the conflicts were professionals trained and/or educated in the principles of unconventional tactics or in revolutionary warfare. The guiding principles evolved from conventional tactics modeled on the European system or from the grand battles of the American Civil War and the two world wars. While American forces did somewhat adopt the requirements of counterrevolutionary war, the underlying professional orientation and the training of the troops were primarily conventional. The American cultural patterns created constraints and limitations regarding the behavior against the adversary, although there were cases of deviant behavior. In the Philippines and in Vietnam, a considerable amount of domestic opposition developed to the behavior of American troops. Even in the Seminole War, there was a public hue and cry when it was learned that the Army was using bloodhounds to track down the Indians.

A major problem faced by American forces in each of the conflicts was collecting intelligence about the adversary and trying to locate the enemy forces. It was perhaps less difficult in the Filipino conflict and against the Moros. The Moros, for example, would eventually make a last stand in their cottas, which could be located rather easily by American forces, although the battles to overrun these Moro forts were usually difficult and deadly. Even in Vietnam, much of the initial intelligence was gained from South Vietnamese sources. Ten years after the war, there was still a great deal of debate about the accuracy and effectiveness of American intelligence in the Vietnam conflict.

The conflict area generally favored the revolutionaries. American forces operating in Florida, for example, were faced with an enemy and a climate and terrain for which they were not prepared. Indeed, they never fully overcame the harshness of the climate and the elusiveness of the enemy. The same holds true with respect to the expedition into Mexico. In the Filipino revolution, the elusiveness of the enemy and the climate were not as foreboding compared to the tactics used by the adversary. In Vietnam, the climate, terrain, and enemy tactics always played a major role in the ability of American forces to react effectively. The use of helicopters overcame much of the difficulty, but in many instances the nature of the war and the involvement of the populace counterbalanced the advantage of American mobility.

American forces, in the main, had overwhelming numbers and superior firepower, and were supported by a reasonably effective administrative and logistical system. Over 10,000 American troops were used to try to defeat the Seminoles, which rarely numbered over 500. In the Philippine and Moro revolutions American forces reached around 75,000. Following the defeat of the Filipino national Army, the American forces were usually able to bring to bear far superior forces. During the Moro phase, Americans were rarely faced with more than 500 to 600 Moros. In Mexico 10,000 American troops were pitted against Villa and his band which rarely numbered over 450. In Vietnam, there were over 500,000 Americans and well over 1 million South Vietnamese military facing about 300,000 of the adversary, at any given time (according to the best available estimates—although today these estimates are being questioned by a variety of people). In every instance the counterrevolutionary forces had overall superiority of firepower and manpower. This was not necessarily the case in specific battles, since the revolutionaries could normally choose the time and place of battle, bringing to bear a superior force, albeit only for a short time. But the essence of manpower was not in the superiority of numbers by the counterrevolutionaries, but in the ability of the revolutionaries to mobilize superior numbers at any given moment. To counter such tactics, counterrevolutionaries usually had to amass an overwhelming number of forces, since they had to be in place or readily available in a variety of locations around the country. Some historians argue that successful counterrevolution requires a ratio of 10 to 1. If this is so, the combined American and South Vietnamese forces had to reach 3 million, for example, if a reasonably successful counterrevolutionary effort was to be undertaken. What made this situation even more difficult was that many Americans could not understand why the American and South Vietnamese forces with their overwhelming numbers could not defeat lesser numbers of the enemy.

Most Americans did not understand the real nature of the conflict, however. The fact that the conflict was asymmetrical and involved a revolutionary/counterrevolutionary environment meant that the center of gravity of the war shifted from the battlefield to the political-psychological arena of the political system. In the main, the revolutionary struggle was against American intrusion. Even in Mexico, the chase to find Villa was soon linked to the American affront to Mexican sovereignty and the Mexican people. In sum, while military forces played an important part in the conflict, the final outcome was very probably a result of the political-psychological fortunes of the protagonists rather than battles won or lost.

Long forgotten were the Seminole Wars in Florida, where conventional military maneuvering and traditional professional perspectives proved inadequate. Forgotten too were the unconventional and bitter struggles in the Philippines, against not only the nationalists but also the Moros. The lessons of the Punitive Expedition into Mexico, though not forgotten, were distorted and transformed into a rehearsal for World War I; the political-social implications of the kind of war fought by Pancho Villa, the Carranzistas, and the Mexican people against Pershing's forces were completely ignored. Faced with similar situations in the post-World War II period, the American military responded as it had in all unconventional wars: it relied on its experience in conventional wars, detaching itself from the more crucial political-social issues which in the final analysis determined the outcome of such wars.

Compounding the problem for the American military was its lack of understanding of revolution and counterrevolution. Those in the military who did understand such wars found it difficult to translate this understanding into American military doctrine. The persistence of a European war orientation and conventional posture, reinforced by traditional views of military professionalism, limited and constrained serious strategic and tactical analyses of counterrevolutionary warfare.

Finally, it seems clear that American forces, for a variety of reasons noted here, were not well prepared to engage in counterrevolutionary struggles. While American forces usually performed well in actual combat, the final outcome of the conflict was linked to how well the American people and those in the revolutionary area responded to the political-psychological issues of the conflict. And it is in this area that American forces were least effective.

NOTES

1. M. M. Cohen, *Notices of Florida and the Campaigns* (Gainesville: University of Florida Press, 1964), p. 145. (A facsimile reproduction of the 1836 edition.)
2. Ibid., p. 222.
3. Clay MacCauley, "Letter of Transmittal, June 24, 1884, to Major J. W. Power," *Fifth Annual Report of the Bureau of Ethnology to the Secretary of the Smithsonian Institution, 1883–1884* (Washington, D.C.: U.S. Government Printing Office, 1887), p. 475.
4. Maurice Matloff, *American Military History* (Washington, D.C.: Office of the Chief of Military History, U.S. Army, 1968), pp. 136–137.
5. John K. Mahon, *History of the Second Seminole War, 1835–1842* (Gainesville: University of Florida Press, 1967), p. 8.
6. Ibid., p. 10.
7. Ibid., p. 14.
8. Cohen, *Notices of Florida*, p. 31.
9. Mahon, *History of the Second Seminole War*, p. 2.
10. The Second Seminole War probably began in the middle of December 1835. Osceola and 80 warriors raided a supply train of wagons under the protection of 30 mounted militia, near the town of Micanopy. The militia withdrew

with eight killed and six wounded, allowing Osceola to plunder the wagons. Less than a week later the Dade massacre occurred. See Virginia Bergman Peters, *The Florida Wars* (Hamden, Conn.: Archon Books, 1979), p. 105.

11. Cohen, *Notices of Florida*, p. 70.

12. Mahon, *History of the Second Seminole War*, p. 106. One of the better accounts of the relationship between the Seminoles and runaway slaves is Daniel F. Littlefield, Jr., *Africans and Seminoles; From Removal to Emancipation* (Westport, Conn.: Greenwood Press, 1977), particularly chapters 1–4.

13. Ibid., p. 125.

14. Ibid., p. 113.

15. Ibid., p. 128.

16. See Mahon, *History of the Second Seminole War*, pp. 227–230, for an account of the battle.

17. Russell F. Weigley, *History of the United States Army* (New York: Macmillan, 1967), p. 160.

18. Ibid., p. 162.

19. Ibid.

20. Mahon, *History of the Second Seminole War*, p. 306.

21. Ibid., p. 322.

22. Ibid., pp. 121–122.

23. Matloff, *American Military History*, p. 161. See also Mahon, *History of the Second Seminole War*, p. 55.

24. John Tebbel and Keith Jennison, *The American Indian Wars* (New York: Harper and Brothers, 1960), p. 219.

25. Weigley, *History of the United States Army*, p. 161.

26. Richard Goldhurst, *Pipe Clay and Drill: John J. Pershing: The Classic American Soldier* (New York: Reader's Digest Press, 1977), p. 101.

27. Richard E. Welch, Jr., *Response to Imperialism: The United States and the Philippine-American War, 1899–1902* (Chapel Hill: University of North Carolina Press, 1979), pp. 32–34.

28. William Thaddeus Sexton, *Soldiers in the Sun: An Adventure in Imperialism* (Freeport, N.Y.: Books for Libraries Press, 1939), p. 79.

29. Ibid., p. 108.

30. Leon Wolff, *Little Brown Brother: How the United States Purchased and Pacified the Philippine Islands at the Century's Turn* (New York: Doubleday, 1961), p. 240.

31. Ibid., p. 289.

32. Uldarico S. Baclagon, *Philippine Campaigns* (Manila: Graphic House, 1952), p. 122. I wish to thank Exequiel R. Sevilla, Jr., a former American Army officer and now a practicing attorney, for bringing this publication to the attention of the author.

33. Sexton, *Soldiers in the Sun*, p. 238.

34. Ibid., p. 121.

35. Wolff, *Little Brown Brother*, p. 241.

36. Ibid.

37. Baclagon, *Philippine Campaigns*, p. 123. See also Welch, *Response to Imperialism*, pp. 33–34.

38. Welch, *Response to Imperialism*, p. 34.

39. Ibid., p. 36.

40. Ibid., p. 166 n. 21.

41. Ibid., p. 32. For a detailed study of this issue see Richard Shelly Hartigan. *Lieber's Code and the Law of War* (South Holland, Ill.: Precedent Publishing, 1983).

42. Baclagon, *Philippine Campaigns*, p. 122.

43. Welch, *Response to Imperialism*, p. 32.

44. Ibid., p. 293.

45. Ibid., p. 289.

46. Ibid., p. 280.

47. Ibid., p. 253.

48. Ibid. For a Philippine perspective, see Renato Constantino with Letizia R. Constantino, *A History of the Philippines: From the Spanish Colonization to the Second World War* (New York: Monthly Review Press, 1975), pp. 231–249.

49. Welch, *Response to Imperialism*, p. 318.

50. Ibid., pp. 317–318.

51. Ibid., p. 318.

52. Ibid., p. 255.

53. Ibid., p. 347.

54. Ibid. For an interpretation of the events surrounding the capture of Aguinaldo from a Philippine perspective, see Usha Mahajami, *Philippine Nationalism; External Challenge and Filipino Response, 1565–1946* (St. Lucia, Queensland: University of Queensland, 1971), pp. 186–187.

55. Constantino, *History of the Philippines*, pp. 250–251.

56. Ibid., p. 280.

57. Ibid., p. 293.

58. Sexton, *Soldiers in the Sun*, pp. 270–271.

59. Ibid., p. 273.

60. Ibid.

61. See, for example, Welch, *Response to Imperialism*, pp. 40–41. For an in-depth analysis of the massacre and its aftermath, see Joseph L. Schott, *The Ordeal of Samar; Above and Beyond* (Indianapolis: Bobbs-Merrill, 1964).

62. Goldhurst, *Pipe Clay and Drill*, p. 101.

63. Wolff, *Little Brown Brother*, p. 363.

64. Goldhurst, *Pipe Clay and Drill*, p. 143.

65. William Addleman Ganoe, *The History of the United States Army* (New York: D. Appleton-Century, 1942), p. 416.

66. Henry F. Graff (ed.), *American Imperialism and the Philippine Insurrection* (Boston: Little Brown, 1969), p. xiv.

67. As quoted in Richard O'Connor, *Black Jack Pershing* (Garden City, N.Y.: Doubleday, 1961), p. 37.

68. Wolff, *Little Brown Brother*, p. 317.

69. Ibid., p. 347.

70. Donald Smythe, *Guerrilla Warrior, The Early Life of John J. Pershing* (New York: Scribner's, 1973), p. 81.

71. O'Connor, *Black Jack Pershing*, p. 56.

72. Haldeen Braddy, *Pershing's Mission in Mexico* (El Paso: Texas Western Press, 1966), p. 13.

73. Ganoe, *History of the United States Army*, p. 424.

74. As quoted in O'Connor, *Black Jack Pershing*, pp. 54–55.

75. Smythe, *Guerrilla Warrior*, p. 92.

76. Braddy, *Pershing's Mission*, p. 38.

77. See Goldhurst, *Pipe Clay and Drill*, pp. 220–226, for a detailed account of the battle. See also Smythe, *Guerrilla Warrior*, p. 273.

78. O'Connor, *Black Jack Pershing*, p. 100.

79. Goldhurst, *Pipe Clay and Drill*, p. 167.

80. Julius W. Pratt, *A History of United States Foreign Policy* (Englewood Cliffs, N.J.: Prentice-Hall, 1960), p. 431.

81. Ibid., pp. 428–429.

82. Ibid., p. 429.

83. Smythe, *Guerrilla Warrior*, p. 218.

84. Ibid., p. 218. See also Haldeen Braddy, *Pershing's Mission*, pp. 3–5.

85. Louis M. Teitelbaum, *Woodrow Wilson and the Mexican Revolution (1913–1916): A History of United States-Mexican Relations* (New York: Exposition Press, 1967), pp. 321–322.

86. Ronald Atkin, *Revolution! Mexico 1910–1920* (New York: John Day Co., 1970), p. 280.

87. Ibid., p. 239.

88. Clarence C. Clendenen, *Blood on the Border: The United States Army and the Mexican Irregulars* (New York: Macmillan, 1966), p. 230.

89. Ganoe, *History of the United States Army*, p. 460.

90. Atkin, *Revolution!*, p. 280.

91. See, for example, Ganoe, *History of the United States Army*, p. 454 and Braddy, *Pershing's Mission*, p. 9.

92. Clendenen, *Blood on the Border*, p. 232.

93. Braddy, *Pershing's Mission*, p. 13.

94. Ibid., p. 16.

95. Goldhurst, *Pipe Clay and Drill*, p. 200.

96. Clendenen, *Blood on the Border*, p. 240.

97. Atkin, *Revolution!*, p. 284.

98. Braddy, *Pershing's Mission*, p. 18.

99. Goldhurst, *Pipe Clay and Drill*, p. 210.

100. Clendenen, *Blood on the Border*, p. 259.

101. Ibid., p. 266.

102. Braddy, *Pershing's Mission*, p. 38.

103. Goldhurst, *Pipe Clay and Drill*, p. 225. See also Braddy, *Pershing's Mission*, p. 55.

104. Clendenen, *Blood on the Border*, p. 273.

105. Atkin, *Revolution!*, p. 289.

106. Ibid., p. 340.

107. For example, Braddy notes that "There are certain parallels between the expedition against Villa and the war in South Viet Nam. Villa employed the same tactics of scattering and concentrating, using the countryside of his native Chihuahua with its mountain hideouts, its opportunities for ambush, as a topographical ally. General Pershing was hedged in, also by political and diplomatic considerations" (p. xiii).

108. Ibid., p. 292.

109. O'Connor, *Black Jack Pershing*, p. 122.

110. Goldhurst, *Pipe Clay and Drill*, pp. 235–236.

111. George M. Kahin and John W. Lewis, *The United States in Vietnam*, revised ed. (New York: Dell Publishing Co., 1969), pp. 405–406.

112. Historically, Vietnam's three major areas had been identified as Tonkin, Annam, and CochinChina. The French colonial regime had a greater impact on CochinChina than on other regions.

113. U.S. Senate Committee on Foreign Relations, "Background Information Relating to Southeast Asia and Vietnam" (5th revised ed.), March 1969, pp. 76–77. Hereafter referred to as Committee Report on Southeast Asia.

114. Ibid., p. 78.

115. See, for example, Bernard Fall, *Street Without Joy: From the Indo-China War to the War in Viet-Nam*, revised ed. (Harrisburg, Pa.: Stackpole Co., 1971); Jules Roy, *The Battle of Dienbienphu* (New York: Harper and Row, 1965); and Vo Nguyen Giap, *Peoples War, Peoples Army* (New York: Praeger, 1962).

116. Bernard B. Fall, *Hell in a Very Small Place; The Siege of Dien Bien Phu* (New York: Vintage Books, 1966), p. 432.

117. See, for example, Chalmers Roberts, "The Day We Didn't Go to War," *The Reporter*, September 14, 1954, pp. 31–35.

118. Matthew B. Ridgway, *Soldier: The Memoirs of Matthew B. Ridgway* (New York: Harper & Brothers, 1956), pp. 277–278.

119. There exists a significant amount of controversy regarding the implications of the Geneva Agreements. The Agreements consisted of two parts, one signed and the other unsigned. The "Agreement on the Cessation of Hostilities in Viet-Nam, July 20, 1954" was signed by the vice-minister of national defense of the Democratic Republic of Viet-Nam and Brigadier General Delteil, for the commander in chief of the French Union Forces in Indo-China. The Final Declaration of Geneva Conference, July 21, 1954, was an unsigned document providing for elections and designating the basis for a final political solution.

120. Kahin and Lewis, *United States in Vietnam*, pp. 456–457.

121. Diem was appointed prime minister by Emperor Bao Dai while the Geneva Conference was in progress. Because of Bao Dai's association with the French, he was badly discredited as far as being leader of an independent South Vietnam was concerned. In 1955 Diem organized a referendum asking the South Vietnamese to choose between him and Bao Dai as chief of state. Although Diem won in an election that appeared rigged, most observers felt that he could have won in any fair election anyway.

122. "America's Stake in Vietnam," American Friends of Vietnam, September 1956, pp. 8–14. As quoted in Wesley R. Fishel (ed.), *Vietnam, Anatomy of a Conflict* (Itasca, Ill.: Peacock Publishers, 1968), pp. 144–148.

123. As quoted in Fishel, *Vietnam*, p. 141.

124. Committee Report on Southeast Asia, p. 122.

125. Jean Lacoutre, *Vietnam: Between Two Truces* (New York: Random House, 1966), p. 28.

126. Joseph Buttinger, *Vietnam: A Dragon Embattled* (New York: Praeger, 1967), 2 vols., p. 978.

127. Kahin and Lewis, *United States in Vietnam*, pp. 108–109. There was some disagreement concerning the impact of the Anti-Communist Denunciation Campaign and of Diem's refusal to conduct elections in 1956. Kahin and Lewis

suggest that Diem's Anti-Communist campaign was so effective that the Communist cadres were decimated and many leaders were lost. As a result, there was an apparent lull in activity against the South following Diem's refusal to hold elections. This is in sharp contrast to Fall's contention and data which reveal that the Communists had embarked on a rather massive plan of assassination and intimidation in 1957–58. Based on an analysis of the strategy of the Northern leaders, the political preparation phase was being implemented in the South combined with small-scale military activity in the form of assassination, sabotage, and intimidation of the populace.

128. Hoang Quoc Viet, et al., "Vietnam Fatherland Front and the Struggle for National Unity," Hanoi, 1956, pp. 6–14.

129. Bernard B. Fall, *Viet-Nam Witness* (New York: Praeger, 1966), p. 283.

130. Thoi-Luan, December 15, as quoted in Fall, *Viet-Nam Witness*, p. 185.

131. As quoted in Fall, *Viet-Nam Witness*, pp. 85–86.

132. Bernard B. Fall, *The Two Viet-Nams: A Political and Military Analysis*, 2d revised ed. (New York: Praeger, 1967), p. 370.

133. Robert Shaplen, *The Lost Revolution: The U.S. in Vietnam, 1946–1966* (New York: Harper Colophon Books, 1966), p. 140.

134. Philippe Devillers, "The Struggle for the Unification of Vietnam," *The China Quarterly*, No. 9 (January-March, 1962): 14–16.

135. "Repression in the South: Law 10/59" as quoted in Marvin E. Gettlemen (ed.), *Vietnam: History, Documents, and Opinions on a Major World Crisis*, (New York: New American Library, 1965), pp. 256–260.

136. Devillers, "Struggle for the Unification," p. 14.

137. Special Report on the VC/NVA Effort in South Vietnam Since 1954, MACV Saigon, 1967, p. 33, unpublished.

138. Paul M. Kattenburg, *The Vietnam Trauma in American Foreign Policy, 1945–75* (New Brunswick, N.J.: Transaction Books, 1980), p. 209.

139. Buttinger, *Vietnam*, Vol. 2, pp. 998–1001.

140. Ibid., p. 1001. For the reaction of the Kennedy Administration, see Roger Hilsman, *To Move a Nation* (New York: A Delta Book, 1967), pp. 514–523.

141. The new constitution which went into effect in April 1967 provided for a popularly elected president and bicameral legislature. The National Assembly, consisting of an upper house (Senate) of 60 and a lower house of 137 representatives, was to be the supreme lawmaking body in South Vietnam. The real power, however, remained with the military.

142. In June 1970 the U.S. Senate repealed the Gulf of Tonkin Resolution. For the text of the Resolution, see Kahin and Lewis, *United States in Vietnam*, p. 477.

143. See, for example, Townsend Hoopes, *The Limits of Intervention* (New York: David McKay, 1969).

144. See, for example, Robert Shaplen, *Time Out of Hand* (New York: Harper and Row, 1969).

145. John Spanier, *American Foreign Policy Since World War II* (New York: Holt, Rinehart and Winston, 1980), p. 149.

146. Major Robert A. Doughty, *Leavenworth Papers: The Evolution of U.S. Army Tactical Doctrine, 1946–76* (Fort Leavenworth, Kans.: Combat Studies Institute, U.S. Army Command and General Staff College, August 1979), p. 32.

147. S.L.A. Marshall, *Vietnam, Three Battles* (New York: Da Capo Press, 1971),

p. 3. Previously published as *The Fields of Bamboo* in 1971, Marshall's account of three battles in 1966 is an excellent portrayal of the kinds of struggles that took place in Vietnam. The futility and frustration are poignantly described in the final pages of the chapter, "By Way of Postlude."

148. John A. Cash, "Fight at Ia Drang, 14–16 November, 1965," in John Albright, John A. Cash, and Allan W. Sandstrum (eds.), *Seven Firefights in Vietnam* (Washington, D.C.: Office of the Chief of Military History, U.S. Army, 1970), p. 3.

149. Ibid., p. 16.

150. Ibid., p. 28.

151. Ibid., p. 40.

152. John Albright, "Convoy Ambush on Highway 1, 21 November 1966," in Albright, Cash, and Sandstrum, (eds.), *Seven Firefights in Vietnam*, p. 41.

153. Ibid., p. 43.

154. Ibid., pp. 57–58.

155. Marshall, *Vietnam, Three Battles*, p. 4.

156. Sam C. Sarkesian, "Viet Nam and the Professional Military," *Orbis* 18, No. 1 (Spring 1974): 255.

157. Jonathan Schell, *The Military Half* (New York: Alfred A. Knopf, 1968), p. 42.

158. See, for example, Michael Herr, *Dispatches* (New York: Avon Books, 1978). See also Allan R. Millett, *Semper Fidelis; The History of the United States Marine Corps* (New York: The Free Press, 1982), pp. 559–606.

159. Ibid., p. 87.

160. One of the best accounts of Special Forces operations in Vietnam is Colonel Francis J. Kelly, *Vietnam Studies: U.S. Army Special Forces, 1961–1971* (Washington, D.C.: U.S. Department of the Army, 1973). See also David J. Baratto, "Special Forces in the 1980s: A Strategic Reorientation," *Military Review*, vol. LXIII, March, 1983, No. 3, pp. 2–14.

161. Ibid., p. 172.

162. As quoted in Harry G. Summers, Jr., Colonel, U.S. Army, *On Strategy: The Vietnam War in Context* (Carlisle Barracks, Pa.: U.S. Army War College, 1981), p. 1.

5

Conclusions and Guidelines for American Policy

While a considerable amount of caution must be exercised in drawing conclusions and generalizations from this study, it is clear that certain guidelines emerge regarding America's role as a counterrevolutionary power. The conclusions presented at the end of each chapter are the bases for these formulations. Although there are differences between the various periods of history covered by the cases studied here and there is danger in forcing historical analogies as well as in designing cause-and-effect relationships, the similarities in the interrelationships among the theoretical components in this study are compelling enough to design guidelines and formulate future directions of American counterrevolutionary policy.

Russell F. Weigley has commented on the U.S. handling of guerrilla warfare with respect to the Seminole War:

A historical pattern was beginning to work itself out: occasionally the American Army has had to wage guerrilla war, but guerrilla warfare is so incongruous to the natural methods and habits of a stable and well-to-do society that the American Army has tended to regard it as abnormal and to forget about it whenever possible. Each new experience with irregular warfare has required, then, that appropriate techniques be learned all over.[1]

How can such historical experiences be translated into strategy and operational doctrines for the future? In light of the low intensity conflicts that are likely to characterize the immediate future, it is important to design guidelines to respond to such conflicts. But these must incorporate the lessons of the past, without necessarily being bound by inappropriate historical analogies. Before we begin to answer the question, there is a need to review the post-World War II period and the concept of "low-intensity" conflicts ranging from surgical-type commando operations to revolution and counterrevolution. The term "special operations" has also emerged from the dustbins of the 1960s.

AMERICAN NATIONAL SECURITY: AN OVERVIEW

Since the end of World War II, American national security policy has been based on a combination of containment and deterrence. While various means have been used to carry out this strategy, the fundamental posture has been based on a balanced military force and nuclear arms. Following the acquisition of nuclear weapons by the Soviet Union and its increasing ability to match American military strength, American national security strategy shifted from nuclear superiority to nuclear equivalency and to a "balance of terror." Much of the American effort was concentrated on Europe and NATO, since the greatest part of the Soviet military threat appeared to be directed against Europe and the United States.

Over the past thirty years therefore, the American military has in the main concerned itself with conventionally postured military forces equipped with nuclear weapons, following a strategy in which massive military forces would be used to deter the Soviet Union. In the course of these 30 years, power positions have changed from American superiority to a relative balance between the United States and the USSR. But equally important, the Soviet Union has developed a highly capable Navy, one that can now roam the oceans, and a military that has developed into a relatively effective instrument for projecting military power to various parts of the globe.

The onset of the Cold War, the rise of the Soviet Union as a superpower, and the power projections by the Soviet Union and others to erode the positions of the United States and the Western Allies ushered in a condition of no war, no peace. In other words, America had to maintain military strength, if for no other reason than to insure that no major wars would occur. It was a condition that Americans had not confronted any time in their history.

It was not all "no war," however. America had been involved to a certain degree in the struggle of the Greek state against Communist insurrection, and with the Philippines against the Huks, and from the sidelines had seen what the French had encountered in Indochina. Americans were to experience at first hand the meaning of limited war when they entered the Korean conflict. Nonetheless, all of these political-military operations were viewed in terms of American perceptions of the world and from the point of view of a military system that was focused on Europe. In brief, Americans did not seriously become involved in unconventional wars during the post-World War II period until Vietnam. And it was in Vietnam that Americans found that the conventional political-military posture would not suffice; at the same time, they were unwilling or incapable of doing those things necessary to "win" in South Vietnam.

The reasons for this situation are many, but there are two underlying causes: the way Americans viewed the world and their own cultural traditions; and the changed international security environment in the post-World War II period. In studying the first reason, we will briefly examine the values and expectations of Americans and how these determine the ways Americans view war. In examining the second reason, we will study how the international system has changed since the end of World War II, the changing nature of war, and how these have affected American national security.

AMERICAN PERSPECTIVES

American Cultural Traditions

From the beginning of the American nation, most Americans have felt that there is a moral basis to democracy. This moral basis transcends both the legal structure of the system and national self-interest. Thus, Americans have felt, rightly or wrongly, that American policy needs to be morally good and ethically proper, seeking to do those things that are good for mankind. Without question there is a degree of arrogance in this view. Nonetheless, it is bound up in American traditions. Moreover, Americans have felt that the form of American democracy is a populous experiment that remains the vanguard of the democratic world.

This moral and self-righteous theme has been a difficult one to reconcile with the real world of international politics. This is particularly true with respect to our use of the military instrument which has normally been resorted to under the label of "making the world safe for democracy" or "punishing international criminals."

Closely linked with this world-view is the idea that democracy must rest on freedom, equality, and the dignity of the individual. "Individualism" has become an ingrained part of our political philosophy. In this respect, most Americans tend to judge their institutions and the political environment in terms of the moral and ethical criteria that foster freedom, equality, liberty, and a higher quality of life.

Throughout American history, the rise of populist movements, the broadening of the franchise, and the concern with quality of life have been reflections of the moral basis of democracy. Granted, rarely does the system work perfectly. At times in our history violent clashes occurred between those whose concern was focused on law and order and those whose concern was on the quality of life and the nature of individual freedom. Nevertheless, American democracy rests on the presumption that the system must work for the individual and reflect a humanistic sensitivity.

In this context, Americans also accept the idea that the military system, indeed all institutions, must reflect society. The values and norms of the military must be within the general guidelines of the American notions of democracy and must provide a sense of "individualism" within the military, with proper attention to freedom, liberty, and equality. Although these must be qualified by the demands of military discipline, the fact remains that their society expects an underlying thread of democracy within its military system.

While there have been a number of periods in American history where the military was isolated from society and developed a more authoritarian and disciplined structure, the post-World War II period moved the military and society closer together for a number of reasons. Throughout most of the post-World War II period, the American military was a mixed system. That is, it was made up of volunteers and those from selective service (draftees). In addition, many individuals entered the services as officers through ROTC programs. Thus, there has always been a constant flow of individuals into and out of the system—individuals who were primarily civilians but entered the military for a relatively short period of time to fulfill their obligations. In such circumstances, there is a constant dynamic interaction between civilian values and military demands. The military, therefore, rarely was isolated from civilian values, attitudes, and life-styles.

Elected officials at the national level also gave increasing attention to the military as the size of the defense budget increased and as international crises developed. The idea of civilian control and the fear of the so-called military industrial complex became a fixed feature of civil-military relations, and with it critical attention was paid to military behavior and practices.

Finally, the changing nature of the military profession, with its focus on technology and managership, broadened career patterns and established skills closely associated with civilian life.[2] Systems analysis, cost overruns, effective managership, mechanical skills, and, later, computer technology moved the center of gravity of the military profession from the traditional warrior view to a more modern technician-manager perspective.

While there were other changes, these illustrate the post-World War II patterns within the military and between society and the military. In any case, the result was the interpenetration of the military and society.

As much as the military penetrated civilian policy circles and life-styles, society penetrated domains that were heretofore exclusively those of the military. Thus, the values of society and the way civilians did business became intertwined with military practices, procedures, and norms.

One major result was that the military could not operate in a vacuum; its doctrine and operational patterns had to be in general accord with society's view of the military. Military men and women were constantly exposed to and socialized into a democratic perception of the world, with far-reaching implications in terms of war.

American Perceptions of War

American cultural traditions have been and are major determinants of how Americans view wars. Until the Vietnam War, Americans always presumed that their country's involvement in conflict had to be based on a moral good. American foreign policy has always been viewed as something that must reflect a moral and ethical purpose. Moreover, Americans felt that war itself was a deviation from normal behavior; most did not accept the view that war was a continuation of politics.[3]

Once Americans were provoked, however, and the United States had to resort to force, the employment of this force was justified in terms of the universal moral principles with which the United States, as a democratic country, identified itself. Resort to the evil instrument of war could be justified only by presuming noble purposes and completely destroying the immoral enemy who threatened the integrity, if not the existence, of these principles. American power had to be "righteous" power; only its full exercise could ensure salvation or the absolution of sin.[4]

Thus, for most Americans, war was entered into only after provocation, and then only with clear political goals in accord with democracy: "As American citizens we expect and desire that our own nation will involve itself in war only under rare circumstances of impelling need, and then only for political ends that are reasonably consistent with its basic political philosophy."[5]

Just as important, Americans expected the behavior of their military on the battlefield to be in general accord with democratic norms. American soldiers were expected to be the "good" guys, exhibiting gentlemanly and chivalrous behavior toward the enemy. While the enemy might use any means to achieve battlefield victory, American soldiers were expected to remain committed to moral and ethical practices.[6]

Underlying these attitudes, the American military as well as civilians perceived war in mainly traditional terms and in accordance with conventional combat. The battles of World War II or the grand battles of the Civil War remained underlying guidelines in preparing for combat. Tanks across the plains of Europe, squadrons of aircraft engaged in air-to-air battles, and aircraft carrier task forces sweeping the seas were part of the general perceptions of how wars would be fought even with nuclear weaponry.

Nothing in the American experience in World War II, Korea notwithstanding, was important enough to radically change this picture—at least until the Vietnam experience. But while Americans held these views, the international order—the security environment and the nature of war—was changing. Unfortunately, America's view of the international world remained fixed in the 1950s.

THE CHANGED INTERNATIONAL SECURITY ENVIRONMENT

The International Order

The United States and the Soviet Union emerged from World War II as superpowers. They had massive military systems, and they were the prime movers behind the defeat of the Axis. But, as we learned earlier, the presumption that the Allies would act in concert in peace as they had in war was quickly proven false. The Soviet Union did not demobilize after World War II, but used its military power as a political instrument, extending its influence throughout Eastern Europe and other parts of the world. By 1947 the United States had recognized that the Cold War had begun in earnest. It was soon recognized that the two superpowers reflected a polarization of the world into those allied with the United States and those allied with the Soviet Union.

At the same time, World War II brought the end of colonialism. By the middle of the 1950s peoples in Africa and Southeast Asia were either proclaiming their independence from colonial powers or were fighting against colonial powers for their independence. With this came a proliferation of nation-states, most of them evolving from the African and Asian colonial empires. The result was the collapse of the European-centered world order. This European order provided a sense of coherency and rationality to diplomacy and behavior of states (regardless of how one views the evils of colonialism). With its collapse, power was dissipated and decentralized throughout various parts of the world. The European view of diplomacy and order gave way to a variety of views of the world and relationships between nation-states. In addition, a number of political forces were unleashed based on nationalism and a drive for economic well-being.

The proliferation of nation-states brought with it an increasingly fragile stability, since most of the new states had yet to develop viable political systems and the necessary economic wherewithal. Independence brought with it a host of political, social, and economic problems. Many of these were the outgrowth of years of colonial rule. Indigenous elites that had gained power had not as yet developed the necessary infrastructure or ideological cohesion to establish reasonably stable political systems. Ethnic hatreds emerged, economic dissatisfaction spread, and social tensions increased. Many of these countries became ripe for revolution. A number of revolutions erupted in Southeast Asia and Africa. From the Mau Mau rebellion in Kenya to the Vietminh fight against the French in Indochina and the Algerian struggle against the French to the Cuban revolution under Castro, it seemed that every region in the world was infected with revolutionary forces.

The international order was also affected by the emergence of China as a major power under Communist rule, the establishment of a Marxist state in Cuba, and the continuing wars in the Middle East which constantly threatened to embroil the United States and the Soviet Union. These events, among others, not only added to the unstable world order, but they also confirmed the decline of the European-centered world order and showed the decreasing ability of the superpowers to maintain influence over world events.

Modern technology has also affected the international security environment. Nuclear weaponry, the sophisticated electronic technology, the increasing sophistication of implements of conventional war, and the availability of modern weapons throughout the world placed a premium on technological capability. For the United States, a great deal of attention is being given to high technology in both civilian and military spheres. High technology not only characterizes the modern industrial world, but has also become a criterion by which the capability of military systems is measured. This compels modern military systems to develop doctrines, organizations, training, and military professions, based on an ever-increasing resort to higher technology. Moreover, modern technology has made available a vast array of weaponry to most states. Even the most backward countries have access to modern implements of war. Similarly, dissident groups throughout the world have relatively easy access to such weapons. These developments increase world tensions as well as the ability of many states and groups to challenge the existing order.

One of the most important developments is the new political awareness of people throughout the globe; through the concepts of nationalism, they have placed a variety of political demands on existing systems and the international community. Combined with the breakdown of the colonial order, this has created a highly sensitive political-social envi-

ronment within most Third World countries. This environment has rejected any notion of European influence or of the attempt by major
powers to control events as had been the case prior to World War II.

A major result of these and other changes has been the breakdown
of the bipolar structure that evolved in the immediate post-World War
II period. Power has become dispersed and decentralized, with the emergence of a number of regional power centers and an increasing number
of states that have acquired nuclear weapons. The world, in a word,
seems to have developed into a chaotic, anarchic, and dangerous place.
Regional organizations and the United Nations appear incapable of dealing with these political and social tensions.

For the United States, these changes have had an important impact
on its ability to initiate policy and/or respond to the changing world
environment. Thus, while the United States continued to view the world
through a 1950 lens with its fixation on Europe, serious problems affecting American national interests developed in non-European areas.
As Michael Howard observes,

Most strategic scenarios today are based on the least probable of political circumstances—a totally unprovoked military assault by the Soviet Union, with
no shadow of political justification, on Western Europe . . . . It need hardly be
said that hostilities breaking out elsewhere in the world are likely, as they did
in Vietnam, to arise out of political situations involving an even greater degree
of political ambiguity, in which our readiness to initiate nuclear war would
appear even less credible.[7]

The Soviet Union was quick to recognize the possibilities of exploiting
tensions and instability in the Third World. The use of proxy forces and
surrogates by the Soviet Union revealed the extent of its planning and
strategy in non-European areas. Reinforced by their willingness to use
military forces in contiguous areas (Afghanistan) and the large number
of "Spetsnatz" forces, Soviet strategy is geared to indirectly challenge
U.S. and Western interests.[8]

Thus, while the United States remains fixed, more or less, on the
threats of the Soviet Union and the European environment, the tensions
of the world environment have shifted their centers of gravity to non-
European areas. To understand the implications of this change and its
consequences to American policy and military strategy, we need first to
examine the nature of conflicts in the post-World War II period.

The Nature of Conflicts and the Conflict Spectrum

Conflicts in the post-World War II period have occurred over a broad
range with varying degrees of intensity, that is, the struggles in the

Middle East, the revolution in El Salvador, the conventional war of the Falkland Islands (Malvinas), and even the incidents of international terrorism. The conflict range is best viewed on a spectrum representing the extremes in the intensity of conflict, with the low end encompassing military assistance and the high end, nuclear war. There is a large area between these extremes that includes middle-range contingencies associated with low-intensity conflict. (See Figure 1.) These cover a range of operations from the armed actions of a few individuals to conflicts short of Korean-type, limited, conventional wars.[9] Most of the conflicts in this middle range are revolutionary and/or counterrevolutionary of varying degrees of intensity. The higher level of low intensity follows a Vietnam pattern, while the lower end identifies revolutions and counterrevolutions similar to the pattern in El Salvador in the middle 1983 period.

Some conflicts are difficult to categorize in clear terms, that is, to distinguish them in low- or high-intensity categories. In Vietnam, for example, during several periods of the war, there were a number of conventional-type battles and some bordered on battles patterned after the Korean War. Similarly, in the Middle East, the Israeli invasion of Lebanon and its actions in Beirut are linked closely to the revolutionary nature of the conflict between the Israelis and the Palestinians. Most of the wars in the Middle East, however, and the Falkland Islands (Malvinas) War are in the limited, conventional war category.

Finally, the conflict spectrum as shown in Figure 1 is not intended to suggest that a clear delineation can be made between types of wars or their intensity. The figure is intended to show broad categories, while focusing on the general nature of each type of conflict. Moving from lower to higher does not preclude a combination of various types of wars. The reasons for this lie partly in American cultural traditions and perceptions of war, and the changed international order. The reasons also rest on the characteristics of low-intensity conflict—particularly conflicts in the middle-range category, that is, revolution and counterrevolution.

Characteristics of Low-Intensity Conflict

Low-intensity conflicts are most likely to occur in non-European areas. Moreover, a number of countries in which such conflicts are likely to occur have a special national security interest to the United States, for example, Central America. These countries also are in the process of modernization, with a number of political, social, and economic problems. Thus, there is an inherent instability associated with the modernization process that breeds revolutionary conflict.

First, low-intensity conflicts tend to be asymmetrical. For the revo-

Figure 1
The Conflict Spectrum

Employment of force: non-combat	*Surgical Opns.	*G.I	G.II	G.III	Vietnam Type	*Lim. Conv. War	*Gen. Conv. War	*Nuc. War

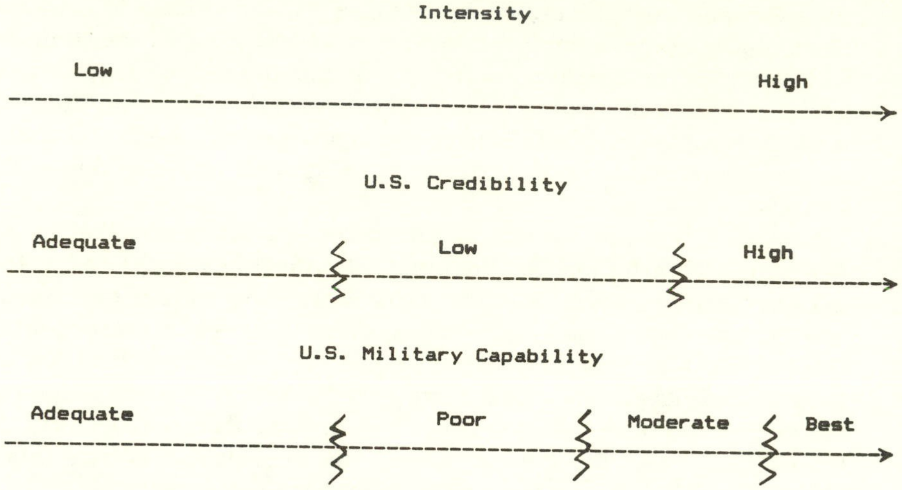

Intensity

Low   High
-->

U.S. Credibility

Adequate   ⌇   Low   ⌇   High
-----------------⌇---------------------⌇------------------------>

U.S. Military Capability

Adequate   ⌇   Poor   ⌇   Moderate   ⌇   Best
-----------------⌇-------------------⌇--------------⌇---------->

Legend

Surgical Opns.=Surgical Operations:Short duration, limited strikes
G.I =   Guerrilla I-Weapons Assistance Teams-Police Training-Advisory
         Teams
G.II =   Guerrilla II-Special Forces Teams-Cadrte for Indigenous Forces
         (Continuation of Guerrilla I)
G.III=   Guerrilla III- Integration of U.S. Combat Units with
         Indigenous Forces (Continuation of Guerrilla I and II)
All Guerrilla classifications include requisite economic assistance

Lim.Conv= Limited Conventional War
Gen.Conv= General Conventional War
Nuc. War= Nuclear War

Adopted from Sam C. Sarkesian, "American Policy and Low Intensity
Conflict: An Overview, " in Sam C.Sarkesian and William L.Scully,
eds., U.S. Policy and Low-Intensity Conflict: Potentials for Military
Struggles in the 1980s (New Brunswick, N.J.: Transaction Books,
1981),p.6.

lutionaries, the struggle is a total one—a struggle for survival. There is,
therefore, a psychological commitment that is enduring and directly
linked to the political-social goals of the revolution and in many instances
to the existence of the people. For the United States, however, such

conflicts are limited, not only in terms of resource commitment, but also in terms of political goals.

Second, low-intensity conflicts are ambiguous, in that it is difficult to separate and distinguish between friends and enemies. Moreover, the highly political-social complexity of the conflict shifts the center of gravity from the actual battlefield to the political-social system. The revolutionary appeal, many times, is more closely related to the moral and ethical principles of American democracy than those of the existing indigenous counterrevolutionary system. This leads to psychological and moral ambiguity in American policy and a lack of clear political goals. In turn, it is difficult in most instances to develop a consensus within the United States for concerted action as a counterrevolutionary force. It is also difficult to develop a clear political-military policy to respond as a counterrevolutionary force.

Third, such conflicts are most likely to be unconventional with political-psychological patterns underlying the purposes of combat.[10] As suggested earlier, the center of gravity of such conflicts is in the political-social system, and not necessarily in the actual battlefield. Given the nature of unconventional war in which combatants and noncombatants are not clearly distinguishable, it is difficult for American forces to conduct military operations with the purpose of finding and defeating the enemy. Trained and organized in conventional terms, the military operational code is oriented toward conventional-type battlefields. The criteria for measuring military operations are fixed in conventional terms, that is, casualties, real estate taken, and weapons captured. In low-intensity conflicts, these may not be meaningful measures in determining who is winning and who is losing. In other words, low-intensity conflicts are beyond the traditional battlefield.

Fourth, low-intensity conflicts usually develop into wars of attrition and are protracted. History shows that democracies have difficulty in reconciling themselves to casualties among their forces over a long period of time, with no measurable criteria for bringing the war to a successful conclusion, particularly in light of the other characteristics of low-intensity wars. It is difficult to maintain a consensus within the body politic to continue a war which has no clear political goals, is characterized by warfare that defies conventional response, and promises to be long and drawn out. The lack of political consensus can be quickly transferred into resistance against the conflict with a negative impact on the morale and effectiveness of American forces engaged in third country operations.

AMERICAN POLICY: CONSTRAINTS AND LIMITATIONS

Low-intensity conflicts create difficult and at times impossible conditions for the success of American political-military policy and for the effective use of the military instrument. The most serious problem is in developing a consensus for American involvement. For the success of American strategy in low-intensity conflicts, the American people must be convinced of its necessity, understand goals and purposes, and provide a continuing consensus on American political-military operations. In other words, there must exist a national will and political resolve to engage and persist in involvement in low-intensity conflicts. Given the characteristics of such conflicts this is a difficult proposition. The trauma of Vietnam, while dissipating, remains immediately below the surface. Even today, the disagreements and debates over the Vietnam memorial, for example, are rooted in the passions and violent disagreements over the Vietnam War. The generation that matured during the Vietnam War is now an important segment of our society penetrating the academic, business, and governmental fields. To presume that the American people have finally put Vietnam behind them is wishful thinking.[11]

The domestic turmoil, tensions, and confrontations evolving out of Vietnam are well known and need no restatement here. The point is that conflicts that have obscure purposes and questionable strategy, challenge moral and ethical norms, and provide no clear criteria for progress are likely to provoke dissent and resistance within democratic societies. The domestic reaction likely to be created by involvement in low-intensity conflicts spills over into the military, negatively affecting its combat effectiveness.[12]

One of the most difficult problems to resolve in terms of low-intensity wars is the American cultural experience. American soldiers socialized in a culture that stresses the importance of human life, the rights of individuals, and moral and ethical behavior patterns will find it extremely difficult to adapt to the foreign cultural environment and to the necessities of military operations responsive to counterrevolutionary requirements. The unconventional nature of low-intensity conflicts usually means that revolutionaries adopt any means to achieve political goals. Thus, political assassination, ambushes, hit and run raids, political and psychological intimidation, and the penetration of the existing political and social systems are the operational mode. Rarely do conventional battles occur or are there conventional measures for military success. The center of gravity shifts to the political-social-psychological arena, where there is rarely a distinction between combatants and noncombatants. There is no such thing as noncombatants in a revolutionary struggle. Such an environment, reminiscent of Vietnam, can easily lead to disillusion, frustration, combat stress without combat, and ultimately to decreasing combat effectiveness and moral disintegration.

American military formations are organized in conventional configurations that are designed to defeat an enemy similarly postured. Thus, the conventional "mind set" spurs conventional organizations and a traditional operational doctrine, even though the U.S. Army, for example, is experimenting with a new light infantry concept with the 9th Infantry Division, in weapons and doctrine. In addition, the formation of the 1st Special Operations Command may be the harbinger of more attention to low-intensity warfare. But the fact remains that organizational innovation and training remain closely wedded to conventional operations or those on the extremely low end of the low-intensity scale, for example, surgical operations or Rapid Deployment Forces type operations. Beneath all of the experimental and innovative layers rests a deep-seated layer of conventional thought and posturing. It seems at this point in time that American military forces organized and trained to fight in conventional operations are likely to be preparing for the wrong enemy in the wrong type of war.[13]

This is not to suggest that American military forces should not be prepared to fight the conventional fight or the high tech conflicts in space. In some instances, conventional forces may be useful in establishing security in counterrevolutionary situations in order to provide the opportunity for political-social-psychological counterrevolutionary efforts to be undertaken. The fact remains, however, that conflicts are most likely to break out in the Third World and to be of a low-intensity variety. Hence, the military must penetrate deeply into the political-social milieu of the populace engaged in revolution and counterrevolution. Moreover, as has been pointed out in this study, the political-military spheres become intermingled, complicating the role of the soldier and raising a host of problems, particularly for the military of a democratic system.

The first step in addressing these difficult problems is to resolve a conceptual problem, that is, the way American civilian and military policymakers and planners view low-intensity conflict. There is no current consensus on the meaning and concept of low intensity. At the same time there is a conceptual problem in dealing with revolutionary and counterrevolutionary wars—the most difficult and most likely conflicts in the decade of the 1980s. The published literature and the terminology employed within American planning circles confuse the concepts associated with revolutionary conflicts. Thus, there are a variety of terms floating around in the literature: wars of national liberation, protracted wars, unconventional war, guerrilla war, insurgency, counterinsurgency, revolution, counterrevolution, internal wars, and even civil war. Nonetheless, three concepts emerge as primary reference points: guerrilla war, insurgency, and revolution.

While some distinction can be made between guerrilla war, revolution, and insurgency, the conceptual ambiguity and semantic confusion between and within these terms obscure precise boundaries and preclude an operationally effective terminology. Faced with these various concepts, one is left with a feeling of frustration. On the one hand, there is intellectual utility at the highest level. On the other hand, it is difficult to apply these perspectives and methodological approaches because of the distinct peculiarities of individual revolutions. This latter criticism is particularly apt in dealing with revolutions in the post-1950 period.

Many use the term insurgency synonymously with guerrilla war and revolution. Insurgency is something more than guerrilla war and less than revolution. It combines armed struggle with political objectives. But political objectives do not include the overthrow of the existing system. More than likely the political objective is a very limited one and the armed struggle is linked specifically with that objective. Shays' Rebellion in Massachusetts, 1786–87, fits the general category of insurgency. Debt-stricken farmers, fearful of losing their land to taxation and bondholders, organized under the leadership of Daniel Shay, a former captain in the Continental Army. Shays' political program was based on tax relief and a moratorium on debts. The ragged army of farmers dispersed tax collectors and broke up court proceedings and sheriff's sales. The rebellion (insurrection) was defeated by an army of state militiamen. The Whiskey Rebellion of 1794 fits the same category. Farmers in western Pennsylvania refused to pay taxes on whiskey. They terrorized tax collectors and the situation threatened to erupt into serious violence. A militia army of 15,000 called up by Congress put down the rebellion without any bloodshed.

In broad terms, revolution is best viewed as the development of an alternative political system while using any means available, especially guerrilla war, to overthrow the existing system and establish a political order whose values, beliefs, and socioeconomic basis differ fundamentally from those in power in the existing system. Revolution encompasses both the political and armed conflict dimension. In this respect, guerrilla warfare is an appendage of the political structure.[14] The purpose of guerrilla warfare is to maintain constant pressure on the armed forces and political effectiveness of the existing system, not only to erode both its credibility and its legitimacy, but also to provide the necessary protection for the revolutionary political organization, allowing it to establish itself as a ruling system. Using this view of low-intensity conflict—revolution and counterrevolution—we can explore the character of a realistic American policy.

A REALISTIC AMERICAN COUNTERREVOLUTIONARY POLICY

In looking back on the history of American involvement in counterrevolution, one is struck by the unlearned lessons of forgotten wars, even though these kinds of wars are the most likely to occur in the foreseeable future. The 1983 conflicts in El Salvador, Nicaragua, Mozambique, and Afghanistan, for example, suggest that the future is now. In this respect, the continuing confrontation between the United States and the USSR must not prevent American civilian and military leaders from understanding the challenges in Third World areas. This means that the design of policies and strategies must evolve from historical insights and an understanding of the historical patterns and continuities of American counterrevolutionary policy.[15]

What may be considered a relatively new development from our past experience is the fact that opportunities have developed for the United States to intervene in support of revolutionaries. In 1983 a number of anti-Marxist revolutions emerged, for example, in Mozambique and Nicaragua, and continued in Afghanistan, providing a new and broader dimension of the revolution/counterrevolution intermix. While the opportunities for furthering American interests have expanded in this regard, so too have the dangers.

Finally, without some recognition of this revolutionary development and America's role, it is easy to fall into the trap (as some journalists and American leaders are prone to do) of presuming that American support of revolution as well as counterrevolution is contradictory. American interests dictate one or the other, or both. It may be in our interest, for example, to support the Afghanistan revolutionaries against the Soviet occupation. It may also be in our interest to support nationalist revolutionaries against the Marxist regime in Nicaragua. Yet, it may also be in our interest at the time of this writing to support the existing system in El Salvador against the revolutionaries. These are not contradictory policies but are dictated by the perceptions of our national interest.

While the study of American policy in support of revolutions is not within the scope of this study, it needs to be noted because of the relationship to counterrevolution. While revolution and counterrevolution are different sides of the same coin, they evolve from similar political-social dynamics and usually pit one section of the population against another. As was noted earlier in this study, counterrevolution is the handmaiden of revolution and usually is a reactive policy. For the intervening power, support of revolution means policy purposes quite different from counterrevolution. The training of individuals and units for revolution, for example, is quite different from the training for counterrevolution. Finally, support of revolutions is usually considered a covert operation and raises fears of nondemocratic activities. For these reasons and more, the study of revolution cannot be simply the reverse side of counterrevolution and vice-versa.

American counterrevolutionary policy appropriate for the modern period should incorporate historical experiences and patterns and be viewed in the context of the revolutionary dimensions in the 1980s. Following through with the purpose of this study, our primary concern is the question of American counterrevolutionary policy. What policy should be adopted? What can be done? What should be done?

The United States must develop a policy aimed at responding to low-intensity conflict for a number of reasons important to American national interests and in accord with the traditions of American concern for the evolution of stable, democratic systems. Few systems in developing areas have established themselves as democratic. On the one hand, to allow externally supported revolutionary systems to exploit the problems of modernization and political change may not be in the best interests of American security. On the other hand, American involvement as a counterrevolutionary force may be counterproductive to the goals of American policy. Counterrevolutionary involvement must be based on careful assessment of the political and social consequences of such involvement, and on careful reading of the direction and purpose of the existing government in the revolutionary/counterrevolutionary area. Even after careful assessment, American involvement in counterrevolution remains a gamble, even if a necessary one in many instances.

In this respect, a realistic policy must be based on the proper balancing and weighing of various elements of American political-military policy and designing a military strategy based on this assessment. There are at least seven factors to consider.

First, the concept of low-intensity conflicts must be explained clearly. Confusing terms, ambiguous definitions, and varying concepts perceived from different institutional settings not only prevent the development of a coherent policy, but also send ambiguous signals to potential enemies while distorting and diminishing America's military effort.[16]

Second, an existing system confronted with revolution must have the potential to develop into a reasonably representative system and must be sensitive to the causes of revolution if it is to have any chance of counterrevolutionary success. This applies both to the existing indigenous system and to the United States as an intervening power. For the United States it means that counterrevolutionary policy must be sophisticated enough to withhold support from repressive systems and yet support those systems that may be authoritarian in the short run but have the potential to develop into a representative one in the long run. This is not an easy proposition. Yet, unless such a posture is adopted, the United States will either find itself in a position of supporting *all* counterrevolutionary systems on the assumption that all revolutions are Communist-inspired, or not supporting *any* counterrevolutionary system on the assumption that democracy must first be established.

Third, counterrevolutionary policy does not necessarily mean that there must be a commitment of American troops or active confrontation with revolutionaries. Economic and military assistance, and low-visibility operations may suffice to reinforce the existing government. The existing system may already have demonstrated a capability to govern and may also have shown the potential to develop into an effective and reasonably representative form of government. With some assistance, it may develop the necessary wherewithal to develop into an effective system.

Fourth, active and visible involvement of American military personnel in counterrevolutionary campaigns will require the support of the American people. This is particularly true if such involvement is protracted. What history shows is that regardless of the attitude of the American people at the initiation of the American involvement, at some stage public opinion may seriously question the effectiveness of policy. To expect the military establishment to become seriously engaged in such policy without continuing public support is to expose it to internal criticism, domestic criticism, and decreased combat effectiveness.

Fifth, American cultural traditions and the premises of American democracy create the kind of military that may not be in the best position to deal with revolutionaries in an alien culture. Historical evidence suggests that revolution and counterrevolution hardly adhere to accepted laws of land warfare. Revolutionaries may use any method to achieve their political goals. To be effective, counterrevolutionaries may need some degree of freedom to operate against the unconventional tactics of the revolutionaries. Yet, the very nature of revolutionary and counterrevolutionary war creates combat conditions that may frequently compel American forces to go beyond democratic proprieties, paralleling the "My Lai" massacre in Vietnam.[17] A protracted and unconventional war can easily lead to a number of My Lai-type incidents. Nonetheless, the American military must maintain some level of moral and ethical behavior in counterrevolutionary wars if it is not to lose the support of the American people. This may mean considerable restraint in battle tactics and behavior, which in turn may have a demoralizing impact on American forces.

Sixth, American military and civilian planners and policymakers must develop a sense of history and keen analytical ability. This is not a purely intellectual exercise. There is a need to learn from history, analyze American involvement and the nature of low-intensity conflict, and translate these into strategy and operational doctrines. Without some sense of historical continuity, Americans are likely to relearn the lessons of history each time they are faced with a low-intensity conflict. But what is more dangerous is the fact that during the relearning process Americans may suffer casualties and develop policy directions that can only lead to defeat.

Finally, low-intensity conflict, particularly counterrevolutionary war, is perhaps the most difficult and frustrating conflict for any democratic system. Involvement in such conflicts cannot be undertaken lightly. For in the long run, they require a civilian policy dimension and military posture that are not bound by traditional mind sets and conventional organization and operations. Political resolve and national will in support of political-military policy must be persistent and enduring—supporting unorthodox and unconventional military operations.

The successful balancing of all of these elements can be done only if American civilian and military policymakers exhibit understanding, sophistication, and maturity regarding the complexities, ambiguities, and political-social dimensions of low-intensity conflict. In turn, this must be translated into a coherent American policy and military strategy, consistent with general democratic norms and understandable to the American public.

If there is any one lesson to be learned from America's counterrevolutionary history, it is that economic development and reasonably effective and just governing institutions and elites will provide the best preventive environment to revolution. In this sense, American policy needs to establish these as national objectives, keeping in mind that in the final analysis American national interests should dictate the overall strategy, even if such strategy necessitates support (hopefully temporary) to systems that are less than democratic. In brief, America appears committed to working through existing systems and with the governing elite. But this should not preclude taking political and economic measures to influence such governing elite to accept at the least some minimum standards of just rule and economic development that aims at the mass of the population.

Underlying all of these elements of American policy is the ends-means dilemma. Democratic norms are based on the notion that no matter how moral and just the ends, the means to carry out policy must be in accord with accepted democratic principles. In simple terms, the ends do not justify the means. Time and again, either directly or indirectly, the ends-means relationships were the underlying causes for American policy problems. From the use of bloodhounds against the Seminole Indians, the water cure in the Philippines, to the use of napalm and actions against civilians in Vietnam, the ends-means dilemma was a constant and often irreconcilable problem for Americans, affecting not only the state of the nation, but also its military posture.

On the one hand, democracy has a right to defend itself and in doing so should be able to employ the most effective and efficient means at its command. On the other hand, the means must be just and in accord with democratic norms. Thus, the best way to counter revolution may violate democratic principles. The means used within the constraints imposed by democracy may not lead to success in counterrevolutionary conflict. And it is the attempt to resolve this dilemma that may seem

too much for a democracy to pay for involvement in counterrevolutionary wars. Yet, not to become involved may in the long run prove more
costly.

NOTES

1. Russell F. Weigley, *History of the United States Army* (New York: Macmillan,
1967), p. 161.

2. See, for example, Kurt Lang, "Technology and Career Management in
the Military Establishment," in Morris Janowitz (ed.), *The New Military* (New
York: Russell Sage Foundation, 1964), p. 77. See also Morris Janowitz, *The Professional Soldier* (New York: Free Press, 1971).

3. The idea that war is a continuation of politics is a Clausewitzian formulation. See, for example, Anatol Rapoport (ed.), *Clausewitz on War* (Baltimore,
Md.: Pelican Books, 1968), p. 119.

4. John Spanier, *American Foreign Policy Since World War II*, 8th ed. (New
York: Holt, Rinehart, and Winston, 1980), pp. 9–10.

5. Bernard Brodie, *War and Politics* (New York: Macmillan, 1973), p. 5.

6. A recent example is *The Challenge of Peace: God's Promise and Our Response,
A Pastoral Letter on War and Peace* (Washington, D.C.: United States Catholic
Conference, May 3, 1983), especially pages 93–95. See also Sam C. Sarkesian,
"Moral and Ethical Foundations of Military Professionalism," in James Brown
and Michael J. Collins (eds.), *Military Ethics and Professionalism: A Collection of
Essays* (Washington, D.C.: National Defense University Press, 1981), pp. 1–22,
and Malham M. Wakin, "Ethics of Leadership," in Sam C. Sarkesian and Thomas
M. Gannon (eds.), *Military Ethics and Professionalism, American Behavioral Scientist*
19, No. 5 (May/June 1976): 573. See also footnote 17.

7. Michael Howard, "The Forgotten Dimensions of Strategy," *Foreign Affairs*
57, No. 5 (Summer 1979): 984.

8. Spetsnatz forces are Soviet "Special Purpose Forces" under the KGB. In
1982 it was estimated that such forces numbered about 200,000, with some
deployed in Afghanistan, Cuba, Nicaragua, and Angola.

9. See, for example, Sam C. Sarkesian, "American Policy and Low Intensity
Conflicts: An Overview," in Sam C. Sarkesian and William L. Scully (eds.),
Potentials for Military Struggles in the 1980s: U.S. Policy and Low Intensity Conflict
(New Brunswick, N.J.: Transaction Books, 1981), pp. 1–15.

10. See Sam C. Sarkesian, *Beyond the Battlefield: The New Military Professionalism*
(New York: Pergamon Press, 1981), pp. 75–87.

11. A number of recently published books provide added dimensions to the
debate on the Vietnam War. See, for example, Michael Maclear, *The Ten Thousand
Day War—Vietnam: 1945–1975* (New York: Avon Books, 1981) and Richard A.
Hunt and Richard H. Shultz, Jr., *Lessons from an Unconventional War: Reassessing
U.S. Strategies for Future Conflicts* (New York: Pergamon Press, 1982).

12. Harry G. Summers, Jr., *On Strategy: The Vietnam War in Context* (Carlisle
Barracks, Pa.: U.S. Army War College, 1981), p. 7.

13. Ibid., p. 1.

14. Bernard B. Fall, *Street Without Joy: Insurgency in Indochina, 1946–63*, 3d revised ed. (Harrisburg, Pa.: Stackpole Co., 1963), p. 356.

15. In a number of regions in the world that are of vital interest to the United States, low-intensity conflicts are likely to occur. See, for example, Frank N. Trager and William L. Scully, "Low Intensity Conflict: The U.S. Response," in Sarkesian and Scully, *Potentials for Military Struggles*, pp. 175–198. See also *Annual Report to Congress, Caspar W. Weinberger, Secretary of Defense, Fiscal Year 1983* (Washington, D.C.: U.S. Government Printing Office, February 8, 1982), pp. II–17 to II–26.

16. See, for example, John Dunn, *Modern Revolutions: An Introduction to the Analysis of a Political Phenomenon* (London: Cambridge University Press, 1972), pp. 1–23.

17. See William R. Peers, *The My Lai Inquiry* (New York: Norton, 1978) and Joseph Goldstein, Burke Marshall, and Jack Schwartz, *The My Lai Massacre and Its Cover-Up: Beyond the Reach of Law? The Peers Commission Report* (New York: Free Press, 1976).

Postscript: A Personal View

In studying historical periods and phenomena, one can leisurely assess, contemplate, and conclude in the comfort and quiet of a scholarly environment. Not caught up in the events of the moment or the stresses and tensions of the period, it is relatively easy to judge the wisdom or lack of it by decisionmakers and movers of history. Such wisdom in hindsight appears to be the nature of much of the work now being done on the American involvement in Vietnam, for example.

There is a need to assess and reassess periods such as the American-Vietnam War. But there is also a responsibility to avoid distortions and misrepresentations by acknowledging the fact that the times were different and those involved in making decisions were caught up in day-to-day events and pressures that in many cases precluded the careful intellectual and operational assessments engaged in years after the event. It is one thing to be able to discern events, separate and analyze cause-and-effect relationships, and formulate proper policy when one is not responsible for the implementation or the consequences of policy, and another thing to be on the "hot seat" knowing that one must make policy and be held responsible for its impact. It is also important to acknowledge that those studying the past can rarely capture the mood and tone of the period in question. This study was undertaken recognizing all of these difficulties. And it is understood that one can rarely escape from his own prejudices and biases, regardless of the effort at objectivity.

The study concluded here reveals that for the United States to have a reasonable chance of success in low-intensity conflicts (revolutionary and counterrevolutionary) in the future, it must focus on the "essence" of such wars. These are rooted in political-social and psychological structures, processes, and interactions. Battles in the pattern of World War II, Korea, or the Falkland (Malvinas) Islands War are not usually major characteristics of low-intensity conflicts.

Western military systems tend to be wedded to the Clausewitzian notion that the center of gravity of wars is the defeat and destruction of the enemy's armed forces.[1] But the true nature of revolution and counterrevolution is more consonant with Sun Tzu's views: "For to win one hundred victories in one hundred battles is not the acme of skill. To subdue the enemy without fighting is the acme of skill."[2] This is not to suggest that armed conflict is not an important part of revolution and counterrevolution. But it is not the *only* part, and in *most* instances it is not the *most* important part. Armed conflict is usually an appendage of the political conflict that is being waged within the political-social milieu of the indigenous system. Thus, political organizers and cadres are more important than battlefield fighters. For the real issue is what political system shall rule, the revolutionary or counterrevolutionary system? As history has shown, in these conflicts those with the biggest battalions, most weapons, and most manpower are not necessarily those that "win." In the Vietnam War, for example, although the Tet Offensive in 1968 was a disastrous military defeat for the Vietcong, it was a major political-psychological victory for them for the very reason that it focused on the political-social milieu and the psychology of the conflict.

In this respect, the revolution has its own morality and ethics. Rarely do these conform to Judeo-Christian norms or those of democracy as interpreted by the United States. The end goal, the success of the revolution, is the ultimate morality. All other things are subordinated to this purpose. Ethics and conflict behavior are guided by this ultimate morality. Thus, American forces operating in such an environment are placed in a difficult moral and ethical position. Committed to Judeo-Christian values and to democratic imperatives, they are at a serious disadvantage in engaging in the type of operations that are likely to provide the best opportunity for "success." Success is made more elusive by the fact that the majority of American political actors tend to view all conflicts through conventional lenses. Thus, it is difficult to change "mind sets" from battlefield victories to the nuances and subtleties of political-psychological battles, or to the terror and fear tactics aimed at the populace.

In this light, U.S. involvement in revolutionary/counterrevolutionary conflict is likely to pose serious policy and operational questions, particularly if American forces become directly involved in the conflict area (assuming a "visible" American presence). Before this policy is adopted, therefore, civilian and military policymakers must analyze American posture, interests, and society to insure a realistic grasp of the costs and consequences of such involvement. They must also determine whether the United States should be or is willing to pay the costs. The costs may be too much to ask of any democratic system, unless it is clear to most of the people that the threat is immediate, serious, and a challenge to the nation itself. The most prudent policy may be to provide adequate economic assistance and military aid short of American "presence" to those states that are in obviously critical areas or have a high potential for revolution. All of this must be tempered by the notion that some revolutions may be true nationalist revolutions against oppressive regimes and deserve American support, and some counterrevolutionary systems may be worth supporting because of their potential for reasonably effective civilian rule. Furthermore, it ought to be recognized that there are few democratic systems or democratic revolutions in the Third World. Moreover, Americans may not have the luxury of standing aside from conflicts in the Third World. Doing nothing may be more dangerous than doing something. America is already involved in one form or another in many Third World areas either through official government relationships, business ventures, and/or psychological linkages with portions of its own population, that is, blacks and Hispanics. Add to this the tensions and dangers of East-West confrontations and a situation emerges with America having no place to hide.

In the final analysis, the basic weakness of American policy and strategy toward the Third World, with particular reference to counterrevolution, is its inconsistency and lack of staying power. This study has pointed out the many moral, ethical, and practical dilemmas facing America when it becomes involved in counterrevolutionary policy. Implicit in this is the fact that the United States has had to relearn lessons time after time. In the process, mistakes were made, and gaps developed between the perceptions and realities of the conflict, making it even more difficult to design proper policy and strategy.

In the post-Vietnam period, America's search for coherency has tended to make American Third World policy and strategy overcautious, bordering on timidity and wrapped in political rhetoric. The moralists tend to castigate American involvement in any area, except in support of a democratic system—even though few such systems exist in the Third World. As a result, America's friends and many of its people are left in a quandary, wondering where, when, and if America will ever stand firm.

Perhaps no better statement can be made in concluding than that by an Army officer who fought in Vietnam. "I don't choose the wars I fight in. . . . When people ask me why I went to Vietnam I say 'I thought you knew. You sent me.' "[3] The strength of any American counterrevolutionary policy must stem from a clear articulation of what we stand for, where and why we intend to stand, and when, if need be, we will fight.

NOTES

1. Anatol Rapoport (ed.), *Clausewitz on War* (Baltimore, Md.: Penguin Books, 1968).

2. Samuel B. Griffith, *Sun Tzu, The Art of War* (New York: Oxford University, 1963), p. 77.

3. As quoted in Harry G. Summers, Jr., *On Strategy: The Vietnam War in Context* (Carlisle Barracks, Pa.: U.S. Army War College, 1981), p. 13.

Select Bibliography

This bibliography lists those books that provide a detailed study of various periods in history, including those that focus specifically on selected American conflicts. Many of these were documented earlier in this volume. In addition, this listing includes a number of books that are excellent background sources as well as those that analyze revolution and counterrevolution, theoretically and practically. Most of these works were not documented earlier. Periodicals and newspaper accounts are not included. In any case, this bibliography is not intended to be a comprehensive list of the many excellent studies that deal with various subjects in this volume. Rather, the intent is to provide a list of representative works, balancing detailed studies with those works that provide a broad view of American history and conflicts.

Albion, Robert Greenhalgh. *Makers of Naval Policy, 1798–1947*. Annapolis, Maryland: Naval Institute Press, 1980.

Albright, John; Cash, John A.; and Sandstrum, Allan W. *Seven Firefights in Vietnam*. Washington, D.C.: Office of the Chief of Military History, U.S. Army, 1970.

Andrews, Wayne (ed.). *The Autobiography of Theodore Roosevelt*. New York: Charles Scribner's Sons, 1958.

Barber, James David. *The Presidential Character*. 2d ed. Englewood Cliffs, N.J.: Prentice-Hall, 1977.

Bell, J. Bowyer. *On Revolt: Strategies of National Liberation*. Cambridge, Mass.: Harvard University Press, 1976.

Berman, Larry. *Planning a Tragedy: The Americanization of the War in Vietnam*. New York: W.W. Norton and Co., 1982.

Braddy, Haldeen. *Pershing's Mission in Mexico*. El Paso: Texas Western Press, 1966.

Brodie, Bernard. *War and Politics*. New York: Macmillan Publishing Co., 1973.

Buttinger, Joseph. *Vietnam: A Dragon Embattled*. 2 vols. New York: Frederick A. Praeger, 1967.

Clendenen, Clarence C. *Blood on the Border: The United States Army and the Mexican Irregulars*. New York: Macmillan Publishing Co., 1966.

Cosmas, Graham A. *An Army for Empire: The United States Army in the Spanish American War*. Columbia: University of Missouri Press, 1971.

Cunliffe, Marcus. *American Presidents and the Presidency*. London: Eyre and Spottiswoode, 1968.

Doughty, Major Robert A. *Leavenworth Papers: The Evolution of U.S. Army Tactical Doctrine, 1946–1976*. Fort Leavenworth, Kans.: Combat Studies Institute, U.S. Army Command and General Staff College, 1979.

Dunn, John. *Modern Revolutions: An Introduction to the Analysis of a Political Phenomenon*. London: Cambridge University Press, 1972.

Evans, Rowland, and Novak, Robert. *Lyndon B. Johnson: The Exercise of Power: A Political Biography*. New York: New American Library, 1966.

Fall, Bernard B. *Street Without Joy: From the Indo-China War to the War in Vietnam*. Revised ed. Harrisburg, Pa.: Stackpole Co., 1971.

————. *The Two Viet-Nams: A Political and Military Analysis*. 2d revised ed. New York: Frederick A. Praeger, 1967.

Ganoe, William Addelman. *The History of the United States Army*. New York: D. Appleton-Century Co., 1942.

Garrity, John A. *The American Nation: A History of the United States*. New York: Harper and Row, 1966.

Gates, John Morgan. *Schoolbooks and Krags: The United States Army in the Philippines, 1898–1902*. Westport, Conn.: Greenwood Press, 1973.

Goldhurst, Richard. *Pipe, Clay and Drill: John J. Pershing: The Classic American Soldier*. New York: Reader's Digest Press, 1977.

Gould, Lewis L. *The Spanish-American War and President McKinley*. Lawrence: University of Kansas Press, 1982.

Graff, Henry F. (ed.). *American Imperialism and the Philippine Insurrection*. Boston: Little Brown and Co., 1969.

Greene, Thomas. *Comparative Revolutionary Movements*. Englewood Cliffs, N.J.: Prentice-Hall, 1974.

Griffith, Samuel B. *Sun Tzu, The Art of War*. New York: Oxford University Press, 1971.

Halberstam, David. *The Best and the Brightest*. New York: Random House, 1972.

Heckscher, August (ed.). *The Politics of Woodrow Wilson: Selections from His Speeches and Writings*. New York: Harper and Brothers, 1956.

Herr, Michael. *Dispatches*. New York: Avon Books, 1978.

Hofstadter, Richard. *The American Political Tradition and the Men Who Made It*. New York: Vintage Books, 1974.

Hunt, Richard A., and Shultz, Richard H., Jr. (eds.). *Lessons from an Unconventional War*. New York: Pergamon Press, 1982.

Karnow, Stanley. *Vietnam: A History*. New York: Viking Press, 1983.

Kelly, Colonel Francis J. *Vietnam Studies: U.S. Special Forces, 1961–1971*. Washington, D.C.: U.S. Department of the Army, 1973.

Kemble, C. Robert. *The Image of the Army Officer in America*. Westport, Conn.: Greenwood Press, 1973.

Leckie, Robert. *The Wars of America*. New York: Harper and Row Publishers, 1968.

Littlefield, Daniel F., Jr. *Africans and Seminoles; From Removal to Emancipation*. Westport, Conn.: Greenwood Press, 1977.

Maclear, Michael. *The Ten Thousand Day War—Vietnam: 1945–1975*. New York: Avon, 1981.

Mahon, John K. *History of the Second Seminole War, 1835–1842*. Gainesville: University of Florida Press, 1967.

Marshall, S.L.A. *Vietnam, Three Battles*. New York: Da Capo Press, 1971.

Matloff, Maurice. *American Military History*. Washington, D.C.: Office of the Chief of Military History, U.S. Army, 1968.

Mayer, J. P. (ed.). *Alexis de Tocqueville, Democracy in America*. New York: Anchor Books, 1969.

McAlister, John T. Jr. *Vietnam: The Origins of Revolution*. Garden City, N.Y.: Doubleday and Co., 1971.

Millett, Allan R. *Semper Fidelis; The History of the United States Marine Corps*. New York: The Free Press, 1982.

O'Connor, Richard. *Black Jack Pershing*. Garden City, N.Y.: Doubleday and Co., 1961.

O'Neill, Bard E.; Heaton, William R.; and Alberts, Donald J. (eds.). *Insurgency in the Modern World*. Boulder, Colo.: Westview Press, 1980.

Papp, Daniel S. *Vietnam: The View from Moscow, Peking, Washington*. Jefferson, North Carolina: McFarland and Co., 1981.

Pearson, Lt. Gen. Willard. *The War in the Northern Provinces, 1966–1968*. Washington, D.C.: U.S. Government Printing Office, 1975.

Peers, Lt. Gen. W.R. *The My Lai Inquiry*. New York: W.W. Norton and Co., 1979.

Peters, Virginia Bergman. *The Florida Wars*. Hamden, Conn.: Archon Books, 1979.

Pratt, Julius W. *A History of United States Foreign Policy*. Englewood Cliffs, N.J.: Prentice-Hall, 1960.

Remini, Robert V. (ed.). *The Age of Jackson*. Columbia: University of South Carolina Press, 1972.

———. *Andrew Jackson and the Course of American Freedom, 1822–1832*. Volume 2. New York: Harper and Row Publishers, 1981.

Roth, Russell. *Muddy Glory; America's 'Indian Wars' in the Philippines, 1899–1935*. W. Hanover, Mass.: Christopher Publishing House, 1981.

Schlesinger, Arthur, Jr. *The Age of Jackson*. Boston: Little, Brown and Co., 1945.

———. *A Thousand Days: John F. Kennedy in the White House*. Boston: Houghton Mifflin Co., 1965.

Sexton, William Thaddeus. *Soldiers in the Sun: An Adventure in Imperialism*. Freeport, N.Y.: Books for Libraries Press, 1979.

Shackley, Theodore. *The Third Option: An American View of Counterinsurgency Operations*. New York: Reader's Digest Press, 1981.

Shaplen, Robert. *Time Out of Hand: Revolution and Reaction in Southeast Asia*. Revised ed. New York: Harper Colophon Books, 1970.

Sharp, Admiral U.S. Grant. *Strategy for Defeat; Vietnam in Retrospect*. San Rafael, Cal.: Presidio Press, 1978.

Sheehan, Neil; Smith, Hedrick; Kenworthy, E. W.; and Butterfield, Fox. *The Pentagon Papers*. New York: Bantam Books, 1971.

Skocpol, Theda. *States and Social Revolutions: A Comparative Analysis of France, Russia, and China*. Cambridge: Cambridge University Press, 1979.

Smythe, Donald. *Guerrilla Warrior, The Early Life of John J. Pershing*. New York: Charles Scribner's Sons, 1973.

Sorenson, Theodore C. *Kennedy*. New York: A Bantam Book, 1966.

Spanier, John. *American Foreign Policy Since World War II*. New York: Holt, Rinehart and Winston, 1980.

Summers, Colonel Harry G., Jr. *On Strategy: The Vietnam War in Context*. Carlisle Barracks, Pa.: U.S. Army War College, 1981.

Thompson, James Clay. *Rolling Thunder; Understanding Policy and Program Failure*. Chapel Hill: The University of North Carolina Press, 1980.

Thompson, Sir Robert. *Defeating Communist Insurgency: The Lessons of Malaya and Vietnam*. New York: Frederick A. Praeger, 1966.

Tompkins, Frank. *Chasing Villa*. Harrisburg, Pa.: Stackpole Co., 1934.

U.S. Army War College. *Study of Military Professionalism*. Carlisle Barracks, Pa.: U.S. Army War College, June 30, 1970.

Utley, Robert M. *Frontier Regulars: The United States Army and the Indian, 1866–1891*. New York: Macmillan Publishing Co., 1973.

Waddell, Colonel Dewey and Wood, Major Norm (eds.). *Air War-Vietnam*. New York: Arno Press, 1978.

Weigley, Russell F. *History of the United States Army*. New York: Macmillan Publishing Co., 1967.

Welch, Richard E., Jr. *Response to Imperialism: The United States and the Philippine-American War, 1899–1902*. Chapel Hill: University of North Carolina Press, 1979.

Westmoreland, General William C. *A Soldier Reports*. Garden City, N.Y.: Doubleday and Co., 1976.

Williams, T. Harry. *Americans at War: The Development of the American Military System*. Baton Rouge: Louisiana State University Press, 1960.

Williams, T. Harry; Current, Richard N.; and Freidel, Frank A. *History of the United States to 1877*. 3d ed. New York: Alfred A. Knopf, 1969.

———. *History of the United States Since 1865*. 3d ed. New York: Alfred A. Knopf, 1969.

Wolff, Leon. *Little Brown Brother: How the United States Purchased and Pacified the Philippine Islands at the Century's Turn*. New York: Doubleday and Co., 1961.

Index

Adams, John, 24, 43
Adams, Samuel, 105
Age of Jackson, 21-22
Age of mass production, 68
Aguinaldo, Emilio, 168, 170; capture of, 174. *See also* Funston, Frederick
America: acquisition of colonies, 56; acquisition of Philippines, 43, 44; attitude on Cuba, 47; attitude towards external world, 3; attitude on Mexican intervention, 66; collapse of consensus on foreign policy, 78; Columbus Raid and, 65; counterrevolutionary experience, 230; defense posture, 2; differences with Filipinos, 174; divisiveness over Vietnam, 78; economic and social changes, (1900-1920), 70; European war and, 64; focus on domestic issues, 42; government expansion, 1880s, 52; Grenada invasion and, 3; growth of federal government, 35; "March on Washington for Peace in Vietnam," 206; mobilization for European War, 69; national security and, 230; neglect of history, 5; "never again" school, 4; 19th century expansion of, 42-43;

Old World and, 57; Pancho Villa and, 65; perceptions of Vietnam War, 231; political cynicism, 52; past unconventional wars and, 3; population (1820-1840), 34; population (1870-1890), 55; population, 1880s, 52; population (1900-1920), 67-68; post-Civil War outlook and, 55; post-World War I period and, 70; post-World War II outlook and, 136-137; post-World War II security posture, 71-72; protest movements in 1890s, 54; socio-economic patterns (1810-1830), 34; Soviet nuclear capability and, 4; standing armies, 105-7; urbanization (1870-1890), 55; Vietnam involvement, 78, 142; Vietnam policymakers and, 4; views on war, 233; world affairs, 19th century, 41-42
American Army: European fixation, 134, 145; first foreign war, 165; Indian wars, 119; isolation and, 135; Korean War and, 140-41; Philippine War and organizational change, 171; professionalism, 130, 135; quality of life, 121; rebuilding period, 134; relationship with Filipi-

About the Author

SAM C. SARKESIAN is Professor of Political Science and Chairman of the Inter-University Seminar on Armed Forces at Loyola University. His previous books are *The Professional Army Officer in a Changing Society* and *Beyond the Battlefield: The New Military Professionalism*. He is the author of numerous articles on political science and military affairs.